CLARENDON LATER ANCIENT PHILOSOPHERS

*Series editors: Jonathan Barnes, University of Geneva
and A. A. Long, University of California, Berkeley*

EPICTETUS

DISCOURSES
BOOK I

EPICTETUS

DISCOURSES
BOOK I

Translated with an Introduction
and Commentary by

ROBERT F. DOBBIN

CLARENDON PRESS · OXFORD
1998

Oxford University Press, Great Clarendon Street, Oxford OX2 6DP
Oxford New York
Athens Auckland Bangkok Bogota Bombay Buenos Aires
Calcutta Cape Town Dar es Salaam Delhi Florence Hong Kong Istanbul
Karachi Kuala Lumpur Madras Madrid Melbourne Mexico City
Nairobi Paris Singapore Taipei Tokyo Toronto Warsaw
and associated companies in
Berlin Ibadan

Published in the United States
by Oxford University Press Inc., New York

British Library Cataloguing in Publication Data
Data available

Library of Congress Cataloging in Publication Data
Epictetus.
[Discourses. Book 1. English]
Discourses. Book I | Epictetus ; translated with an introduction
and commentary by Robert F. Dobbin.
— (Clarendon later ancient philosophers)
Includes bibliographical references and indexes.
1. Ethics—Early works to 1800. 2. Philosophy—Early works to
1800. I. Dobbin, Robert F. II. Title. III. Series.
B560.E5D63 1998 188—dc21 97-51410
ISBN 0-19-823664-6

1 3 5 7 9 10 8 6 4 2

Typeset by Graphicraft Typesetters Ltd, Hong Kong
Printed in Great Britain
on acid-free paper by
Bookcraft (Bath) Ltd
Midsomer Norton, Somerset

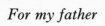

For my father

PREFACE

Epictetus has historically been one of the most widely read philosophers. He also attracted a good deal of attention from scholars in the early modern era. But in our century he has been much less studied. That, fortunately, is beginning to change, as the revival of interest in later Greek philosophy has caught up with him and again made him the focus of scholarly activity. Although Epictetus might regard this improvement in his academic fortunes a bit cynically, given his insistence that philosophy should be practised, not just read, my book is nevertheless intended to further the trend and assist others in rehabilitating this recently neglected author.

Epictetus wrote for the public, which accounts for his traditional popularity. The *Discourses* are not dull treatises, but sermons (or 'diatribes') enlivened with all the resources that ancient rhetoric had at its command. In this respect they resemble the work of other philosophers of the early Empire such as Dio Chrysostom and Maximus of Tyre. Like their work, the *Discourses* benefit, I think, from a commentary that is not just philosophical but philological as well. The appearance of this volume in the Clarendon Later Ancient Philosophers series ensures that the philosophical will predominate, which I think is the right emphasis in any case. But I have tried to furnish the literary or cultural background to certain passages, and I hope readers looking for purely philosophical edification will know enough in such places to skim.

I wish to thank Jonathan Barnes and Tony Long, the editors of the series, for their comments on earlier drafts of the book. I owe a particular debt to Tony for his help over the years, and for fostering my research into Epictetus. Christopher Gill read the whole book as it neared completion, and made many suggestions for improvement. I also received valuable help from David Sedley, Benson Mates, Daniel Warren, and Menachem Luz. John Strohmeier has been a friend and a supporter of the work from the beginning. My thanks to all of them. My greatest thanks are due to my father, to whom the book is dedicated.

R. F. D.

Berkeley, August 1997

CONTENTS

LIST OF ABBREVIATIONS

DK   H. Diels and W. Kranz, *Die Fragmente der Vorsokratiker* (3 vols., 6th edn., Berlin, 1951–2).

EK   L. Edelstein and I. G. Kidd (eds.), *Posidonius* (2 vols., Cambridge, 1972, 1988).

Guthrie   W. K. C. Guthrie, *A History of Greek Philosophy* (6 vols., Cambridge, 1962–81).

LS   A. A. Long and D. N. Sedley (eds.), *The Hellenistic Philosophers* (2 vols., Cambridge, 1987). References such as LS 34G indicate a specific passage in their collection; LS 2. 207, however, designates a volume and page number, and refers to the editors' comment on the passage.

PIR^2 *Prosopographia Imperii Romani* (2nd edn., Berlin and Leipzig, 1933).

SVF   H. von Arnim, *Stoicorum Veterum Fragmenta* (4 vols., Leipzig, 1905–23). Citations of the form *SVF* 3. 92 indicate the volume number, followed by the number of the fragment. Citations such as *SVF* 2. 333. 29–30 indicate the volume, followed by the page, then the line number(s).

INTRODUCTION

1. Epictetus' Life

Little is known with certainty about the life of Epictetus. Most of the tradition about him derives from the *Discourses* themselves. The tenth-century lexicon called the *Suda* gives a thumb-nail biography: 'From Hierapolis in Phrygia. Slave of Epaphroditus, who was one of the bodyguards of the emperor Nero. Lame in the leg from rheumatism. Settled in Nicopolis in Epirus. Lived until the accession of Marcus. Wrote a great deal.' At 1. 9. 29 and 1. 19. 21 of the *Discourses* Epictetus confirms that he had been a slave. An ancient inscription indicates that he was born into slavery, since his mother had been a slave.[1] Epictetus refers to his lameness at 1. 8. 14 and 1. 16. 20. The majority of ancient sources ascribe it to something more dramatic than rheumatism, however. They blame it on Epictetus' cruel master (presumably Epaphroditus), and never fail to mention the quintessentially 'Stoic' way in which he endured the ill treatment;[2] but this tradition may assume that personal experience lies behind the advice he gives at 1. 19. 8. Epaphroditus is mentioned at 1. 1. 20, 1. 19. 19, and 1. 26. 11. He was not 'one of the bodyguards of the emperor Nero', however, as the *Suda* would have it, but Nero's secretary in charge of receiving petitions. He later served Domitian in the same capacity.[3]

We cannot be certain whether Epictetus (hereafter simply 'E') was the slave of Epaphroditus, and therefore in Rome, as early as the reign of Nero. But he was definitely there during the Flavian period, when he studied under the philosopher Musonius Rufus.[4] At 1. 9. 29 he indicates that he was still a slave when he heard Musonius lecture. Sources report that he moved to Nicopolis when Domitian, probably in 92 or 93, announced a wholesale expulsion of philosophers from Rome.[5] By that time he had evidently gained

---

[1] The inscription is quoted in Schenkl 1916: p. vii.   [2] Ibid., pp. vi–ix.
[3] Cf. Suetonius, *Nero*, 49. 5; *Domitian*, 14. 2.   [4] Cf. 1. 1. 27 and 1. 9. 29.
[5] Gellius, 15. 11 (= Testimonium X, Schenkl); Simplicius, *In Ench.* 153b (= Test. LI, Schenkl). On the date of the expulsion see A. N. Sherwin-White, 'Pliny's Praetorship Again', *JRS* 47 (1957): 126–30.

his freedom. Nicopolis was a city founded by the emperor Augustus on the Bay of Actium in north-west Greece (Epirus), to commemorate his victory over Antony. It is the site of the *Discourses*, and there is no evidence that E ever returned to Rome or settled anywhere else.

E's dates cannot be determined precisely. His birth and background are obscure. That he was alive during the reign of Trajan (98–117) is assured from 4. 5. 17, where coinage bearing that emperor's likeness is referred to. In 3. 7 E converses with a *corrector*, an official of senatorial rank assigned to the Greek East. Most scholars assume that this is the Maximus twice mentioned in the discourse (at §§3 and 10), and further identify him with the Maximus to whom Pliny the Younger addresses *Ep.* 8. 24, concerning his appointment 'to arrange the affairs of the free cities in Greece'.[6] As the letter can be dated to around 108, we evidently have a *terminus post quem* for E's death.

The *Suda* says that E lived into Marcus' reign (161–80). But for this to be true, he could not have been much more than 20 when Domitian expelled him from Rome. (There is no evidence that he was one of the ancient *makrobioi*, those who lived into extreme old age.) And it is unlikely that by the age of 20 he had achieved sufficient fame as a philosopher to attract the emperor's notice. The association with Marcus probably derives from the latter's admiring mention at 1. 7, 7. 19, etc., of the *Meditations*. The fourth-century orator Themistius implies that E was alive under the Antonines, which could mean Marcus, or could mean Marcus' predecessor Antoninus Pius, who acceded in 138.[7] According to another late source, E was friendly with Hadrian, who ruled from 117 to 138.[8] Whatever his relations with the emperor—and the condescension shown philosophers by the good ruler, which Hadrian preeminently represented, is too much of an ancient topos for this tradition to be completely trustworthy—it is not impossible that E was at least alive during his reign. At 3. 13. 9, he alludes to the *pax Romana*, with which Hadrian especially was associated.

---

[6] See *PIR²* M 399.   [7] Themistius, *Or.* 5, 63d (= Test. XXX, Schenkl).
[8] Aelius Spartianus, *Life of Hadrian*, 16. 10 (= Test. XXVII, Schenkl). Spartianus is one of the authors of the *Historia Augusta*, which was composed some time in the fourth or early fifth century. There survives a (spurious) conversation between E and Hadrian known as the *Altercatio Hadriani et Epicteti*, evidently a product of the Middle Ages; see Schenkl 1916: p. xxvi.

Schenkl put E's dates at *c*.50–*c*.138, based on the assumption that he was alive under Hadrian, and dead before the age of 90.[9] This is certainly consistent with the available evidence. But in view of the lateness of these sources, and the evident unreliability of some, I would prefer a simple *floruit* of AD *c*.110. Anything more precise is misleading. If we are to associate E with contemporary events, it is most important for our purposes to focus on those that influenced his thought. Of particular importance in this connection is the resistance that certain Stoics offered the Roman emperors in the second half of the first century AD. See the references at 1. 1. 18–32, 1. 2. 19–24, and 1. 25. 22 to the opposition of Helvidius Priscus and others to Nero, Vespasian, and Domitian. The physical force that these tyrants represented served as a correlative to the Stoic concept of fate, and helped shape E's doctrine that moral character is the only thing within our power. This background of conflict also helps to account for the embattled nature of his philosophy.

The earliest independent testimony to E's fame is credited to the orator Favorinus, a protégé of Hadrian. Aulus Gellius reports that he heard E lecture, on the popular theme of the failure of so-called philosophers to practise what they preach (*Attic Nights*, 17. 19. 1–6 = E fr. 10 Schenkl). Gellius (1. 2. 6) further reports that the cultural benefactor Herodes Atticus (*c*.101–77) considered E 'the greatest of the Stoics'. His writings were evidently well known and widely circulated soon after his death. Gellius quotes him again 'from the fifth book of the *Discourses*' at 19. 1. 14–21, indicating that some of the *Discourses* have been lost, since only four books have come down to us. The emperor Marcus Aurelius refers to the *Discourses* several times in his *Meditations*, written in his last years, and they are acknowledged to be a major influence on his work; at 7. 19 he exalts him in the company of Socrates and Chrysippus. The physician-philosopher Galen, a contemporary of Marcus, wrote a book, now lost, defending E against criticisms by Favorinus.[10] Another author worthy of note is Origen (*c*.185–254). E is cited six times by name in his writing, and deserves to be considered a significant influence on him as well; see comment ad 1. 1. 12. At *Contra Celsum* 6. 2 he reports that E was more popular in his day than Plato, whom only philologists still read. That his popularity continued into late antiquity is attested by the massive commentary on the *Enchiridion*

---

[9] Schenkl 1916: p. xlii.   [10] Galen, *Lib. prop.* 11 (= Mueller 2. 120).

(a digest of the *Discourses*) written by the Neoplatonist philosopher Simplicius in the sixth century AD. This, the first commentary on E, is cited occasionally in my own.[11]

2. Philosophical Position and Style

The modern view of E's philosophical position was largely established by Adolph Bonhöffer, in two books published over a century ago: *Epictet und die Stoa* (1890) and *Die Ethik des Stoikers Epictet* (1894). Both books use the *Discourses* as the basic text for expounding old Stoicism.[12] Bonhöffer's approach was dictated in part by reasons of convenience. None of the old Stoic texts survive whole (except Cleanthes' short *Hymn to Zeus*), and von Arnim's collection of the fragments had not yet appeared. Since E wrote in Greek, he could be used to explain Stoic terms without having to translate them from the Latin of Cicero or Seneca. Marcus Aurelius also wrote in Greek. But Marcus' thought was known to be contaminated by alien philosophical traditions, and is not as comprehensive.[13] E, moreover, seems devoted to the old Stoics. At 1. 4. 31 he praises Chrysippus as one 'who has discovered and illuminated the truth and brought it forth for all men'—a tribute that recalls Lucretius' praise of Epicurus at *De Rerum Natura*, 5. 13–19, and seems to reflect the same exclusive attachment to him as Epicureans had to their own founder. When he refers to 'the philosophers' (as at 1. 18. 1), he almost always means the Stoics, as if they were the only ones worthy of the name.

Bonhöffer's books continue to be valuable, because his method was mainly sound. As Aulus Gellius (19. 1. 14) put it, 'The *Discourses* of the philosopher Epictetus undoubtedly agree with the writings of Zeno and Chrysippus.' But Bonhöffer went too far in trying to make his work conform in all respects. It is now recognized that E's philosophical background is complicated. First of all,

---

[11] Simplicius' commentary is available in a new edition by Ilsetraut Hadot (Leiden, 1996).

[12] Bonhöffer's method is laid out in the foreword to the 1894 book, pp. iii–vi.

[13] Logic, for example, hardly figures in his thought. See Rist 1982: 23–45; and Barnes 1997: 1–11.

we have to account for the influence of Musonius Rufus, E's teacher.
Musonius was a Stoic, who explored in an original manner problems
of ethics in action, such as whether parents should always be obeyed,
whether women should engage in philosophy, and what relation
ideally obtains between a husband and wife. E engages few of these
same topics. But, broadly speaking, his discourses are also works of
practical ethics, rather than theory. Both philosophers' primary aim
is to persuade listeners to think and act in a definite way. Roman
Stoicism generally is dominated by practical ethics, and it is reasonable to suppose that Musonius was a major influence in getting E to
share this orientation.[14]

Bonhöffer (1894: p. iv) suggested that Musonius brought E to his
interest in Cynicism. This is largely conjecture, because Musonius
(unlike E) never discusses Cynicism directly (although he refers to
Diogenes the Cynic in Discourse 9, 'That Exile is Not an Evil').
Nevertheless, the idealization of the Cynic teacher that we find in
E reflects the same interest in practical guidance that Musonius
represents; the Cynic is a normative figure whose work is directed
at making people better by leading them to philosophy. E's admiration for Cynicism (however he came by it) is clear from 3. 22, 'On
Cynicism'. The fact that 3. 22 is the only extant discourse devoted
to the subject indicates that it does not permeate his outlook, however. In fact, one of the points made there is that the vocation of
Cynic is only for a few, whereas E often asserts that philosophy—
the Stoic philosophy he normally expounds—should be practised
by everyone (cf. 1. 26. 5–7; 2. 25, etc.). He also believes that logic
is essential (cf. 1. 7. 12), whereas Cynics disparaged it. Other differences between the Stoic and Cynic outlooks are discussed in the
commentary to 1. 6. 35–6 and 1. 24. 6–9.

An influence of a more pervasive kind is represented by Plato. E
cites him more than sixty times, always with admiration or respect.
One of his refrains is that it is necessary to distinguish between
'what is in our power' and what is not. He sometimes defines these
respectively as *prohairesis* (on which see below) and the body. Related to this is his belief that matter acts as a force for evil and limits
the scope of god's power. Both ideas are basically Platonic; see comment on 1. 1. 7–11. These are only a couple of areas in which his

[14] So Bonhöffer 1890: 3 and Souilhé i: p. vii.

effect on E's thought is evident; see comment ad 1. 3 and 1. 9 for additional examples in Book I. The subject has been treated at length by Amand Jagu (1946).

Related to this is E's admiration for Socrates, since he is credited with some of the views we now regard as Platonic, including contempt for the body. Socrates is cited more than fifty times in the *Discourses*; he is E's great personal exemplar. He esteems him above all for his adherence to principle in the face of physical force and death, as shown by his behaviour in the *Phaedo* and *Apology*. He is thus transformed into a Stoic *avant la lettre*, who demonstrated in his life (and death) the timeless truth of Stoic philosophy. But he is also invoked as an authority in doctrinal matters, such as the importance of defining terms (1. 17. 12). Socrates figures prominently in chapters 9, 12, and 29 of Book I. The role that he plays in E has been explored in detail by Döring 1979: 43–79; see in addition Long 1988: 150–1.

Then there is the matter of 'Middle Stoicism', meaning the direction given Stoicism by Panaetius and Posidonius. They were Greek philosophers active in Rome in the second and first century BC, respectively. None of their writings survive, and the extent of their influence, especially in Posidonius' case, is still debated. Bonhöffer, for his part, was of the view that they might as well not have existed so far as E was concerned,[15] and it is true that he never mentions them by name. But Panaetius' focus on social roles and personality as determinants of moral behaviour certainly prepared for E's version of the same thing,[16] and in the comment on 1. 4. 5–9 I argue that his influence may go further. As regards Posidonius, Karl Reinhardt (1921) demonstrated the extent to which Discourse 1. 14 of E is indebted to him. Posidonius also introduced Platonic elements into Stoicism, and the Platonic strain in E no doubt reflects this at second hand; see comment ad 1. 1. 7–11, 1. 9. 10–17, 1. 12. 5, etc.

E betrays other influences. In 1. 22 he borrows Sceptic arguments. Ancient scepticism began in earnest in the third century BC in the New Academy of Arcesilaus. It was given new life in the first century BC by the ex-Academic Aenesidemus, under the name of neo-Pyrrhonism. Debate raged between Stoics and Sceptics of both types, as reflected in the writings of Cicero and Sextus Empiricus.

---

[15] See Bonhöffer 1894: pp. iii–iv.
[16] See LS 1. 368. Alesse (1994: 267–78) explores this and other connections between E and Panaetius.

True to his school, E combats the Sceptics directly in 1. 5. But another, less direct way to counter one's opponents, one common in the philosophical polemic of the Hellenistic and Roman periods, was to appropriate elements from them and make them one's own. This, I think, is the strategy essayed in 1. 22.

The indirect strategy also lies behind E's use of the word 'prohairesis'. This, the principal term of his ethics, derives from the Aristotelian tradition, as I have argued elsewhere.[17] The neo-Aristotelian movement dates from the rediscovery of Aristotle's works in the first century BC. From that time commentaries on his work begin to appear. These commentaries body forth a distinct philosophy based on Aristotle whose significance is better appreciated now, thanks to their ongoing appearance in English translations.[18] Like the Sceptics, neo-Aristotelians developed their thought largely in opposition to Stoicism, the dominant philosophy of the day. Controversy in their case often centred on the question of whether the Stoic doctrine of fate left room for human free will. The commentators defined free will in terms of *prohairesis*, a word featured prominently in Aristotle's ethics (cf. *EN* 3. 1–5; *EE* 2. 10). E's use of his opponents' chief weapon in this connection can be interpreted as a pointed response to their attacks. Further discussion will be found in the commentary on 1. 1. 23.

Finally, in qualification of Bonhöffer's assumption that E's thought depends entirely on the old Stoics, we should consider the possibility that he is sometimes simply original. There is no precedent, for instance, Stoic or otherwise, for his doctrine of the three *topoi* (fields of study). Although it is made up of older elements, this teaching as a whole has no exact parallel: see 1. 4.

Thus, what we have in E is not a fossilized philosophy, but Stoicism of its time. It is eclectic in absorbing elements from different traditions, and reflects what Seneca says at *Ep.* 33. 3–4 about Stoic pride in its school's independence of thought: Stoics defined themselves in opposition to other schools by their very willingness to admit elements from them if they appeared true and consistent with their own.[19] But E is eclectic with a difference, when compared

---

[17] Dobbin 1991.

[18] In the series *The Ancient Commentators on Aristotle* (Ithaca, NY, 1987–), under the general editorship of Richard Sorabji.

[19] For the issues touched on here, see the papers collected in Dillon and Long 1988.

with Seneca and Marcus. There is never any question in his case
of his primary allegiance. He does not adopt some of the most distinctive elements of Middle Stoicism, such as Posidonius' complex
psychology. And most of his borrowings from alien traditions, such
as 'prohairesis', are intended to defend Zeno and Chrysippus at
points where they were perceived as vulnerable. He updates traditional Stoicism by co-opting rival theory when it threatened to subvert it. Despite the Platonic colouring of some of his arguments,
overall he deserves to be classed as the sole representative among
Roman Stoics of what I would call 'neo-orthodoxy'.

My assumption, then, is that we should comment first in the
light of old Stoicism, but that part of the job is to identify secondary influences. We must also try to elucidate E's arguments. He is
not always easy to follow, in part because his writings are *kommatikoi*
('chopped', 'abrupt'), as Simplicius described them (*In Ench.* 3b).
This is mainly an effect of the diatribe style. More than 100 years
after Hermann Usener identified it as a distinct genre, the diatribe
is still difficult to define.[20] What seems clear is that it developed to
convey philosophy, at least ostensibly, to the masses; it was a marriage of philosophy and rhetoric. Already the old Stoics are credited
with works entitled *Diatribai*, and one ancient account of Chrysippus'
style can serve to characterize the style as a whole: 'Wake up and hear
what Chrysippus himself aims at. Is he content to give information,
expound the facts, make definitions and lay everything out? No. He
expands on everything as far as possible, he exaggerates, anticipates
objections, repeats himself, defers matters, retraces his path, gives
descriptions, makes divisions, introduces characters and puts what
he has to say into other people's mouths.'[21] Vivid and abrupt, full of
apostrophes, rhetorical questions, and objections from an imaginary interlocutor: these are the diatribe's recognized features. It was
favoured mainly by Cynics and Stoics, and E is considered a prime
practitioner. Simplicius already refers to his writings as 'diatribes'
(*In Ench.* 1a), and the *Discourses* continue to be otherwise known by
this name.

[20] On the diatribe, see Usener 1887: p. lxix; Griffin 1976: 13–16, 412–15, 508–9;
A. E. Douglas, 'Form and Content in the *Tusculan Disputations*', in J. G. F. Powell
(ed.), *Cicero the Philosopher* (Oxford, 1995), 197–218.
[21] Fronto, *De Eloq.* 2. 17. For diatribes among the old Stoics cf. SE *PH* 3. 245;
DL 7. 175.

One frequently runs across the prejudice that one diatribe of E is much like any other. In fact, the reader will find a range of topics treated in this, the first book: preconceptions (Chapter 22), the doctrine of 'sympathy' (Chapter 14), the compatibility of free will within a determinist framework (Chapter 1), moral progress (Chapter 4), providence (Chapters 6 and 16), and many others. I actually find Book I philosophically the richest of the four, which is one reason why a detailed commentary on it can serve almost as a complete guide to E's thought—certainly more so than one on the *Enchiridion*, which, despite Simplicius' decision to comment on it, and its reputation as a digest of E's philosophy, really only succeeds in reducing him to his most sententious. To comment on all four books, on the other hand, would be too long and repetitive. The *Discourses* in general are valuable for the way they interweave various themes, demonstrating, in a way that the old Stoic fragments cannot, the coherence of the Stoic system.

It is conventional to divide Greek authors of the Imperial period into those whose writing reflects the tradition of Greek as written and spoken in their own day (e.g. Strabo and Marcus) and those who reproduce the Greek of a bygone era, the classicizing or archaizing authors (e.g. Philostratus, Dio Chrysostom, Arrian). E clearly belongs to the first group, since he writes in Koine, the current and popular form of the language. With his forcefulness and willingness to express himself in a contemporary idiom, E retains some of the qualities of the Classics precisely because he was not enslaved to them. This is what Simplicius says in the introduction to his commentary on the *Enchiridion* (2a–b):

The aim of this book, if it should find an audience not content just to hear it, but prepared to obey and respond to the words, and apply them in practice, is to render our soul free. . . . The style of discourse is very active and stimulating, so as to prick and arouse those not too inert, or stultified, to an awareness and correction of their personal faults. Some, to be sure, will be more affected than others. But if anyone is left altogether cold by these *Discourses*, then I suppose only the tribunals of Hades will affect him.

It is true that E has traditionally been judged more remarkable for vigour than for subtlety. But my commentary tries to correct that prejudice as well.

For other surveys of E's thought, see Hershbell 1986 and C. Gill in Hard 1995: pp. xvii–xxvii.

3. Authorship[22]

The *Discourses* are prefaced by a letter written by Arrian (full name, Lucius Flavianus Arrianus Xenophon) to one Lucius Gellius. In his youth, apparently, Arrian was a student of E's. Under Hadrian he was governor of Cappadocia. He wrote a biography of Alexander the Great, a history of India, and other works.[23] His letter begins:

I neither composed the *Discourses* of Epictetus—however it is one composes such things—much less did I deliver them myself, seeing as I have already said that I did not compose them. Whatever I heard him say, these very things I tried, so far as I could, to transcribe *verbatim*, to preserve for myself a record for later time of this man's thought and frank expression. They are such as one might by chance be moved to say to someone else spontaneously, not as one might compose for others to come upon later. This being the case, somehow, I don't know how, without my knowledge or co-operation, they have fallen into the public's hands.

There are a couple of things to note about Arrian's letter. He clearly means to locate the *Discourses* within the Socratic tradition of personal, oral teaching. He therefore has to establish a pretext for their appearance in print, and he offers two: (1) he had transcribed them as a personal *aide-mémoire*; (2) they were already circulating in this form, so he has simply consented to make them more widely available. Now, Socrates' teaching is known to us mainly through the dialogues of Plato and the *Memorabilia* of Xenophon. The *Discourses*, then, would seem to belong to that tradition. But, as Radt points out (1990: 364–5), Arrian denies in so many words that they do. When he says 'I neither composed the discourses of Epictetus—however it is one composes such things' he effectively disavows the role Plato and Xenophon played *vis-à-vis* Socrates.

There are reasons for not completely believing Arrian, however. First, in an age when stenographic techniques were primitive and reserved to a class of civil servant,[24] it would have been virtually impossible for him to transcribe E's statements with the degree of fidelity he claims for them. Second, although his version of events presupposes that he was personally present at the delivery of the

[22] On the question of authorship see Stellwag 7–16; Souilhé i: pp. xiv–xix; Wirth 1967; Stadter 1980: 20–8; Long 1982b: 989–90; Hershbell 1986: 2152–3; Radt 1990; I. Hadot 1996: 152–60.

[23] On Arrian see S. Follet, 'Arrien de Nicomédie', in R. Goulet (ed.), *Dictionnaire des Philosophes Antiques*, i (Paris, 1989), 597–604.

[24] See Radt 1990: 367 n. 3.

Discourses, this is not consistent with the ostensible setting of some of them: thus 1. 11 represents a conversation between E and a Roman official; cf. also 1. 15, 2. 14, and 3. 7. Arrian would not have had access to this type of private interview. The veracity of a few of them has also been challenged.[25] They seem too clearly modelled on the dialogues with prominent citizens in which Plato and Xenophon have Socrates engage.

On this basis Wirth (1967) has argued that, despite Arrian's protest, the *Discourses* do in fact conform to the model of Xenophon's *Memorabilia*, and that they are in consequence largely his own work. But Wirth's thesis has not been widely accepted either. The reason is that Arrian's attested writings are so different in style and content. The *Discourses* are written in Koine, whereas the *Anabasis* and *Indika* are Atticizing in style. And Stoicism hardly figures in these other works.[26] No one doubts that Arrian did hear E lecture, and as a man of letters commended the *Discourses* to the world at large by writing a foreword. But the majority of scholars believe that his attested works are sufficiently different that we can accept his claim to the extent of assuming that he did not in fact compose the *Discourses* the way Xenophon did the *Memorabilia*, or Plato the Socratic dialogues.

Stellwag had earlier arrived at what is in a sense a conclusion opposite to Wirth's, but based on the same considerations. Rather than identify Arrian as the author, however, she preferred to believe that E wrote the *Discourses* himself. The *Suda*, after all, says that he 'wrote a great deal'. It has been pointed out that this ignores the fact that E is always referred to in the third person in the *Discourses*. But this is not a serious objection. Plato (*Apol.* 34a) and Xenophon (*Mem.* 1. 3), among others, also refer to themselves in this way.

The consensus today is (1) that lack of evidence makes it impossible to determine precisely how the *Discourses* came to be written, but (2) that they reflect the thought of E, not Arrian or anyone else. The ancient testimony all supports the latter assumption, and most scholars are content to leave it at that. But I must say that I side with Stellwag. The *Discourses* have traditionally been treated as the actual words of the master, which is how Arrian intended it to be. But the objections to supposing that he wrote them—either in the

---

[25] See Millar 1965: 143; Hahn 1989: 71 n. 22.

[26] See Bosworth 1988: 135–45, who argues that E's teaching is at odds with Arrian's admiring biography of Alexander.

strong sense that Wirth defends, or only in the weak sense that Arrian himself alleges—are compelling. And they are evidently not the impromptu dissertations they purport to be. Most are too polished to be 'such as one might by chance be moved to say to someone else spontaneously'. And a few, such as 1. 29, 3. 22, and 4. 1, are clearly too long for *ex tempore* delivery (much less *verbatim* transcription). I suspect that E is responsible for composing the *Discourses* as we have them, but that he tried to preserve the dramatic context from which they probably developed. Near parallels for what I am suggesting can be found among other Roman Stoics. The *Discourses* of Musonius are supposed to reproduce his lectures, but this has been challenged, and on similar grounds.[27] Seneca strived to give his *Letters* the appearance of personal correspondence, but this too is acknowledged to be pretence; they were intended from the start for a wider audience.[28] The same may be true of Marcus' *Meditations*.[29] I suspect that E committed his thoughts to writing, in the form of diatribes, in a like effort to reach an audience beyond his immediate time and place. Arrian's foreword played its part in putting this slight deception across.

It is true, as indicated, that the *Discourses* are abrupt in style, which is what we would expect of *ad hoc* homilies. But this is a conscious effect. Diatribes share in a kind of rhetoric that was anti-rhetorical in so far as it eschewed artifice and affected to be spontaneous, concerned with content to the exclusion of style. This derives from a prerogative claimed by philosophers since Socrates (Pl. *Apol.* 17 sq., *Rep.* 394d) to say whatever comes into their head, a trait that distinguishes their manner of address from the polished rhetoric of the orator. As Aelius Aristides writes, 'Wherever the *logos* goes, there I am obliged to follow' (*Panath.* 17; cf. *Panath.* 151; Dio Chrys. 7. 1, 12. 16, 12. 38). This became, of course, a style of rhetoric in its own right, one patronized especially by Stoics, who were distrustful of traditional rhetoric.[30]

In E's case there was special reason to affect this unstudied, oral character, because, as indicated, it probably did have some foundation in fact. Internal evidence suggests that E's students performed

[27] See A. Jagu, *Musonius Rufus: Entretiens et Fragments. Introduction, Traduction et Commentaire* (Hildesheim, 1979), 9–10.

[28] See Griffin 1976: 416–19.   [29] See Rutherford 1989: 9–10.

[30] See Atherton 1988: 424–5; Russell 1992, ad Dio Chrys. 7. 1; and my comment ad 1. 8.

logical exercises and explication of classic Stoic texts. (Cf. 1. 10. 8 and 1. 26. 1 and 13, with comment.) External evidence suggests that these elements dominated instruction in most philosophical schools of the Imperial period, but also that they were supplemented by oral teaching on the part of the master.[31] Arrian's letter indicates that E engaged in the latter practice, and this, so far, is uncontroversial. But it is not incompatible with the assumption that he then took charge of effecting his lectures' transition to print. In the process he was careful to preserve their dramatic context, producing another example of literary, or 'secondary' diatribe.[32] He also positioned himself as an heir to the tradition of oral teaching represented by Socrates, one of his intellectual masters.

4. The Text, Modern Editions, and the Translation

The oldest manuscript of the *Discourses* is Codex Bodleianus Graecorum Miscellaneorum 251 (S). It is dated to the end of the eleventh century or the beginning of the twelfth. It is the archetype of all remaining MSS, and the basis of all recent texts. See note ad 1. 18. 9–11 for how its primacy came to be recognized. For a full account of the *deteriores* see Souilhé 1948 vol. i, pp. lxxv–lxxxi. Another authority sometimes cited in the commentary is the 'codex' of John Upton. This is known from citations in Upton's own commentary, published in London between 1739 and 1741. The 'codex' was a copy of the first printed edition of the *Discourses* (published by Victor Trincavelli in Venice in 1535), annotated with alternative readings derived from a manuscript other than S, along with the textual notes of Hieronymus Wolf and other early editors. Upton's readings are of limited independent value.

The textual notes in the commentary usually indicate where the translation assumes readings that depart from S, in so far as these are known to me from the critical apparatus of modern editions. My preferred readings often agree with one or more of these editions. But such agreements, or disagreements, have not always been registered. Those with an interest in the text should use the notes in conjunction with the text and apparatus of Schenkl or Souilhé (on whom see below).

---

[31] See Hahn 1989: 67–8; Barnes 1993; Lakmann 1995: 216–20.
[32] Compare the diatribes of Teles, which no one doubts Teles penned himself.

The most important modern editions are, first, that of Hieronymus Wolf, published in Basel between 1560 and 1563, which included a Latin translation and commentary. The five-volume edition of Johannes Schweighäuser (1799–1800) represented a milestone in Epictetan studies. It comprised a new Greek text with Latin translation, a commentary, an edition with translation of Simplicius' commentary on the *Enchiridion*, and a commentary, in turn, on Simplicius. The commentary on the *Discourses* in the second volume has some of the qualities of a variorum edition, and helpfully incorporates many of Wolf's notes. My few citations of Wolf derive from these cross-references.

The edition of Heinrich Schenkl in the Teubner series (1894, 2nd edn. 1916) marked a decisive advance in being the first based on S. Its value is enhanced by the inclusion of an *index verborum* that in coverage and attention to detail is a monument of scholarship and an essential tool for anyone doing serious work on E. All my references to Schenkl are to the 1916 edition. William Oldfather's Loeb edition (1925–8) is based on the text of Schenkl, but displays some welcome independence. The Budé version of Joseph Souilhé (1948–65) maintains the high editorial standards that E has commanded in modern times. It is notable for the number of its emendations. The editor realized that S, although the most authoritative MS, is frequently corrupt.

The text of E remains in need of work; for an example of what can still be accomplished, see Radt 1990: 368–73. My few textual notes are intended to contribute modestly to that effort, in addition to indicating in doubtful cases what text the translation assumes.

E has been as fortunate in his translators as in his editors. My translation is original. But I have consulted those of Elizabeth Carter, Oldfather, Souilhé, Cesare Cassanmagnano, and Robin Hard. And I am occasionally indebted to all of them. In general, my translation tries to steer a middle course between literalness and fluency. In this connection, one element in E's vocabulary deserves special mention. 'Prohairesis' is a key term of E's ethics, but, depending on context, can be rendered in various ways. 'Moral character' or 'choice' are the translations I favour, but part of the power of the word is its polyvalence, and different renderings have been resorted to as needed. In most cases the commentary alerts the reader to the appearance of the word in the original Greek.

TRANSLATION

CHAPTER 1

Concerning What Is In Our Power and What Is Not

[1] Among capacities in general you will find none that is self-critical, and therefore none that is self-approving or self-disapproving either. [2] To what extent is the art of grammar critical? Only so far as judging literature is concerned. Music? Only so far as judging song. [3] So does either of them criticize itself? Not at all. Now, if you are writing to a friend, grammar will tell you that you require such-and-such letters; but whether you should write to your friend in the first place, grammar will not say. Music is no different in regard to song. Whether you should sing now and play the lyre, or not sing and not play, it will not say. [4] What, then, will? The faculty that examines both itself and all the rest. And what is that? The faculty of reason. For it alone takes thought for itself, what it is, what it can do, and how valuable it has come to be—as well as taking thought for other faculties. [5] For what else says that a piece of gold is beautiful? It does not say so itself. Obviously, it must be the faculty that uses such impressions. [6] What else is there that judges music, grammar, and the other arts, evaluating their uses and deciding when to use them? Nothing.

[7] As was fitting, therefore, the gods have put in our power only the supreme and most powerful thing, the power of making correct use of impressions. The others they did not put under our control. [8] Was it because they refused? For my part, I think that, had they been able, they would have entrusted us with the others too. But they were completely unable. [9] For since we are on earth, and tied to such a body and such associates, how was it possible in respect of these things not to be hindered by externals? [10] But what says Zeus? 'Epictetus, if it were possible, I would have made both your body and your possessions free and unimpeded. [11] But as it is, make no mistake, the body is not yours, but is clay cunningly compounded. [12] And since I could not give you this, I have given you a part of myself, the power of impulse and repulsion, of desire and avoidance—in a word, the power of using impressions. If you care for this and put your interest there, you will never be impeded,

never thwarted; you will not groan, will not blame or flatter anyone. [13] Well, does this seem insignificant to you?' 'Far from it.' 'Are you, then, content with this?' 'I pray to the gods that I may be.'

[14] But although we can care for, and attach ourselves to, one thing only, we choose instead to care for and cling to many things: the body, possessions, brother, friend, child, slave. [15] And being tied to many things, we are weighed down and dragged along with them. [16] And so, if the weather forbids us to sail, we sit down and fidget and keep peering about. 'What wind is blowing?' 'The north wind.' 'What good is that to us? When will the west wind blow?' 'When it wants to, or when it pleases Aeolus. For god has not made you steward of the winds, but Aeolus.' [17] 'What, then, must we do?' 'Make the best of what is in our power, and use the rest according to its nature.' 'And what is its nature?' 'However god wishes it.'

[18] 'Must I be beheaded now, and alone?' Well, would you like everyone to be beheaded so that you can feel better? [19] Won't you hold out your neck as Lateranus did at Rome, when ordered by Nero to be beheaded? For he held out his neck and was struck, but since the blow was weak, he shrank back a little, then stuck it out again. [20] And also before that, when Epaphroditus the freedman of Nero approached a certain man and asked him about the grounds of his offence, the man replied: 'If I wish anything, I will inform your master.'

[21] What should we have ready at hand in such circumstances? What else but knowledge of what is mine and what is not mine, what I can do and what I cannot do? [22] I must die. But must I die groaning? I must be fettered. And crying too? I must be exiled; but does anyone keep me from going with a smile, cheerful and serene? [23] 'Reveal your secrets.' I refuse, for this is in my power. 'But I will fetter you.' What do you mean, man? My leg you will fetter, but not even Zeus can conquer my moral choice. [24] 'I will throw you into prison.' My body, you will. 'I will behead you.' Did I ever say that my neck was the only neck that couldn't be severed? [25] These are the things you ought to practise if you study philosophy, these the things you ought to write down every day, and exercise yourself in.

[26] Thrasea used to say, 'I would rather be killed today than banished tomorrow.' [27] What did Rufus say to him? 'If you choose death because it is the heavier of two evils, what folly of choice! But if as the lighter, who has given it to you? Are you not willing to

practise being content with what has been given you?' [28] And
what was it Agrippinus used to say? 'I am not a hindrance to myself.'
Someone told him, 'You are being tried in the Senate. Good luck.'
[29] But it was eleven in the morning, and he was in the habit of
taking a cold bath and exercising at that hour. 'Let us be off and
exercise.' [30] Someone told him as he was exercising that he had
been condemned. 'To exile', he said, 'or death?' 'To exile.' 'And
my estate, what of that?' 'It has not been confiscated.' 'Well then,
let us go to Aricia and lunch there.' [31] This is what it means to
have practised what ought to be practised, to render desire and
aversion free from any injury or mishap. [32] I must die. If now,
then I die; if later, then now I will lunch, since the hour for lunch
has arrived—and I will die later. How? As befits one who is returning what belongs to another.

CHAPTER 2

How a Man May Preserve his Proper Character in Every Circumstance

[1] To the rational animal the only unbearable thing is what is
unreasonable, while what is reasonable is bearable. [2] Blows are
not by nature unbearable. 'How so?' Just consider: Spartans are
whipped having once learned that it is reasonable. [3] 'But to be
hanged—isn't that unbearable?' Well, whenever one feels that it is
reasonable, he goes and hangs himself. [4] In short, if we pay attention, we will find mankind distressed by nothing so much as by the
unreasonable, and attracted to nothing so much as the reasonable.

[5] But different people consider different things reasonable and
unreasonable, just as with things good and bad, or profitable and
unprofitable. [6] It is for this reason especially that we need education, to learn how to bring our preconception of the reasonable and
unreasonable into conformity with nature. [7] But for this we consult not only the value of externals, but also what is in accordance
with our character. [8] For one person it is reasonable to hold a
chamber-pot, since he only considers that, if he does not, he will be
beaten and deprived of food, whereas if he does hold it, nothing

harsh or painful will happen to him. [9] But for another man it is not only unendurable to hold the thing himself, he cannot even bear that someone else should do it. [10] If you ask me, then, 'Shall I hold the pot or not?', I will tell you that getting food is preferable to being deprived of it, and being whipped is worse than not being whipped. So that if you compare your interests by these criteria, then go ahead and hold the pot. [11] 'But it would not be worthy of me.' That is an additional consideration which you alone bring to the question, not me. You are the one who knows yourself, how much you are worth in your own eyes, and at what price you sell yourself. For different men sell themselves at different prices.

[12] For this reason, when Florus was wondering whether to enter Nero's festival and make a personal contribution, Agrippinus said to him, 'Enter.' [13] And when Florus asked, 'Why don't you enter yourself?', he answered, 'I do not even consider the possibility.' [14] For when a man once stoops to the consideration of such questions as the value of externals, he is close to having forgotten his own proper character. [15] What is it you ask me? Is death or life preferable? I answer, Life. Pain or pleasure? I answer, Pleasure. [16] 'But unless I take part in the tragedy, I will be beheaded.' Go ahead then, and participate—but I refuse. [17] Why? Because you regard yourself as merely one thread in the robe. Consequently, your job is to consider how to conform with other men, just as the white thread does not wish to appear in any way conspicuous in relation to the other threads. [18] But I want to be the purple, that small and brilliant part that causes the rest to appear fair and attractive. Why, then, do you say to me, 'Be like the rest'? For how in that case could I be the purple any more?

[19] Helvidius Priscus saw this, and having seen it, acted on it. When Vespasian sent him word not to enter the Senate, he replied: 'You can disqualify me as a Senator, but so long as I remain one, I must enter.' [20] 'Well then, enter, but keep quiet.' 'Do not ask me for my opinion, and I will keep quiet.' 'But I must ask you for your opinion.' 'And I must answer what seems to me right.' [21] 'Yes, but if you speak, I will kill you.' 'When did I ever say that I was immortal? You will do your part, and I mine. It is yours to put me to death, mine to die without flinching; yours to exile me, mine to depart without complaining.' [22] What good, then, did Priscus accomplish, who was but a single man? Well, what good does the purple do to the robe? What else, but that it stands out conspicuous

in it as purple, and represents a good example to the rest? [23] If Caesar had told another man in such circumstances not to enter the Senate, he would have said: 'I am grateful that you can spare me.' [24] Such a man, in fact, the emperor would not even have kept from entering, knowing that he would either sit like a jug or, if he did speak, would say only what he knew Caesar wanted to hear, and would pile on more besides.

[25] A certain athlete, at risk of dying unless his genitals were amputated, acted similarly. When his brother, who was a philosopher, approached and asked him, 'Well, brother, what do you intend to do? Are we going to cut off this part, and once again enter the gymnasium?,' he refused to submit, but steeled himself and died. [26] When someone asked, 'How did he do this, as an athlete or as a philosopher?,' Epictetus replied: 'As a man—one who had performed and been acclaimed at the Olympic games, who was at home in such a place, not just rubbed down at Bato's wrestling school.' [27] But another would even have had his neck cut off, if he could have lived without his neck. [28] This is what it means to have consideration for one's character, so great is its weight with those accustomed to introduce it into their deliberations. [29] 'Come Epictetus, shave off your beard.' 'If I am a philosopher, I will not shave it off.' 'But I will cut off your neck.' 'If that will do you any good, then do so.'

[30] Someone asked: 'How then shall each of us become aware of what is in keeping with our character?' How is it that the bull, when the lion attacks, alone perceives his own capacities, and thrusts himself forward to protect the whole herd? Or isn't it clear that along with the possession of a certain capacity comes the awareness thereof? [31] So whoever of us has such a capacity will not be unaware of it. [32] But a bull does not become a bull all at once, any more than a man becomes heroic. He must put up with a winter training, must prepare himself, instead of jumping rashly into situations that do not become him.

[33] Only consider at what price you sell your freedom of will. If nothing else, man, at least don't sell it cheap. The great and exceptional thing perhaps belongs to others, to Socrates and his kind. [34] 'Why, then, if we are endowed by nature for such greatness, do we not all achieve it?' Well, do all horses become fast? Are all dogs hunters? [35] What then—if I lack talent, should I for that reason give up the effort? [36] By no means. Epictetus will not be better

than Socrates. But if I am no worse, that is enough for me. [37] For I will not be Milo either, and nevertheless I do not neglect my body. Nor will I be Croesus, and nevertheless I don't neglect my possessions. In a word, we do not abandon any discipline out of despair of becoming the best.

CHAPTER 3

From the Thesis that God is the Father of Mankind, How May One Proceed to the Consequences?

[1] If one could whole-heartedly believe, in the way one should, that we are all primary creatures of god, and that god is father of both gods and men, I imagine that he will think nothing mean or lowly about himself. [2] If Caesar adopts you, no one will put up with your pretension; but if you know that you are the son of god, will you not be elated? [3] But as it is, we do nothing of the sort. But since these two elements have been conjoined in our creation, the body, which we have in common with animals, and mind and reason, which we have in common with the gods, some incline to the former relationship, miserable and mortal, while a few incline toward this divine and blessed one.

[4] Since it is necessary that every man should treat each thing in accordance with his beliefs about it, those few who think that they are born for fidelity, respect, and assurance in the use of impressions entertain no mean or ignoble thoughts about themselves. Most people, however, do just the opposite. [5] 'What am I? A miserable little man.' And, 'My poor, wretched flesh!' [6] Wretched indeed, but you also have something superior to the flesh. Why then do you abandon this, and cleave to that?

[7] Because of this kinship, some of us incline to it and become like wolves, faithless, treacherous, and vicious; others like lions, wild, savage, and untamed. But most of us become like foxes, the sorriest of the lot. [8] For what else is a slanderous, malicious man than a fox, or something even meaner and less dignified? [9] Take care, then, and see to it that you do not turn out like one of these pitiful creatures.

CHAPTER 4

On Progress

[1] He who is making progress, having learned from the philosophers that desire is for good things and avoidance is toward bad things, and having also learned that impassivity and a good flow of life are not otherwise attained than through unerring desire and unfailing avoidance—such a person has removed desire from himself altogether, or else deferred it to another time, and exercises avoidance only toward things within the sphere of choice. [2] For if he tries to avoid anything outside the sphere of choice, he knows that sooner or later he will stumble on to something contrary to his aversion, and come to grief. [3] But if virtue holds this promise—to secure happiness, impassivity, and a good flow of life—then progress toward virtue must surely be progress toward each of these other states as well. [4] For wherever the perfection of something tends, progress is always an approach toward the same thing.

[5] How, then, do we acknowledge virtue to be a thing of this sort, and yet seek and display progress in other things? What is the product of virtue? A good flow of life. [6] Who, then, is making progress? The man who has read many of Chrysippus' books? [7] Is virtue no more than this, to have made the acquaintance of Chrysippus? For if this is what it is, then progress is admittedly nothing other than learning a lot of Chrysippus. [8] But we are now agreed that virtue produces one thing, while declaring that the approach to it, progress, is something else. [9] 'This person is already able to read Chrysippus by himself.' You are making good progress, by the gods—progress indeed! [10] 'Why do you mock him?' And why do you distract him from the consciousness of his own faults? Are you not willing to show him the product of virtue, that he might know where to look for progress? [11] Seek it there, poor fellow, where your work lies. And where is your work? In desire and avoidance, that you may not fail of your desires or fall into what you would avoid; in impulse and repulsion, that you may not err; in attention and suspension of judgement, that you may become infallible. [12] But the first topics are the first and most

necessary. If you seek to be faultless while trembling and moaning, how are you making progress?

[13] Show me, then, evidence of your progress. Just as if I were talking to an athlete and said, 'Show me your shoulders,' and he said, 'Look at my jumping weights.' Get out of here with you and your jumping weights! I want to see the end result of the jumping weights. [14] 'Take the treatise *On Impulse* and see how well I have read it.' Slave, that is not what I am looking for, but how you actually use impulse and repulsion, desire and avoidance; how you apply yourself, prepare yourself, and practise intention; whether it is in accordance with nature or not. [15] If you are acting in harmony, show me that, and I will say that you are making progress. Otherwise, be off, and besides commenting on books, write such a book yourself. [16] And what will you gain thereby? Don't you know that a whole book costs five denarii? Is the commentator, then, worth more than five denarii? [17] Never look for your work in one place and your progress in another.

[18] Where, then, is progress? If any of you renounces externals and turns his attention to his moral character, cultivating and perfecting it, so as to bring it in line with nature: elevated, free, unhindered, unimpeded, trustworthy, and honourable; [19] and has learned that whoever desires or avoids things not in his power can be neither faithful nor free, but must of necessity shift and fluctuate right along with them, and must subject himself to other people who can furnish or deprive him of these things; [20] and if, again, from the time he gets up in the morning, he keeps and preserves these tenets, bathing as a faithful man, eating as an honourable man, in every situation equally practising his principles as the runner does when he applies the principles of running, or a singer those of musicianship. [21] This, then, is the man who in truth is making progress, and has not left home in vain.

[22] But if he is wholly intent on reading books and works only at that, and has left home for it, I tell him to return home at once and not neglect his affairs there, [23] for the goal to which he has set out is nothing. But this is the proper goal, to practise how to remove from one's life sorrows and laments, and cries of 'Alas' and 'Poor me', and misfortune and disappointment; [24] and to learn what death is, and exile, and prison, and hemlock, in order to be able to say while in prison, 'Dear Crito, if this is how the gods want it, then let it be so,' instead of 'Poor me, an old man, did I keep my grey

hairs for this?' [25] Who says such things? Do you suppose that
I will name someone humble or obscure? Does not Priam say it?
Does not Oedipus say it? All kings say it. [26] For what else are
tragedies but the sufferings of men who have admired externals,
rendered in this or that kind of verse? [27] If one had to be deceived
in order to learn that of externals and things outside our power none
concern us, I for one would consent to a deception from which I
would live with a smooth current of life and without annoyance.
What you prefer you will see for yourself.

[28] What, then, does Chrysippus provide us with? 'That you
may know', he says, 'that these things are not false which issue in
the good flow of life and impassivity, [29] take my books and you
will know how conformable and harmonious with nature are the
things that render me impassive.' The great good fortune! The
great benefactor who has pointed the way! [30] Now, to Triptolemus
all men have set up altars because he has given us cultivated foods;
[31] but to him who has discovered and illuminated the truth and
brought it forth for all men—not the truth that pertains just to
living, but to living well—who of you has set up an altar, or a
temple, or erected a statue, or venerated god, for that? [32] Because
the gods gave us the vine, or barley, we offer them sacrifice. But
because they brought forth such fruit in the human mind, whereby
they intended to show us the truth about happiness—shall we fail
to render god thanks for that?

CHAPTER 5

Against the Academics

[1] If a man objects to truths that are all too evident, it is not easy
to find an argument with which to change his mind. [2] This is due
neither to his strength nor to the teacher's weakness. When a man
caught in an argument hardens to stone, how can you reason with
him any longer? [3] Now there are two kinds of petrifaction: that of
the intellect and that of the sense of shame, when a man assumes a
belligerent stance, resolved neither to assent to self-evident truths
nor to leave the combatants. [4] Most of us dread the deadening of

the body, and will do anything to avoid it. But about the deadening of the soul we do not care at all. [5] Even in the case of the soul, we regard a man as badly off if he cannot follow or comprehend anything. But if his sense of shame and respect are deadened, we go so far as to call this strength of character.

[6] 'Do you apprehend that you are awake?' 'No, no more than when I dream and have the impression that I am awake.' 'Does one impression differ in no way from the other?' 'None.' [7] Can I reason with such a person any longer? What fire or iron can I apply to him, to make him aware that he is deadened? He senses it, but pretends he does not: he is even worse off than a corpse.

[8] One man does not notice the contradiction; he is badly off. Another man notices it, but is not moved and does not make progress; [9] he is even worse off. His sense of respect and shame have been excised, and his reason—not excised, but brutalized. [10] Am I to call this strength of character? Far from it, unless I am to call by the same name the strength of catamites that permits them to say and do in public whatever they please.

CHAPTER 6

On Providence

[1] From everything that happens in the universe it is easy to praise providence, if one has within him two things: the faculty of taking a comprehensive view of the things that happen to each person and a sense of gratitude. [2] Otherwise, one man will not see the usefulness of what has happened, and another, even supposing that he does see it, will not be grateful for it. [3] If god had made colours, but had not fashioned the faculty of sight, what good would it have been? None at all. [4] Conversely, if he had made the faculty, but not made objects in such a way as to be amenable to the power of sight, in that case too, what good would it have been? None at all. [5] And if he had indeed made both of these, but had not made light? Even then, it would have been of little use. [6] Who, then, has fitted that to this and this to that? And who has fitted the sword to the scabbard, the scabbard to the sword—no one? [7] But from the construction of manufactured objects we are accustomed to state

that the work is certainly that of some craftsman, and has not been constructed at random. [8] Does each of these, then, proclaim its craftsman, while visible things and sight and light do not? [9] And the male and the female, and the passion of each one for intercourse with the other, and the faculty that uses the parts constructed for this purpose—do these not reveal their craftsman, too?

[10] Well, so much for these examples. But the constitution of the intellect, whereby when we meet with sensible objects, we do not merely have their forms imprinted upon us, but also make a selection from among them, and subtract and add, and make these sorts of combinations through them, and, what is more, pass from certain things to others somehow connected—are not even these sufficient to impress people, and induce them not to leave a craftsman out of account? [11] Or, let them explain to us what causes each of these things, and how it is possible for objects so wonderful and so craftsmanlike to come into being randomly and haphazardly.

[12] Well, then, is it in our case alone that these things are found? Many indeed are the things found in our case alone, of which the rational animal had peculiar need; but you will also find many in common between us and the irrational animals. [13] Do they also, then, understand what happens? By no means. For use is one thing, understanding another. God had need of animals that use impressions; he had need of us because we understand their use. [14] And so for them it is enough to eat, drink, sleep, copulate, and whatever else satisfies members of their kind. But for us, to whom he also gave the faculty of understanding, [15] such things are not enough. Unless we act appropriately, systematically, and conformably with our nature and constitution, we will not gain our respective ends. [16] For of beings whose constitutions are different, the functions and ends diverge correspondingly. [17] So for the being whose constitution is made for use alone, mere use suffices; but where the capacity to understand their use supervenes, unless this faculty be exercised, the being will fail to attain its end. [18] And so of animals, one is constituted by god to be eaten, another to serve in farming, another to produce cheese, another for some other, related service. To perform such functions, what need do they have of understanding external impressions and being able to differentiate among them? [19] But god has brought man into the world to be a spectator of himself and of his works, and not merely a spectator, but an interpreter too. [20] Therefore it is disgraceful for man to

begin and end where animals do. He should begin where they do, but end where nature has fixed his end. [21] Now, she ended with contemplation and understanding, and a manner of life in conformity with nature. [22] See to it, then, that you do not die having never been a spectator of these things.

[23] But you travel to Olympia to behold the work of Pheidias, and you each regard it as a misfortune to die without seeing such sights. [24] But when there is no need to travel at all, and where you are already, and Zeus is present in his works—will you not desire to contemplate *these* things and understand them? [25] Will you never perceive either who you are, or for what you have been born, or the purpose for which this vision has been given to you? [26] 'But some unpleasant and difficult things happen in life.' And don't they happen in Olympia? Don't you grow hot? Aren't you crowded? Don't you bathe poorly? Don't you get soaked when it rains? Don't you have your fill of noise and shouting, and other discomforts? [27] But I imagine that, setting all this beside the value of the spectacle, you endure and put up with it.

[28] Haven't you received faculties that enable you to bear whatever happens? Have you not got magnanimity? Courage? [29] Have you not received the power of endurance? And why should I care any longer about whatever happens if I have magnanimity? What will upset or disturb me, or seem annoying? Will I fail to use my faculty to that end for which I have received it, but groan instead and lament over events as they occur? [30] 'Yes, but my nose is running.' What have you hands for, slave? Is it not that you may wipe your nose? [31] 'Is it reasonable, then, that there should be running noses in the world?' [32] And how much better for you to wipe it, than find fault!

Or how do you think Heracles would have turned out, if such a lion had not appeared, and a hydra, and a stag, and a boar, and certain vicious and savage men, whom he drove out and cleared the world of? [33] And what would he have been doing in the absence of such enemies? Is it not obvious that he would have wrapped himself in a blanket and slept? In the first place, then, he would never have become Heracles while snoring away his whole life in luxury and ease. And even if he had, what good would it have done him? [34] What would have been the use of those arms of his, and of his strength in general, of his endurance and nobility, if there had not been such circumstances and occasions to stir and excite him? [35] Well, but should he have furnished these himself, and searched for a lion to bring into his country, and a boar and a hydra? [36] That would have been foolishness and idiocy. But when they were found and did appear, they proved useful to show off and exercise Heracles.

[37] Come then, now that you are aware of all this, contemplate the faculties that you have, and having done that, say: 'Bring, Zeus, what circumstance you please. For I have a constitution given me by you and resources to distinguish myself whatever comes to pass.' [38] But no. You sit fearful lest certain things happen, lamenting, grieving, and groaning about whatever is already taking place. And then you reproach the gods. [39] For what else can be the consequence of such meanness of spirit than impiety? [40] And yet god has not merely given us faculties with which we can bear all that happens without being humbled or broken, but, as befitted a king and a true father, he has given them to us free from restraint, compulsion, and hindrance. He has put the whole matter in our control, without even reserving to himself any power to prevent or hinder. [41] Although you have these faculties free and entirely your own, you do not use them; nor do you realize what you have, and from whom. [42] Instead, you sit moaning and complaining, some of you blinded toward the giver, not acknowledging your benefactor; others directing accusations and complaints against god from sheer meanness of spirit. [43] And yet I will show you that you have resources and a disposition for courage and magnanimity; show me in turn what grounds you have for censure and laying blame.

CHAPTER 7

On the Utility of Changing Arguments, Hypothetical Arguments, and the Like

[1] Most men do not know that attention to changing and hypothetical arguments and those that conclude by way of questioning, and to all such arguments generally, has a bearing on proper function. [2] For we look for how the good man will behave and acquit himself correctly in every matter. [3] Let them therefore say that the good man will not submit to question and answer, or, if he does,

that he will not care whether in questioning and answering he behaves carelessly or at random. [4] Or if they do not accept either alternative, they must concede that we should investigate the topics with which question and answer are chiefly concerned.

[5] For what does reason purport to do? Establish what is true, eliminate what is false, and suspend judgement about what is doubtful. [6] Is it enough, then, to learn this only? 'It is enough,' one says. Well, is it enough if you wish to avoid error in the use of money, to be told to accept genuine drachmas, and reject counterfeit ones? 'It is not enough.' [7] What more is necessary? 'What else but a faculty of testing and distinguishing genuine drachmas from counterfeit ones?' [8] And so too in the case of reason, in addition to what was said, it is also necessary to learn how to test and distinguish what is true, false, and unclear. 'It is necessary.' [9] What else does reason purport to do? 'Accept the consequences of what you have correctly granted.' [10] Then is it enough, in this case too, to know this? 'It is not enough, but one must learn how one thing is consequent upon another, and how sometimes something follows one thing, and sometimes it follows several things together.' [11] Then surely this too must be acquired by the man intent on acquitting himself intelligently in matters of reason—both when he undertakes to define and demonstrate each point himself, and when he follows the demonstrations of others, refusing to be misled when they utter sophisms as though they were proving something. [12] And so there has developed among us study and training in conclusive arguments and logical schemata, which have proved necessary.

[13] Now, there are cases where we have rightly granted the premisses, and such-and-such is the result; although it is false, it is nevertheless the result. [14] What, then, is it appropriate for me to do? [15] Accept the falsehood? How can I? Say I erred in granting the premisses? That is not allowed either. Say it does not result from what was granted? But neither is this allowed. [16] What, then, should I do in such cases? Well, just as it is not enough to have borrowed money to establish that you are still in debt, but you must still stand by the loan, and it must not be repaid yet; so in this case it is not enough to have granted the premisses to establish that we must allow the conclusion: we must stand by what was granted. [17] Now, if the premisses remain what they were when we granted them, then we are under every necessity of abiding by what was granted and accepting the consequences. [18] But if they do not

remain as they were, we can refuse to accept them. [19] For this conclusion no longer holds for us, nor is it appropriate to us, since we have retracted our concession of the premises. [20] Therefore, we ought to study premises of this kind, in particular their changes and alterations, such that in the very process of questioning, answering, drawing conclusions, and the like, they undergo modifications and cause the ignorant to become confused when they don't see what follows. [21] Why? So as not to behave in this matter in an inappropriate, haphazard, or chaotic manner.

[22] It is the same with hypotheses and hypothetical arguments. It is sometimes necessary to posit a hypothesis as a basis for the subsequent argument. [23] Then, should we grant every hypothesis that is proposed, or not? [24] And if not every one, then which ones? And once we have admitted a hypothesis, should we abide by the admission come what may, or should we sometimes repudiate it? Should we accept what is consistent with it, and reject what is in conflict? 'Yes.' [25] But someone says, 'I will make you accept the hypothesis of something possible and lead you on to an impossibility.' Will the wise man refuse to engage with such a person, and avoid all examination and joint discussion? [26] Who but he, though, is adept in argument, expert in question and answer, and proof against sophisms and deceit? [27] Or will he engage with him, but take no thought for how to avoid comporting himself in argument recklessly and at random? How, then, will he be the sort of man we imagine him to be? [28] But in default of such training and preparation, can he maintain coherence in argument? [29] Let them show that he can, and all these principles become superfluous; they are absurd and inconsistent with our preconception of a good man.

[30] Why are we still lazy, indifferent, and dull? And why do we look for excuses not to toil and work on our own reason? [31] 'Why, if I err in such matters, I haven't killed my father, have I?' No, slave, for there was no father there for you to kill. What, then, did you do? You committed the only mistake there was to commit. [32] For you know, I myself once said that to Rufus when he reproached me for not discovering the omission in a certain syllogism. I said, 'It's not like I burned down the Capitol.' And he said, 'Slave, the omission here *is* the Capitol.' [33] Or are these the only crimes, burning down the Capitol and killing your father? But to use one's impressions recklessly, carelessly, and at random, to fail to analyse an argument as either valid proof or fallacy, and, in a word, not to see what is

appropriate and inappropriate in one's own case in the matter of
questioning and answering—is there no blame in all of this?

CHAPTER 8

That Capacities are Treacherous for the Uneducated

[1] In as many ways as it is possible to vary terms that are equivalent to each other, in just so many is it possible to vary the forms of
proofs and enthymemes in arguments. [2] Like in this way: 'If you
borrowed money and did not repay, you owe me the money'; 'it is
not the case that you borrowed and did not repay and yet do not
owe me the money.' [3] And no one should do this more capably
than the philosopher. For if the enthymeme is an incomplete syllogism, it is plain that he who has been trained in the complete
syllogism must be no less adept in the incomplete one.

[4] 'Why, then, do we not train ourselves and each other in this
argument?' [5] Because at present, although we are not trained in
these matters, or distracted from the study of morals (by me, at any
rate), still we make no progress toward moral virtue. [6] What, then,
must we expect, if we should adopt this additional pursuit, particularly as this would not only be a pursuit that would distract us from
more necessary studies, but would also be no small cause of vanity
and presumption? [7] For the power of proof and persuasion is great,
especially if it should be trained, and acquire in addition a certain
elegance of language. [8] In general, every capacity when acquired
by the weak and uneducated carries with it the danger of making
them arrogant and conceited. [9] For what means remain to persuade
a young man who excels in these matters not to become an append-
age to them, but they to him? [10] Will he not trample on all such
advice, and strut before us elated and puffed up, not enduring it
if anyone should take hold of him and remind him what he has
abandoned and where he has erred?

[11] 'Well, then, wasn't Plato a philosopher?' Yes, and wasn't
Hippocrates a physician? 'But you see how Hippocrates expresses
himself.' [12] Yet, is it in respect of being a physician that Hippocrates expresses himself so well? Why, then, do you confuse qualities
that are incidentally united in the same people? [13] If Plato had

been handsome and strong, should I also strive and endeavour to become handsome or strong, as if this were necessary for philosophy, since a certain philosopher was at the same time handsome and a philosopher? [14] Are you not prepared to see and distinguish in what respect men become philosophers, and what qualities pertain to them incidentally? If I, for instance, were a philosopher, would you too have to become lame? [15] Well, then, do I make light of these capacities? Not at all; no more than I do the capacity of sight. [16] But if you enquire of me what the good is in man's case, I can tell you only that it is moral character of a certain kind.

CHAPTER 9

How from the Fact that We are Akin to God Should One Proceed to the Consequences?

[1] If what is said by the philosophers concerning the kinship of god and men is true, what other course remains for men than to do as Socrates did, never replying to anyone who asked him where he was from, 'I am Athenian', or 'I am Corinthian', but, 'I am a citizen of the world'. [2] For why say, 'I am Athenian', rather than just name the corner where your miserable body was thrown at birth? [3] Or is it clear that you prefer the superior designation that includes not only that corner, but your whole family, and all the ancestry that preceded you, and on this basis call yourself Athenian, or Corinthian? [4] Anyone, though, who has come to understand the administration of the universe, has learnèd that the supreme and greatest and most inclusive government is the one composed of men and god. He knows that from god have descended the seeds of being, not only to his father or grandfather, but to all things born and engendered on the earth, but chiefly to rational beings, [5] since they alone are equipped by nature to share in god's society, being entwined with him through reason. [6] And why shouldn't he call himself a citizen of the world and a descendant of god? And why will he fear anything that happens? [7] Is kinship with Caesar or any of the other great ones at Rome sufficient to live in security and honour, fearing nothing, while having god as our maker and father and caretaker—won't this deliver us from grief and fear?

[8] 'And how am I to eat, if I have nothing?' And what about slaves, what about fugitives—what is it they put their trust in when they desert their masters? In their lands, their servants, their silver plate? No, in themselves instead. And yet they do not lack for food. [9] And will our philosopher be forced to depend on others to shelter him when he goes abroad, instead of relying on himself? And will he be worse off and more cowardly than beasts, who are all self-sufficient and supplied with proper food and the way of life appropriate to, and in agreement with, their nature?

[10] But I for my part think that the older man should not be sitting here plotting how to keep you from thinking small, or reaching mean and humble conclusions about yourselves. [11] Rather, if there are young men among you who appreciate their kinship with the gods, and realize that we have these chains fastened upon us— the body, possessions, and whatever for their sake are required for our maintenance and sustenance in life—I should be keeping them from the desire to get rid of all these things as so many worthless and bothersome encumbrances, and return to their kind. [12] And this is the effort that ought to absorb your teacher and mentor, if he really were one. And for your part you would come to him saying, 'Epictetus, we can no longer endure being tied to this poor body, giving it food and drink, resting and cleaning it, and having to associate with these people and those on account of it. [13] Are not such things indifferent, and nothing to us? And is not death no evil? Aren't we akin to god, and haven't we come from him? [14] Let us return from where we came, let us be freed, finally, from these chains that encumber us and weigh us down. [15] Here we find robbers and thieves and courts, and tyrants, so-called: they imagine that they have some power over us because of our poor body and its possessions. Let us show them that they have power over no one.' [16] Then it would be my part to say: 'Men, wait upon god. Whenever he gives the sign and frees you from this service, then you are free to return to him. But for now be content to remain in the place where he has stationed you. [17] Short indeed is the time of your sojourn, and easy for those of your convictions. For what tyrant, thief, or court of law can daunt those who make so little of the body and its possessions? Stay, do not depart on unreasonable grounds.'

[18] Some such advice ought to pass from a teacher to the youth of good parts. [19] But as it is, what happens? A corpse is your

teacher, and corpses are you. Whenever you have eaten your fill today, you sit whining about tomorrow, where your food will come from. [20] Slave, if you get it, you will have it; otherwise you will depart this life: the door stands open. Why do you grieve? What place is there anymore for tears? What occasion for flattery? Why should one man envy another? Why should he admire those who have many possessions, or those in power, especially if they be strong and prone to anger? [21] For what will they do for us? The things they have power to do will be of no concern to us; and as for the things we care about, these they are powerless to affect. Who, then, will rule over someone with such convictions? [22] How did Socrates stand in regard to these matters? How else than as one convinced of his kinship to the gods. [23] 'If you say to me now,' he said, ' "We will release you on these conditions, that you no longer engage in these dialogues that you have engaged in thus far, nor give trouble to our young men and our old," [24] I will answer that it is absurd to suppose that, if a general of yours stationed me at a post, I should maintain and defend it, choosing to die a thousand times rather than desert it, but if god has stationed us to a certain place and way of life, we ought to abandon that.' [25] This is a man who was a kinsman of the gods indeed. [26] But we think of ourselves as bellies, entrails, and genitals, because we have fear, we have desires. We flatter those able to assist us in such matters, and we fear them.

[27] A certain man asked me to write to Rome for him because he had met with what most people consider misfortune. Whereas he had once been distinguished and rich, later he lost everything, and was living here. And I wrote on his behalf in a submissive manner. [28] But when he had read the letter, he handed it back to me, saying, 'I wanted your help, not your pity; nothing really bad has befallen me.' [29] Similarly, Rufus used to test me by saying, 'Your master is going to do thus and such to you.' [30] And when I would reply, 'Such is the lot of man,' he would say, 'Will I still petition him when I can get the same things from you?' [31] For in fact it is foolish and vain to try and obtain from another what one can get from oneself. [32] Since, therefore, I can get greatness of soul and nobility from myself, am I to get a farm and money, or some office, from you? No, I will not be so insensible of what I myself possess. [33] But when a man is timid and cowardly, what else is there to do but write letters on his behalf as if he were dead? 'Please grant

us the body of so-and-so together with his paltry pint of blood.'
[34] For, really, such a person is but a carcass and a pint of blood,
nothing more. If he were anything more, he would realize that no
man is ever unfortunate because of another.

CHAPTER 10

To Those who have Applied Themselves
to Advancement at Rome

[1] If we philosophers had applied ourselves to our activity as earn-
estly as those old men in Rome do to their interests, perhaps we too
would be getting somewhere. [2] For I personally know a man older
than myself who is now in charge of the grain supply in Rome.
When he passed through here on his return from exile, what things
he said to me as he ran down his former life, proclaiming that,
when he got back, he would in future apply himself to nothing
more than spending the rest of his life in peace and tranquillity.
'For how much time, in fact, remains for me?' [3] And I used to say
to him, 'You won't do it. As soon as you get a whiff of Rome, you
will forget all this.' And I added that if the least access to court were
granted him, he would push his way in joyfully, giving thanks to
god. [4] 'Epictetus,' he said, 'if you find me putting even one foot
inside the court, think as little of me as you please.' [5] What, then,
did he do? Before he arrived in Rome, letters from Caesar reached
him. He no sooner received them than he forgot all those things,
and since then it's been one thing after another. [6] I wish I could
stand by him now and remind him of the words he said while
passing through here, and add, 'How much more clever a prophet I
am than you!'

[7] What then am I saying? That man is an animal unfit for
action? Not at all. But why are we not active ourselves? [8] Take
me, for instance. When day begins, I remind myself a little what
author I am to read. Then I think to myself: 'But what does it matter
how so-and-so reads? First let me get my sleep!' [9] And yet what
comparison is there between the affairs of those men and ours? If
you pay attention to what they do, you will see. And what is that

but voting on resolutions, consulting together, deliberating about a bit of grain, a patch of land, or other such sources of profit? [10] Is it the same thing, then, to receive a petition from someone that reads, 'Please allow me to export a bit of grain,' and this: 'Please learn from Chrysippus what the administration of the universe is, and what place the rational animal has in it. Consider, too, who you are, and what the good and evil in your case is.' [11] Is this to be compared with that? Do they demand the same amount of application? [12] Is it equally shameful to neglect the one as the other?

Well, are we the only ones who are lazy and nonchalant? [13] No, you young men are far more so. For you know, we old men, whenever we see youth at play, become eager to join in the game ourselves. How much more would I be inspired to join you in serious work, if I found you alert and enthusiastic for the job.

CHAPTER 11

Of Family Affection

[1] When he was visited by a magistrate, Epictetus enquired of him about several particulars, and asked if he had both children and a wife. [2] When the man replied that he had, Epictetus enquired further, 'How do you enjoy it?' 'I'm miserable,' the other replied. [3] So Epictetus asked: 'How so? For men do not marry and beget children in order to be miserable, but rather to be happy.' [4] 'But', the man replied, 'I am so miserable concerning my poor children that the other day, when my little daughter was sick and seemed in danger of her life, I could not bear even to remain with her, but had to desert her and go off, till someone came and told me she was better.' [5] 'Well,' said Epictetus, 'do you think you acted rightly in this case?' 'I acted naturally,' the man replied. 'But convince of me of this,' Epictetus said, 'that you acted naturally, and I will convince you that everything that happens in accordance with nature happens rightly.' [6] 'This is what all, or at least most, of us fathers go through.' 'I don't deny that,' Epictetus said. 'The point at issue between us is whether it is right. [7] For by your reasoning we ought to say that tumours also exist for the good of the body, because they exist, and flatly declare that to do wrong is in accordance with nature,

because nearly all, or at least most of us, do wrong. [8] What you must do is show me how it is in accordance with nature.' 'I cannot,' the man said. 'Why don't you show me instead how it is not in accordance with nature, nor happens rightly?'

[9] And Epictetus said: 'Well, if we were disputing about things white and black, what criterion would we invoke to discriminate them?' 'Sight,' the man replied. 'And what about things hot and cold, and hard and soft—what then?' 'Touch.' [10] 'Therefore, since we are disputing about what is in accordance with nature and happens rightly or not rightly, what criterion do you think we should admit?' 'I don't know,' the man said. [11] 'And yet ignorance in the case of the criterion of colours, smells, and flavours is perhaps no great harm. But in the case of things good and bad, things in accordance with and contrary to nature for man—does the harm to one who is ignorant seem small to you?' 'No, very great harm.' [12] 'Come, tell me: is everything judged good and appropriate by people, rightly so judged? Is it possible that all the opinions that the Jews, Syrians, Egyptians, and Romans have about food, are right?' 'How is it possible?' [13] 'But I suppose it is quite necessary, if the opinions of the Egyptians are right, that those of the others are wrong. And if those of the Jews are right, then those of the others are not.' 'Of course.' [14] 'And where there is ignorance, there is also want of learning and instruction in the most necessary things.' The man agreed. [15] 'You then,' said Epictetus, 'since you know this, for the future will apply yourself and put your mind to nothing else but learning the criterion of things in accordance with nature, and using this to judge particular cases.

[16] 'But in the present matter I have this much to contribute toward what you need. [17] Does family affection seem to you to be in accordance with nature, and good?' 'Certainly.' 'Well, can it be the case that family affection is in accordance with nature, and good, while what is rational is not good?' 'By no means.' [18] 'So what is rational is not in conflict with family affection?' 'I don't think so.' 'For otherwise, if they were in conflict, one would be in accordance with nature, while the other would be contrary to nature. Isn't that so?' 'It is.' [19] 'Whatever, then, we find to be at the same time affectionate and rational, this we confidently declare to be right and good.' 'Agreed.'

[20] 'Well, then, to leave your sick child and to go away is not rational, and I don't suppose that you will gainsay that. But it

remains for us to consider if it is consistent with family affection.'
'Yes, let us consider.' [21] 'Well, then, since you had an affectionate
disposition toward your child, did you do right when you ran off
and left her—and has the mother no affection for the child?' 'Certainly she has.' [22] 'Should the mother, then, also have left her,
or not?' 'She should not have.' 'And the nurse, does she care for
her?' 'She does.' [23] 'Should she also have left her, then? 'By no
means.' 'And her attendant, does he not care for her?' 'He does.'
'Should he, then, have deserted her also? And should the child have
been left alone and without help on account of the great affection
of you, the parents, and of those about her, and should she have
died in the hands of those who neither loved nor cared for her?'
'Certainly not.' [24] 'Now, this is senseless and unfair, not to allow
those who have equal affection with yourself to do what you think
appropriate for yourself to do, because you have affection.' 'It is
strange.' [25] 'Come, then, if you were sick, would you wish your
relations, your very children and wife, in addition to the rest, to be
so affectionate as to leave you alone and deserted?' 'By no means.'
[26] 'And would you wish to be so loved by your own that, because
of their too great affection, you would always be left alone in sickness? Or for this reason would you rather pray, if it were possible,
to be so loved by your enemies as to be left alone by them? And
if this is so, the result is that what you did can by no means be
considered affectionate anymore.

[27] 'Well then, was it nothing that moved and induced you to
desert your child? That is unlikely. But it might be the sort of thing
that moved a man at Rome to cover his head while the horse he
favoured was running. Then, when his horse unexpectedly won, he
needed sponges to be revived. [28] What, then, is the cause of your
behaviour? The precise explanation, perhaps, does not belong to
the present occasion. But it is enough to be convinced of this, that if
what the philosophers say is true, we must not look for it anywhere
outside ourselves. Rather, in all cases it is one and the same thing
which is the cause of our doing or not doing something, of saying
or not saying something, of being elated or depressed, of avoiding
or pursuing something: [29] the very thing which is now the cause
to me and to you—to you of coming to me and now sitting and
listening, to me of saying these things. And what is that? [30] Is it
anything but our judgement about what is right?' 'Nothing else.'
'If we had seen things differently, what else would we be doing but

what seemed right to us? [31] So this was the cause of Achilles'
lamentation—not the death of Patroclus, for another man does not
suffer so when his companion dies—but because it seemed right to
him to do so. [32] And this was the same thing that caused you to
flee, that it seemed right to you; and conversely, if you remain, it
will be because it seemed right to you. And now you are off to
Rome, because it seems right to you; and if you change your mind,
you won't go. [33] In a word, then, neither death, nor exile, nor
pain, nor anything of the sort is the cause of our doing anything or
not doing it, but our opinions and suppositions.

[34] 'Do I convince you of this or don't I?' 'You do convince me,'
the man said. 'As the causes are in each case, so also are the effects.
[35] So when we do anything incorrectly, from this day forward
we shall ascribe it to nothing else than the opinion from which we
did it; and it is this we shall try to remove and excise, more than
tumours and abscesses from the body. [36] And in like manner we
shall declare it to be the selfsame cause of the things we do correctly. [37] And we shall no longer blame either slave or neighbour,
wife or child, as causes of evil to us, being persuaded that, if we do
not conceive things to be so-and-so, we do not behave accordingly.
And we, not externals, are masters of what things appear best to
us.' 'Correct,' the man said. [38] 'So from now on we shall inspect
and examine nothing as to its nature or condition, whether that be
land, slaves, horses, or dogs—but only opinions.' 'Hopefully,' the
other said. [39] 'So you see that you must become a student—that
creature everyone mocks—if you intend in earnest to make examination of your opinions. [40] That this does not happen overnight,
you know as well as I.'

CHAPTER 12

On Satisfaction

[1] Concerning gods there are some who say that the divine does
not even exist, and others who say that it exists, but is inactive,
negligent, and takes thought for nothing. [2] A third group says it
exists and takes thought, but only for great things in the heavens,

not for anything on earth. A fourth group says that it takes thought
for things on earth and for human affairs, but only in a general way,
not for the interests of individuals. [3] And there is a fifth group,
among them Odysseus and Socrates, who say 'I cannot make a move
without your noticing'.

[4] Before all else, then, it is necessary to enquire about each of
these opinions, whether it is soundly or unsoundly held. [5] For if
the gods don't exist, how can it be our goal to follow the gods? And
if they exist, but take thought for nothing, how will this goal be
sound? [6] Or even supposing that they exist and take thought, if
there is no communication from them to mankind, and by Zeus, to
me personally, how again is the goal sound? [7] The educated man,
then, after considering all these things, submits his will to him who
administers the universe, as good citizens do to the law of the state.
[8] He who is being educated should come to education with this
thought: 'How can I personally follow the gods in all things, and
how can I be satisfied with the divine administration, and how can
I become free?' [9] For he is free to whom everything happens in
accordance with his choice, and whom no one can hinder.

[10] What then? Is freedom insanity? Far from it. For insanity
and freedom are not compatible. [11] 'But I want everything that
seems best to me to happen, however it came to seem so.' [12] You
are mad, you are out of your mind. Don't you know that freedom is
a noble and precious thing? But for me to randomly desire that those
things should happen which randomly seemed best, this appears to
be not only not noble, but even of all things most shameful. [13] For
how do we proceed in writing? Do I desire to write the name 'Dio'
as I wish? No, but I am taught to want to write it as it ought to
be written. And what is the case with music? The same. [14] And
what in general, where it is the case of any art or science? Otherwise, it would not be worth the trouble to learn anything, if it were
amenable to each person's desires. [15] And is it only here in the
case of the greatest and most important thing, freedom, that I am
permitted to wish at random? Not at all. But this is just what getting an education means, to learn to wish for each thing to happen
as in fact it does happen. And how does it happen? As the one who
administers them has ordained. [16] He ordained that there be
summer and winter, abundance and dearth, virtue and vice, and all
such opposites for the harmony of the whole. And he gave to each
of us a body and bodily parts, and possessions, and companions.

[17] Mindful, therefore, of this dispensation we should go to be instructed, not in order to change the hypotheses—for this is neither given to us, nor is it better that it should be so—but in order that, seeing how things concerning us are in their nature, we may maintain our will in conformity with what happens. [18] For can we escape from mankind? And how is that possible? But if we associate with them, can we change them? And who gives us that power? [19] What then remains, or what method can we find of dealing with them? Such a one that, while they will act as they see fit, we will remain in accord with nature none the less. [20] But you are impatient and peevish, and if you are alone, you call it desolation, while if you are with other men you call them plotters and thieves, and you blame your own parents and children and brothers and neighbours. [21] When you are alone, you should call it tranquillity and freedom, and think of yourself as the equal of the gods. When you are among many, don't call it a mob, a tumult, or a vexation, but a feast and a festival, and on that basis accept it with good grace.

What, then, is the punishment of those who do not accept? To be just as they are. [22] Is someone dissatisfied with being alone? Let him be in desolation. Is someone dissatisfied with his parents? Let him be a bad son, and complain. Is someone dissatisfied with his children? Let him be a bad father. [23] 'Throw him in gaol.' What gaol? Where he is already, for he is there against his will; and wherever someone is against his will, there he is in prison. Thus Socrates was not in prison, for he was there willingly.

[24] 'But that my leg should be crippled!' Slave, so you find fault with the world on account of one poor leg? Won't you surrender it for the sake of the whole? Won't you renounce it? Won't you gladly return it to the one who gave it? [25] Will you be malcontent and aggrieved at the ordinances of Zeus, which he with the Fates who were present and spinning the thread of your destiny, defined and ordained? [26] Don't you know how small a part you are compared to the whole? I mean with respect to the body; for as to the mind you are not inferior, or less than the gods. For the greatness of reason is measured not by its length or height, but by its judgements.

[27] Won't you choose, then, to place the good there, in that respect in which you are equal to the gods? [28] 'Poor me, I have such a father and mother.' What then? Was it given to you to choose them beforehand, saying, 'Let such and such a man have intercourse with such and such a woman at this hour, in order that I may be

born'? It was not given. [29] But your parents had to come first, then you had to be born as you were. Of what sort of parents? Of such as they were. [30] What then? They being such as they are, is no recourse available to you? Well, let us suppose you were ignorant of the reason you possessed the faculty of sight; you would be wretched and unhappy if you closed your eyes when colours are brought before you. Aren't you even more wretched and unfortunate in that you have nobility and greatness of mind to deal with these things, and don't know it? [31] Things appropriate to the power you have are brought before you, but you turn that power aside, at the very moment you ought to have it awake and alert. [32] Do you not rather give thanks to the gods for putting you above what they did not actually put in your power, and making you responsible only for what is in your power? [33] As for parents, the gods have released you from accountability, for brothers they have released you; for the body they have released you; and for property, death, and life. [34] What did they make you responsible for, then? For the only thing in your power, the proper use of impressions. [35] What then? Do you draw upon yourself matters for which you are not responsible? That is to create trouble for yourself.

CHAPTER 13

How Each Thing May be Done in a Manner Pleasing to the Gods

[1] When someone enquired how it was possible to eat in a manner pleasing to the gods, he said, 'If it is done justly and with discretion, equitably and with restraint and self-control—isn't that pleasing to the gods?' [2] When you have asked for warm water, and the slave ignores you; or if he hears you, but brings in tepid water; or if he is not even to be found in the house; then to refrain from anger and not to explode—isn't that pleasing to the gods? [3] 'But how is one to put up with such people?' Slave, won't you put up with your own brother, who has Zeus as his ancestor and is a son born of the same seed as yourself, and has the same noble descent? [4] But if you have been placed in a position above others, will you straightway set yourself up as a tyrant? Don't you remember who you are and

who you command, that they are kinsmen, brothers by nature, offspring of Zeus? [5] 'But I have a bill of sale for them, and they have none for me.' Don't you see that it is to the earth, to the pit, to these wretched laws of the dead, that you are looking, and not to the laws of the gods?

CHAPTER 14

That the Deity Oversees All Men

[1] Someone asked him how one could be convinced that every-thing done by him is overseen by god. 'Do you not think', he said, 'that all things are united as one?' 'I do,' said the other. [2] 'Do you not think that what is on earth feels the influence of that which is in heaven?' 'I do,' he said. [3] 'For how else does it come about that, with such regularity, as if by god's command, when he commands the plants to flower, they flower, and to shoot, they shoot, and to bear fruit, they bear fruit, and to ripen, they ripen? And again, when he bids them drop their fruit, shed their leaves, withdraw within themselves and remain in peace and quiet, they remain in peace and quiet? [4] And how else does it happen that at the waxing and waning of the moon and the approach and recession of the sun we see among the things on earth so great an alteration and change to the opposite? [5] Or could it be the case that while plants and our own bodies are so closely bound up with the universe, and share so intimately in its affections, yet the same is not much more true of our souls? [6] But if our souls are so bound up with god and joined together with him, as parts and fragments of his being, does not god perceive their every movement as a movement of that which is his own and connate with himself?

[7] 'And yet you have the power to think about the divine admin-istration and about each divine thing, and at the same time about human affairs, and you have the faculty of being moved by thou-sands of matters simultaneously, both in your senses and in your intelligence; and you assent to some while you dissent from others, or suspend judgement about them; [8] and you preserve in your soul so many impressions derived from so many different matters. And when stirred by them, your mind moves to the conceptions

corresponding to the initial impressions; and so from thousands of matters you derive and retain arts, one after another, and memories. [9] And is god not able to oversee all things and be present with, and enjoy a certain communication with, them all? [10] Yet the sun is capable of illuminating so large a portion of the universe, and of leaving unilluminated only the small space which is no larger than can be covered by the shadow which the earth casts; and is god, who created the sun, which is only a small portion of himself in relation to the whole, and which he causes to revolve—is he not able to perceive all things?'

[11] 'And yet', someone objects, 'I cannot follow all these things at one and the same time.' 'But does anyone go so far as to say that you possess a faculty equal to that of Zeus? [12] Nevertheless, he has stationed by each man's side as a guardian his *daimon*, and has committed the man to its care, a guardian who does not sleep and is not to be deceived. [13] For to what other guardian, better or more careful, could he have committed each of us? So when you close your doors and make darkness within, remember never to say that you are alone. [14] For you are not: god is within, your own *daimon* is within. What need do they have of light to see what you are doing? [15] It is to this god that you ought to swear allegiance, as the soldiers do to Caesar. For they, in order to receive their pay, swear to put the safety of Caesar before all else. And will you, who have been counted worthy of blessings so numerous and so great, be unwilling to swear or abide by your oath? [16] And what will you swear? Never to disobey under any circumstances, never to bring charges, never to find fault with anything he has given, never to do or experience with a bad grace anything that is inevitable. [17] Can the soldier's oath in any way be compared to yours? There they swear never to prefer another before Caesar; but we swear to prefer ourselves above all else.'

CHAPTER 15

What Philosophy Professes

[1] When a man was consulting him how to persuade his brother to be angry with him no longer, Epictetus said, [2] 'Philosophy does

not promise to secure for a man any external thing. If it did, it would take on something outside its proper subject-matter. For as wood is the material of the carpenter, and bronze that of the sculptor, so the subject-matter of the art of life is each person's own life.' [3] 'Well, what about my brother's life?' 'That, in turn, belongs to his own art of living, but with respect to yours it is one of the externals, similar to land, similar to health, similar to reputation. Philosophy promises none of these things. [4] In every circumstance I will keep the ruling principle in accord with nature.' 'Whose ruling principle?' 'His in whom I exist.' [5] 'How, then, do I keep my brother from being angry at me?' 'Bring him to me and I will speak to him, but I have nothing to say to you about his anger.'

[6] The man consulting with Epictetus said, 'What I want to know is this, how can I keep in accord with nature even if my brother will not be reconciled to me?' [7] 'Nothing great comes into being suddenly, since not even a bunch of grapes or a fig does. If you say to me now, "I want a fig," I will reply to you that it takes time. First let it flower, then put forth fruit, then ripen. [8] If, then, the fruit of a fig-tree is not brought to completion suddenly and in an hour, would you possess the fruit of a man's mind in so short a time and so easily? Do not expect it, even if I told you so myself.'

CHAPTER 16

On Providence

[1] Do not wonder if the things necessary for the body stand ready at hand for other animals, not just food and drink, but also a place to sleep, and the fact that they have no need of shoes, bedding, or clothing, while we stand in need of all these things. [2] For in the case of creatures born not for their own sake but for service, it was not advantageous to have created them in need of other things. [3] After all, consider what it would be like for us to have to take thought not only for ourselves, but also for our sheep and asses, how they are to be clothed and shod, how they are to eat and drink. [4] But just as soldiers appear at the ready before their general—clothed, armed, and shod—and it would be strange if the brigadier

had to go around shoeing and clothing the regiment; so too, nature has created animals which are born for service ready for use, equipped, and in need of no further attention. [5] So it is that a single small child armed only with a stick can drive an entire flock of sheep.

[6] But as it is, we first neglect to give thanks for not having to bestow on animals the same attention as we do on ourselves, and then we complain to god on our own account. [7] Yet, by Zeus and the gods, one single event would suffice, at least for one who is reverent and grateful, to recognize providence. [8] And do not speak to me now of great things; take the mere fact that milk is produced from grass, and cheese from milk, and wool from skin. Who is it that has made or conceived these things? 'No one,' he says. Oh, the great obtuseness and temerity!

[9] Let us leave aside the works of nature, and consider its secondary effects. [10] Is there anything more useless than the hairs on the chin? But hasn't nature made use even of these in as becoming a manner as possible? Has it not through them distinguished the male from the female? [11] Does not the nature of each one of us declare at once from afar, 'I am a man: on this basis approach me, on this basis talk to me. Look for nothing further, just consider the tokens.' [12] Again in the case of women, just as in their voice nature has mingled a softer note, so too it has removed the hair from their chins. But no, you say: 'The animal ought to have been left without distinguishing mark, and each of us should announce on his own account, "I am a man."' [13] But how fair and becoming and noble the token is! How much fairer than the cocks' comb, how much more magnificent than the lions' mane! [14] For this reason we ought to preserve the signs of god, we should not do away with them or, so far as in us lies, confuse the sexes that have been thus distinguished.

[15] Are these the only works of providence in our case? Hardly. Indeed, what language is adequate to praise them or present them fairly? For if we had sense, is there anything else we ought to be doing both in public and private than singing and praising god, and rehearsing his benefits? [16] Should we not sing a hymn to god while digging and ploughing and eating? 'Great is god, that he has given us these instruments with which we work the earth. [17] Great is god, that he has given us hands, and a gullet, and belly, and ability to grow unconsciously, and to breath while asleep.' [18] This is what we ought to sing on every occasion, and especially the greatest

and divinest hymn, that he has given us the power to understand
these things and use them methodically.

[19] Well then, since most of you are blind, shouldn't there be
someone who fills this office, and on behalf of the rest of you, sings
the hymn of praise to god? [20] What else am I, a lame old man,
capable of doing but singing a hymn of praise to god? If I were a
nightingale, I would do the duty of a nightingale, if a swan, that of
a swan. But as it is, I am a rational being, and I must praise god.
[21] That is my task, I do it, and will not desert the post, so long
as it is given me to occupy it. And I invite you to join me in this
same song.

CHAPTER 17

Concerning the Necessity of Logic

[1] Since reason articulates and processes everything else, and itself
should not remain unarticulated, what should it be articulated by?
[2] Obviously, it must be by itself, or by something else. Now, that
will be reason, or something greater than reason, which is impossible. [3] If it is reason, what, in turn, will articulate it? If itself, well,
the other reason can do the same. If we require another reason to
perform the service, the process will be endless and unceasing.

[4] 'Yes, but it is more important that we tend to passions, and
opinions, and the like.' So, you want to be told about them? Very
well, listen. [5] But if you say to me, 'I don't know whether you
argue fairly or foully,' or if I use a word in an ambiguous sense, and
you say to me, 'Distinguish,' I won't put up with you, but will say,
'No, the other is more important. . . .' [6] That is why, I suppose,
they place logic first: for the same reason that, before the measure-
ment of grain, we put investigation of the measure. [7] And if we
don't first specify what a bushel is, and what a scale is, how then
will we be able to measure or weigh anything? [8] So, in this case,
unless we have apprehended and defined the thing by means of
which all else is apprehended, how can we investigate and apprehend anything else? How is it possible? [9] 'Yes, but a bushel con-
tainer is wooden, and bears no fruit.' [10] But it measures grain.

'And matters of logic are fruitless.' We will even see about that. But even if this be granted, it is enough that logic examines and distinguishes the other things, and, as it were, measures and weighs them. [11] Who says so? Only Chrysippus, Zeno, and Cleanthes? Doesn't Antisthenes say so? [12] And who is it that wrote, 'The beginning of education is the examination of terms'? Doesn't Socrates say so? And about whom does Xenophon write, that he used to begin with the examination of terms, what each meant?

[13] Is this, then, the great and admirable thing, to understand or interpret Chrysippus? Who says that? What, then, is the admirable thing? To understand the will of nature. [14] Well, then, do you understand it alone and by yourself? What more, then, do you require? For if it is true that all men err unwillingly, and you have apprehended the truth, then you must be on the right path already. [15] 'But in fact I do not understand the will of nature.' Who, then, interprets it? People say 'Chrysippus.' [16] I go to find out what that interpreter of nature has to say. I begin not to understand what he is saying, and look for one to explain. 'Look and consider what this means'—just as if it were written in Latin! [17] What right, then, does the interpreter have to be proud? Not even Chrysippus has cause, if he only explains the will of nature, and does not follow it himself; how much less the one who interprets him. [18] For we do not need even Chrysippus on his own account, but in order to understand nature. Nor do we need the diviner on his own account, but because we think that through him we will grasp the future and the signs sent by the gods. [19] Nor have we need of the victim's entrails for their own sake, but because the signs come through them. And we do not admire the crow or the raven, but god, who gives signs by means of them.

[20] So I go to this interpreter and diviner, and I say, 'Please examine the victim's entrails, for what they signify for me.' [21] He takes and spreads them out, and explains: 'Man, you have a power of choice incapable by nature of being forced or compelled. This is what is written in the entrails. [22] I will demonstrate this for you first in the case of assent. Can anyone prevent you from assenting to the truth?' 'No one.' 'Can anyone force you to accept what is false?' 'No one.' [23] You see that in this area you have a power of choice that is free of hindrance, force, or obstruction. [24] Come, is it any different in the sphere of desire and impulse? And what can defeat an impulse except another impulse? What can defeat a desire

or aversion except another desire or aversion? [25] 'But if someone applies the fear of death, he compels me.' It is not the thing
applied that compels you, but the fact that you would rather do
something of the sort than die. [26] Again, therefore, your decision
compelled you—that is, choice compelled choice. [27] For if god
had so arranged his own part, which he has given to us as a fragment of himself, that it could be hindered or constrained by himself
or by anyone else, he would no longer be god, nor would he be
caring for us as he ought. [28] 'This is what I find', says the diviner,
'in the victims; these are the signs sent to you. If you wish it, you
are free. If you wish it, you will blame no one, you will accuse no
one; everything will happen according to plan, both yours and god's.'
[29] This is the prophecy for which I go to the diviner and philosopher, not admiring him because of his interpretation, but admiring the interpretation itself.

CHAPTER 18

That We Should Not Be Angry with Wrongdoers

[1] If what the philosophers say is true, that all men have one principle, as in the case of assent the feeling that a thing is so, and in the
case of dissent the feeling that it is not so, and, by god, in the case of
suspending judgement, the feeling that a thing is unclear, [2] and
also in the case of impulse toward anything the feeling that a thing
is to my advantage; and that it is impossible to judge one thing
advantageous and desire another, and to judge one thing proper
and have an impulse toward another—why then are we angry with
the multitude? [3] 'Thieves', he says, 'are what they are, and gaolbirds.' What does 'thieves and gaolbirds' mean? They are mistaken
about what is good and evil. [4] So should one be angry with them,
or pity them? Just point out their mistake, and you will see how
they mend the error of their ways. If they don't see the light, they
have nothing superior to their opinion.

[5] 'Well, shouldn't this thief and adulterer die?' [6] Say rather,
'Shouldn't this person who is mistaken and deceived about the
most important things, and blinded, not in the faculty of vision

which distinguishes white and black, but in the faculty of reason which distinguishes good and evil—shouldn't he die?' [7] And if you put it this way, you will realize how inhuman what you say is, and how like it is to saying, 'Shouldn't this blind man be killed, and this deaf one?' [8] For if loss of the most important things involves the greatest harm, and if the most important thing in each person is the right moral choice, and one is deprived of this, why are you still angry with him? [9] Man, if you must be affected in a way contrary to nature by the evil of another, pity, do not hate, him. Drop this readiness to hate and take offence. [10] Don't utter those words which most fault-finders do: 'These damned, blasted fools!' Fine. How in the world did you suddenly become so wise as to be angered at others?

[11] Why, then, are we angry? Because we attach such import-ance to the things that they take from us. So, don't attach import-ance to your clothes, and you are not angry with the thief. Don't attach importance to the beauty of your wife, and you are not angry with the adulterer. [12] Know that the thief and the adulterer have no place in the things that are yours, but in those that belong to others and are not in your power. If you dismiss those things and set them at nought, with whom are you still angry? But as long as you set store by these things, be angry with yourself rather than with the thief and the adulterer.

[13] For just consider: You have beautiful clothes; your neighbour does not. You have a window, and wish to air them. He does not know what man's good consists in, but imagines that it means having beautiful clothes, the very thing that you imagine too. [14] Then, shall he not come and carry them off? When you show a bit of food to hungry men and then gobble it down alone, don't you want them to snatch at it? Don't provoke them; don't have a window; don't air your clothes.

[15] Something similar happened to me the other day. I kept an iron lamp by my household shrine. Hearing a noise from my win-dow, I ran down. I found that the lamp had been stolen. I reasoned that the one who had lifted it had felt something he couldn't resist. So what? 'Tomorrow', I said to myself, 'you will find one of earth-enware.' [16] For a man loses what he has. 'I lost clothes.' Yes, because you had clothes. 'I have a pain in the head.' You don't have a pain in the horns, do you? For grief and loss relate only to what we have.

[17] 'But the tyrant will chain—.' What? Your leg. 'He will chop off—.' What? Your neck. What will he neither chain nor chop off? Your moral choice. For this reason the ancients advise, 'Know yourself.' [18] And so we ought to exercise ourselves in small things and, beginning with them, proceed to the greater. [19] 'I have a pain in the head.' Do not say, 'Alas!' 'I have a pain in the ear.' Do not say, 'Alas!' I do not say that it is not permitted to groan; only do not groan in the centre of your being. And if your slave is slow in bringing a bandage, do not cry out and fidget and say, 'Everybody hates me.' For who would not hate such a person? [20] So put your trust in these opinions and walk upright, free, not trusting to the size of your body, like an athlete. For a man should not be invincible in the way an ass is.

[21] Who, then, is invincible? He whom nothing non-moral disconcerts. I then go through each of the circumstances and scrutinize them, as with an athlete: 'He survived the first round; what will he do in the second? What if it is hot? What if it is the Olympics?' [22] And so here too: 'If you throw money in his way, he will turn up his nose. What if it's a pretty girl? What if it's dark? What if you tempt him with reputation? Or abuse? Or applause? Or death?' All these he can overcome. [23] What, then, if he feels hot because he's inebriated? What if he's melancholy-mad? Or asleep? This is the invincible athlete as far as I'm concerned.

CHAPTER 19

How One Should Behave toward Tyrants

[1] If a man possesses some superiority, or even thinks that he does when he doesn't, it is quite inevitable that such a man, if he is uneducated, will become puffed up as a result. [2] The tyrant, for instance, says, 'I am more powerful than anyone.' And what can you give me? Can you secure me desire free from hindrance? How can you? Do you have it yourself? What about aversion that does not get what it would avoid—do you have that? Infallible impulse? [3] What claim do you have to that? Well, on board ship do you trust yourself or the one who has knowledge? In a chariot, whom do you trust but the one who knows? [4] And what of the other skills?

Just the same. In what, then, does your power consist? 'All men care for me.' Yes, and I care for my writing tablet, washing and wiping it; and for the sake of my oil flask I drive a nail in the wall. Does that mean that these things are superior to me? No, but they are useful in some respect. What of my donkey—do I not care for that? [5] Do I not wash its feet? Do I not comb it? Aren't you aware that all men care for themselves, but care for you as they would for their donkey? Who, then, cares for you as a man? Show me that. [6] Who wants to be like you, who wants to emulate you, the way they emulated Socrates? 'But I can cut off your head.' Good point. I had forgotten that I ought to care for you as for fever or cholera, and erect an altar to you on the model of the altar of Fever in Rome.

[7] What is it, then, that disturbs and confounds the multitude? The tyrant and his guards? Hardly. What is by nature free cannot be disturbed or hindered by anything but itself. [8] It is a man's own opinions that disturb him. For whenever a tyrant says to someone, 'I will chain your leg,' the man who values the leg says, 'No, have mercy'; while the man who values his moral character says, 'If it seems the better course for you, then chain it.' 'You don't care?' 'I don't care.' 'I will show you that I am master.' [9] 'How can you do that? Zeus has set me free. Or do you think that he was going to permit his son to be enslaved? Of my corpse you are master, that you can take.' [10] 'So when you approach me, it is not me that you are attending to?' 'No, but myself. And if you want me to say that I am attending to you too, I will say that I attend to you as to my pot.'

[11] This is not selfishness, this is the nature of the animal: he does everything for his own sake. For even the sun does everything for its own sake, and so, for that matter, does Zeus. [12] But when Zeus wishes to be 'Rain-giver', and 'Fruit-giver', and 'Father of gods and men', you see that he cannot accomplish these acts or earn these epithets except by consulting the common interest. [13] And, in general, Zeus has so constituted the nature of the rational animal that he can attain none of his proper goods without contributing to the common interest. [14] And so it is no longer anti-social to do everything for one's own sake. [15] Well, what did you expect? That a man would stand aloof from himself and his own interest? And how can there any longer be one and the same principle for all beings: namely, appropriation to themselves?

[16] What follows then? When people hold absurd opinions about things that lie outside the sphere of moral choice, regarding them as

good and evil, it is quite inevitable that they flatter tyrants. [17] And if only it were tyrants alone, and not their flunkies too! How does a man become wise immediately after Caesar puts him in charge of his chamber-pot? Why at once do we say, 'Felicio has spoken to me wisely'? [18] I wish he were cast off his dung-heap, that you may think him a fool again. [19] Epaphroditus once owned a slave who was a shoemaker, whom he sold because he was useless. Then, as luck would have it, he was bought by one of Caesar's household and became shoemaker to Caesar. You should have seen how Epaphroditus flattered him! [20] 'How is my good Felicio, pray?' [21] Then if one of us asked, 'What is the master doing?', he would be told, 'He is with Felicio, deliberating about something.' [22] Yet, had he not sold him because he was useless? [23] Who, then, had suddenly made him wise? This is to honour something other than what lies within the sphere of moral choice. [24] Someone is raised to the office of tribune. All who meet him congratulate him. One kisses his eyes, another his neck, and his slaves kiss his hands. He goes home and finds lamps being lit. [25] He climbs the Capitol and offers sacrifice. Now, who ever offered sacrifice for having good desires? Or because his impulses were in accord with nature? For wherever we place the good, for that we thank the gods.

[26] A man was talking with me today about a priesthood of Augustus. I say to him, 'Let the thing alone, friend. You will go to great expense for nothing.' [27] 'But those who draw up contracts', he says, 'will write my name there.' 'Do you expect to stand by, then, and say to those who read them, "That's my name they're writing down"? [28] And even if you can stand in front of all of them now, what will you do when you're dead?' 'My name will survive me.' 'Write it in stone, and it will survive. Outside of Nicopolis, however, who will remember you?' [29] 'But I will wear a crown of gold.' 'If you are quite set upon a crown, take one of roses and put it on. You will look more elegant in that.'

CHAPTER 20

About Reason, How It Investigates Itself

[1] Every art and faculty investigates certain things specifically. [2] When, therefore, it is of like kind with what it investigates, it

necessarily investigates itself as well. When it is dissimilar, it cannot investigate itself. [3] So, for example, the art of shoemaking has to do with leather, but itself is entirely distinct from the material of leather. Therefore, it does not investigate itself. [4] Again, the art of grammar has to do with written speech. Is it written speech itself? By no means. Therefore it cannot investigate itself. [5] Now, for what purpose has reason been given by nature? For the proper use of impressions. And what is it itself? A composite of certain impressions. Thus it comes naturally to investigate itself. [6] Again, what things does wisdom profess to contemplate? Things good, bad, and indifferent. And what is wisdom itself? Good. And what is folly? Bad. Do you see, then, that it naturally investigates itself and its opposite? [7] Therefore, the first and most important duty of the philosopher is to test and distinguish impressions and to admit none that is untested.

[8] You see in the case of coinage, where our interest appears to be somewhat at stake, how we have also devised an art, and how many means the tester employs to test the coin: sight, touch, smell, finally hearing. [9] He lets the denarius fly and listens to the sound, and is not satisfied with one hearing, but after repeated listenings becomes a veritable musician. [10] Thus, wherever we think that error and accuracy make a difference, there we take considerable care to recognize what is liable to deceive. [11] But where it is merely the case of our ruling principle, we yawn and nod, content to accept every impression. For here the loss we suffer is not as evident. [12] So when you wish to know how complacent you are about things good and bad, and how serious about things indifferent, just consider how you feel about physical blindness on the one hand, and mental delusion on the other, and you will realize how far you are from feeling as you ought about things good and bad.

[13] 'But this requires a lot of preparation, and much work, and learning.' So what? Do you expect to acquire the most important art in a short time? [14] And yet the principal doctrine of the philosophers is itself very short. If you want to know, just read the works of Zeno, and you will see. [15] For what is long in the statement that 'The end is to follow the gods, and the essence of the good is the proper use of impressions'? [16] Say, 'So what is god, and what is an impression? And what is individual nature, and what is the nature of the whole?' Now it is long.

[17] If, then, Epicurus comes and says that the good ought to lie in the flesh, again it becomes long, and one must hear lectures on

what the dominant principle in us is, and the substantial and the essential. If the good of the snail is not likely to be in the shell, what is the likelihood in man's case? [18] And you yourself, Epicurus, what do you have that is superior? What is the thing in you that deliberates, that examines each thing, that decides in the case of the flesh itself that it is dominant? [19] And why do you light your lamp and labour for us, and write so many books? Is it that we may not be ignorant of the truth? Who are we? And what are we to you? Thus the argument becomes long.

CHAPTER 21

To Those who Want to be Admired

[1] When someone has his proper station in life, he does not look for help without. [2] Man, what do you hope for yourself? For my part, I am content if my desires and aversions are in accordance with nature, if I exercise impulse and refusal in accordance with nature, and my purpose, design, and assent likewise. Why, then, do you walk before us as if you had swallowed a spit? [3] 'I wish that all who meet me would admire me, and follow me around, shouting, "The great philosopher!"' [4] Who are these people by whom you wish to be admired? Aren't these the same people whom you are in the habit of calling mad? Well, then, do you wish to be admired by lunatics?

CHAPTER 22

Concerning Preconceptions

[1] Preconceptions are common to all men. And preconception does not conflict with preconception. For who of us does not assume that the good is beneficial and choiceworthy, and in all cases to be strived after and pursued? Who of us does not assume that justice is fair and appropriate? Where, then, does conflict arise? [2] In applying

preconceptions to particular cases. [3] As when one person says, 'Well done, he is a brave man,' but another says, 'No, he is out of his mind.' This is the source of men's conflict with each other. [4] This is the conflict among Jews, Syrians, Egyptians, and Romans —not that what is holy should be preferred above all and in all cases pursued, but whether it is holy, or unholy, to eat this particular joint of pork.

[5] This is the conflict you will find between Agamemnon and Achilles. Call them before us. What do you say, Agamemnon? Shouldn't we do what is proper and appropriate? 'Of course we should.' [6] And what do you say, Achilles? Don't you agree that what is appropriate ought to be done? 'I agree to that above all.' Very well, then, apply your preconceptions. [7] It is just here that conflict starts. One says, 'I should not have to return Chryseis to her father.' The other says, 'You'd better.' Obviously one is apply-ing his preconception of the appropriate wrongly. [8] Again, one says, 'Fine, if I have to give Chryseis back, then I should take a prize from one of you.' The other says, 'You don't intend to take my beloved, do you?' 'Yours,' the other says. 'Shall I, then, be the only one . . . ?' 'Well, am I alone to go without . . . ?' Thus conflict arises.

[9] What, then, does it mean to get an education? It means learn-ing to apply natural preconceptions to particular cases in accord-ance with nature. And further, it means making the distinction that some things are in our power while others are not. [10] In our power are moral character and all its functions; not in our power are the body, the parts of the body, possessions, parents, brothers, children, country, and associates in general. [11] Where, then, shall we place the good? To what thing should we apply it? To what is in our power. [12] Is health, then, not a good thing, and soundness of one's faculties, and life? No? Nor children, parents, or country? Who will put up with you if you say so? [13] So let us transfer the designation 'good' to these things. Is it then possible to be happy when harmed and deprived of such goods? 'It is impossible.' And to maintain the right relation with one's associates? How is that possible? For I naturally incline to my own interest. [14] If it is in my interest to have land, it is in my interest to steal it from my neighbour. If it is in my interest to have a coat, it is in my interest to steal it from a bath. This is the source of wars, factions, tyran-nies, plots. [15] How then shall I render my duty to god? For if

I am harmed and come to grief, I conclude that he takes no heed of me. What have I to do with him, then, if he cannot help me? Again, what have I to do with him if he allows me to be in the state I am? So I begin to hate him. [16] Why, then, do we build temples, or statues to god, as for evil spirits like Fever? And how can god any longer be Saviour, and Rain-bringer, and Fruit-bringer? If, indeed, we set the essence of the good here, all these things follow in consequence.

[17] What, then, shall we do? This is a subject of enquiry for the man who truly philosophizes and is in travail of thought. Now I do not see what is good and bad. Aren't I crazy? [18] But suppose I set the good among the things subject to moral choice; everyone will laugh at me. Some white-haired old man wearing many gold rings on his fingers will come up to me shaking his head, and say: 'Listen to me, son. One ought of course to philosophize, but one should also keep one's head: this is all nonsense. [19] You learn a syllogism from the philosophers, but you know better than the philosophers what you ought to do.' [20] 'If I know, then why do you rebuke me?' What should I say to this slave? If I ignore him, he explodes. [21] So I must say to him, 'Humour me as you would someone in love. I am not in control of myself, I am crazy.'

CHAPTER 23

Against Epicurus

[1] Even Epicurus understands that we are by nature social, but having once placed our good in the husk, he is no longer able to say anything else. [2] For again, he is vehement that we ought not to admire or accept anything which is detached from the nature of good; and he is right so to insist. [3] How, then, are we suspicious, if we have no natural affection for our children? Why do you dissuade the wise man from bringing up children? Why do you fear that he may thereby be involved in sorrow? [4] For are you involved in sorrow on account of your house-slave Mouse?

Well, what's it to him if his little Mousling, raised in his home, comes bawling to him? [5] But he knows that if once a child is born, it will no longer be in our power not to love it or care for it. [6] For this reason he says that a man of sense will not engage in politics either, for he knows what things a politician should do. Well, it is true, if you are going to behave as if you were among flies, there's nothing to prevent you.

[7] But as if he did not know these things, he dares to say, 'Let us not raise children.' But a sheep does not desert its own offspring, nor a wolf; and does a man desert his? [8] What do you want? Would you have us be as foolish as sheep? Not even they desert. As savage as wolves? Not even they desert.

[9] Come, who takes your advice when they see their little child fallen and crying on the ground? [10] For my part, I imagine that your mother and father, even if they had divined that you were going to say such things, would not have exposed you.

CHAPTER 24

How We should Struggle with Circumstances

[1] It is circumstances that show what men are. So, when a difficult circumstance befalls you, remember that god, like a trainer of wrestlers, has matched you with a tough young man. [2] 'For what purpose?,' he says. That you may become an Olympic victor. But it does not happen without sweat. In my view, no one has a better circumstance than you have, if you are willing to make use of it as an athlete uses a young opponent. [3] And now we are sending you as a spy to Rome. But no one sends a cowardly spy, who, if he only hears a noise and sees a shadow somewhere, comes back running in terror, saying that the enemy is already at hand. [4] So now if you too should come back and say to us, 'Things are frightful in Rome: death is terrible, exile is terrible, abuse is terrible, poverty is terrible; [5] fly, my friends, the enemy is near,' we shall answer, 'Off with you, prophesy to yourself. We have made only one mistake: we tried to send a spy such as you.'

[6] Diogenes, who was sent as a spy before you, gave us a different report. He says that death is no evil, for it is not shameful either. He says that ill repute is the empty noise of madmen. [7] And what

sorts of things this spy has said about pain, about pleasure, about poverty! He says that to be simply clothed is better than any purple robe, and that to sleep on the bare ground is the softest bed. [8] And he gives as proof of each thing his assurance, his serenity, his freedom—then too his gleaming, well-knit little body. [9] 'There is no enemy near,' he says; 'all is quiet.' 'How is that, Diogenes?' 'Look,' he says, 'I am not hurt, or wounded, I am not in retreat from anyone, am I?' [10] This is a proper spy. But you come and tell us one thing after another. Won't you be off again, and take a closer look, without the trepidation?

[11] 'What then shall I do?' What do you do when you leave a ship? You don't carry off the rudder or the oars, do you? What, then, do you carry off? What is yours: your oil flask and wallet. And now, if you are mindful of what is yours, you will never lay claim to what is another's. [12] He says to you, 'Remove your scarlet hem.' 'There's my scarlet hem.' 'Remove this, too.' 'See, I have only my toga.' 'Remove your toga.' 'See, I am naked.' [13] 'But you arouse my envy.' 'Then take my whole poor body.' Do I still fear the man at whose command I can discard the poor body?

[14] 'But he will not leave his estate to me.' What then? 'I forgot that none of these things was mine.' How then do we call them mine? As we call the bed in the inn mine. If, then, the innkeeper at his death leaves you the beds, fine. But if he leaves them to someone else, he will have them, and you will look for another. [15] And if you don't find one, you will sleep on the ground. Only rest easy, and snore away, mindful that tragedies have their place among the rich, and kings, and tyrants. But no poor man swells a tragedy, except as one of the chorus. [16] Kings begin in prosperity: 'Deck the halls.' Then about the third or fourth act: 'O Cithaeron, why did you receive me?' [17] Slave, where are your crowns, where is your diadem? [18] Your guards can't help you now.

So when you approach one of these persons, remember this, that you are approaching a tragic figure—not the actor, but Oedipus himself. [19] 'But so-and-so is happy, he walks around with an entourage.' And I also mingle with the crowd and walk around with an entourage. [20] The chief thing to remember is that the door is open. Don't be more timid than little children, but just as they say, whenever a thing does not please them, 'I will play no longer,' so do you, when things seem to you of such a kind, say, 'I will no longer play,' and be rid of it. And if you stay, don't complain.

CHAPTER 25

On the Same Theme

[1] If these things are true, and we are not silly, or pretending that man's good and evil lie in moral character, and that all other things are nothing to us, why are we still disturbed, why are we still frightened? [2] No one has authority over the things we prize, and we despise the things that others do control. What, then, is our difficulty?

[3] 'But tell me what to do.' What am I to tell you to do? Hasn't Zeus told you? Hasn't he given you what is your own, free from hindrance and constraint, and what is not your own, subject to hindrance and constraint? [4] What commandment, then, what instructions did you have when you came from there? 'Guard by every means what is your own; do not desire what belongs to another.' Trustworthiness is your own, decency, and a sense of shame. Who, then, can deprive you of these? Who besides yourself will hinder you from using them? And how do you hinder yourself? When you value things that are not your own, you lose what is your own. [5] When you have these directions and commandments from Zeus, what sort do you still desire from me? Am I better than he, or more to be trusted? If you keep these, do you require any others besides? [6] But hasn't he commanded them? Bring your preconceptions to bear, bring the proofs of the philosophers, bring what you have often heard, and often said yourself, bring what you have read, what you have practised.

[7] How long, then, is it fit to keep these precepts, and not break up the game? [8] As long as it goes on agreeably. In the Saturnalia a king is chosen by lot, for this is the game that has been agreed upon. The king commands: 'You, drink; you, mix the wine; you, sing; you, leave; you, come here.' I obey, lest the game be broken up on my account. [9] But: 'You, suppose that you are in a bad way.' I do not so suppose—and who will force me to suppose? [10] Again, we contracted to re-enact the quarrel of Agamemnon and Achilles. Agamemnon says to me, 'Go to Achilles, and tear Briseis away.' [11] I go. 'Come back.' I come back.

For as we behave in the matter of hypothetical arguments, so should we behave in life. 'Let it be night.' So be it. 'Well, then, is it day?' No, for I accepted the hypothesis that it is night. [12] 'Let it be that you suppose it to be night.' So be it. 'Now, suppose that it *is* night.' [13] That is not consistent with the hypothesis. So here also: 'Let it be the case that you are unlucky.' So be it. 'Are you then unfortunate?' Yes. 'Well, then, are you wretched?' Yes. 'But suppose that you are also in a bad way.' That is not consistent with the hypothesis; and another forbids me from thinking so.

[14] How long, then, must we submit to such rules? As long as it is profitable; that is, as long as I maintain what is fitting and appropriate. [15] Now, some men are severe and ill-tempered, and they say, 'I cannot dine with this man, if I have to hear him every day explaining how he fought in Mysia: "I told you, brother, how I climbed the hill; then I withstood another siege."' [16] Another says, 'I prefer to dine and to hear him babble as long as he likes.' [17] It is for you to compare these values; only do nothing in a depressed mood, or as one afflicted, or supposing that you are in a bad way. For no man compels you to do that. [18] Is there smoke in the house? If there isn't too much, I will stay. If it is excessive, I leave. For one should remember and hold fast to this, that the door is open.

[19] 'Do not live in Nicopolis.' I do not live there. 'Nor in Athens.' Nor in Athens. 'Nor in Rome.' Nor Rome. 'Live on Gyara.' [20] I do. But living in Gyara seems like a whole lot of smoke. I repair to the place where no one can keep me from residing. For that residence is open to all. [21] And the last garment, that is the poor body—further than this, no one has any power over me. [22] That is why Demetrius said to Nero, 'You threaten me with death, but nature threatens you.' [23] But if I honour my body, I have given myself up to be a slave; if I honour my little estate, I also make myself a slave. [24] For at once I bear witness against myself as to what I may be captured by. As in the case of a snake, if it draws in its head, I say, 'Hit that part of him that he protects,' so you may be sure that whatever you choose to protect, your master will attack you at that point. [25] If you remember this, whom will you still flatter or fear?

[26] 'But I want to sit with the senators.' Don't you see that you are crowding yourself, you are making trouble for yourself?

[27] 'How else am I to get a clear view in the theatre?' Man, give up being a spectator, and you won't be troubled. What is the problem? Or wait a little, and when the spectacle is over, seat yourself in the senators' seats and sun yourself. [28] For remember, in general, we make trouble for ourselves, we hem ourselves in; that is, our opinions trouble and hem us in. [29] What does it mean to be reviled, for instance? Stand by a stone and revile it; and what have you done? If, then, someone listens like a stone, what will the reviler gain thereby? But if the reviler has the vulnerability of the one who is reviled as a point of vantage, then he accomplishes something.

[30] 'Strip him.' What do you mean, 'him'? Take his garment, and strip that. [31] 'I have insulted you.' 'A lot of good may it do you!' This was what Socrates practised, and for this reason he always had the same countenance. But we prefer to practise and study anything rather than how to be free and unimpeded.

[32] 'Philosophers speak in paradoxes.' Is there nothing paradoxical in the other arts? And what is more paradoxical than to cut someone's eye, that he may see? If someone said this to a man ignorant of medicine, wouldn't he laugh at the person who told him it? [33] What wonder, then, if in philosophy, too, many of its truths appear paradoxical to the inexperienced?

CHAPTER 26

What is the Law of Life?

[1] As a person was reading the hypothetical arguments, Epictetus said: 'This also is a hypothetical law, that we must accept what follows from the hypothesis. But even more is this a law of life, that we must act in conformity with nature. [2] For if in every matter and circumstance we wish to guard what is in accordance with nature, it is obvious that in everything we ought to make it our aim that the consequent does not escape us, and that we do not admit the contradictory. [3] Philosophers, then, train us first in theory, which is easier, then in this way lead us on to more difficult things. For here there is nothing that distracts us from following what is

taught, but in the matters of life many things divert the attention. [4] He is ridiculous, then, who says that he wishes to begin with the matters of life. For it is not easy to begin with more difficult things.

[5] 'And this is the justification we should use to parents who are upset because their children study philosophy. "Very well, father, I do wrong and do not know what is proper and suitable for me to do. If this can neither be learned nor taught, why do you blame me? But if it can be taught, teach me; and if you cannot, allow me to learn from those who profess to know. [6] For what do you suppose? That I voluntarily fall into evil and miss the good? Of course not. What, then, is the cause of my doing wrong? Ignorance. [7] Don't you want me, then, to get rid of my ignorance? Whom did anger ever teach the arts of navigation or music? Do you suppose, then, that your anger will teach me the business of life?"

[8] 'Only a person evincing such an intention is allowed to say such things. [9] But if someone merely wishes to display at a party his knowledge of hypothetical arguments, and he reads them and attends philosophers for this reason—for what other object does he act than to earn the admiration of some senator sitting next to him? [10] For the really great matters are there, and treasures here are accounted trifles there. For this reason it is difficult for a man to be master of his impressions where the things that disturb the judgement are great. [11] I know a man who cried as he clung to the knees of Epaphroditus, and said that he was in misery, for he had nothing but a million and a half left. [12] What did Epaphroditus do? Did he laugh at him, as you are laughing? No, but he said with amazement, "Poor man, how did you keep silence, how did you endure it?"'

[13] When Epictetus interrupted the person who was reading the hypothetical arguments, and the person who had set the reading began to laugh at him, Epictetus said: 'You are laughing at yourself. You did not train the young man beforehand, nor did you ascertain whether he was able to follow these arguments. But you use him as a reader! [14] Well then,' he said, 'if a mind has not the aptitude to understand the judgement concerning a conjunctive argument, do we trust it to bestow praise, to assign blame, to form a judgement about things good or bad? And if it thinks ill of anyone, is the latter concerned? If it esteems anyone, is the latter elated —when in such small matters it cannot draw the inference?'

[15] 'This, then, is the beginning of philosophy, recognizing the condition of one's ruling principle. For after a person realizes that it is weak, he will no longer want to employ it on things of the greatest difficulty. [16] But as it is, some people cannot swallow even a crumb, but they buy a whole treatise and set themselves to ingest that. And for this reason they vomit it up or get indigestion; then come colics, fluxes, and fevers. [17] Such people ought to consider what their capacity is. In the realm of theory it is easy to refute an ignorant person. But in the affairs of life no one offers himself to be refuted, and we hate the person who refutes us. [18] But Socrates said not to live the unexamined life.'

CHAPTER 27

In How Many Ways Impressions Arise, and What Aids We Should Provide Against Them

[1] Impressions come to us in four ways: for either things are and appear so; or they are not, and they do not appear to be; or they are, and do not appear to be; or they are not, and yet appear to be. [2] And so in all these cases the duty of an educated man is to judge correctly. But whatever it is that troubles us, to that we ought to apply a remedy. If the sophisms of the Pyrrhonists and the Academics are what trouble us, we must apply the remedy to them. [3] If it is the plausibility of things, which makes some things appear to be good when they are not, let us seek the remedy there. If it is habit that troubles us, we must try to seek a remedy for that. [4] What aid, then, can we find to combat habit? The opposite habit. [5] You hear laymen saying, 'Poor man, he is dead.' 'His father perished, his mother.' 'He was cut down in his prime, and in a foreign land.' [6] Give heed to the opposite words, distance yourself from these statements, check one habit with the contrary one. Against sophistic arguments one should have logic, and practice, and exercise in it. Against the plausibility of things one should have clear preconceptions polished and ready to hand.

[7] When death appears to be evil, one should have ready the fact that it is a duty to avoid evil things, and that death is necessary.

[8] For what am I to do? Where am I to escape it? It may be that I am not Sarpedon, the son of Zeus, so that I can say in his heroic way: 'I wish to go, and either win the prize for valour myself, or give another the opportunity of winning it. If I cannot succeed in anything myself, I will not begrudge another the chance to do something heroic.' This may be beyond us. But isn't that within our reach? [9] And where am I to escape death? Inform me of the country, of the people, safe from death, to whom I can resort. Inform me of the magic charm. I cannot escape death. [10] Can I not escape the fear of it, or am I to die moaning and groaning?

For the origin of passion is this: to wish for something, and not get it. [11] Hence, if I am able to change externals in accordance with my wish, I change them. If not, I am ready to maim the person who prevents me. [12] For, by nature, man cannot endure being deprived of the good, or falling into evil. [13] Then, at last, when I can neither change things nor maim whoever prevents me, I sit down and moan, and abuse whom I can, Zeus and the other gods. For if they do not care for me, what are they to me? [14] 'Yes, but you will be impious.' How will I be any worse off than I am now? To sum up, remember that unless piety and self-interest coincide, piety cannot be saved in any respect. Doesn't this seem cogent?

[15] Let the Pyrrhonist and the Academic come and face us. 'For my part, I have no leisure for these things, nor can I side with convention. [16] If I had a problem with a bit of land, I would have called in someone else to support my cause. With what, then, am I satisfied in this case?' [17] How, indeed, perception takes place, whether through the whole or a part, perhaps I cannot explain, for both opinions puzzle me. But that you and I are not the same person, I am quite certain. [18] How so? When I want to swallow something, I never carry it to your mouth, but to my own. When I want to take bread, I never take a broom, but I always go to bread as to a target. [19] And you yourselves who do away with the evidence of the senses, do you do anything different? Who of you, when wanting to enter a bath, ever went into a mill? [20] What then? Should we not, to the best of our ability, support the maintenance of convention and guard against the things that threaten it? [21] Who denies that? But that is the business of one who can, who has leisure. The person who is groaning, anxious, and inwardly broken in spirit should devote his time to something else.

CHAPTER 28

That We Should Not Be Angry with Men, and What Are the Small Things and the Great among Men

[1] What is the reason that we assent to anything? The fact that it appears to be so. [2] It is not possible, therefore, to assent to what appears not to be so. Why? Because that is the nature of the mind: to assent to the truth, reject what is false, and suspend judgement in doubtful cases. [3] What is the proof of this? Feel, if you can, that it is now night. 'Impossible.' Don't feel that it is now day. 'Impossible.' Feel or don't feel that the stars are even in number. 'Impossible.' [4] When anyone, then, assents to what is false, know that he was unwilling to assent to it as false; for, as Plato says, every soul is unwillingly deprived of the truth. [5] But it seemed to him that the false was true. Well, in the sphere of actions, what do we have corresponding to the true and the false? 'What is proper and improper, the advantageous and the disadvantageous, what is incumbent upon me and what is not, and the like.' [6] Can someone, then, think that something is advantageous to him, and not choose it? 'He cannot.'

[7] But what of her who says,

> 'I know what evils I intend to do
> But *thumos* is the master of my purposes'?

It is just this, that the gratification of her *thumos* in taking vengeance on her husband she regards as more profitable than saving her children. [8] 'Yes, but she is deceived.' Show her clearly that she is deceived, and she will not do it. But so long as you do not show it, what else has she to follow but that which appears true? Nothing. [9] Why, then, are you angry with her, because the poor woman has gone astray in the greatest matters, and has changed from a human being into a snake? Why do you not, if anything, pity her? As we pity the blind and lame, why do we not pity those who are blind and lame in respect of the most important things?

[10] Whoever, then, remembers this clearly, that the measure of every man's action is his impression—now this impression may be right or wrong; if right, the man is blameless; if wrong, the man

himself pays the penalty. For it is impossible that one man goes wrong, while another suffers the consequences—whoever remembers this will not be angered at anyone, will not be aggrieved with anyone, will not revile, blame, hate, or censure anyone. [11] 'So you infer that such momentous things have this as their origin, the impression?' This and nothing else. [12] The *Iliad* is nothing but an impression and the use of impressions. Paris got an impression to carry off Menelaus' wife, and an impression came to Helen to follow him. [13] Now, if Menelaus had got the impression that it was a gain to be deprived of such a wife, what would have happened? We would have lost not only the *Iliad*, but the *Odyssey* as well.

[14] 'Do matters of such moment depend on anything so small?' What do you call 'matters of such moment'? Wars and factions and deaths of many men and destruction of cities—what is there great in all of that? Nothing. [15] Why, what is there great in the death of many oxen and many sheep and the burning and destruction of many nests of swallows and storks? [16] 'Is there any similarity?' A great one. Men's bodies perished in the one case, bodies of oxen and sheep in the other. The paltry dwellings of men were burned, and so were nests of storks. [17] What is there great or dreadful in all that? Or else show me in what respect a man's house and the nest of a stork differ in respect of being a habitation. [18] 'Is there any similarity between a stork and a man?' As far as the body is concerned, a great similarity, except that the measly houses of men are made of beams and bricks, while the nest of a stork is composed of sticks and mud. [19] 'Does a man, then, differ in no way from a stork?' Yes, of course, but not in these respects. [20] Look, and you will find that he differs in others. See whether it is not in understanding what he does, in his social instinct, his faithfulness, his sense of respect, security from error, and intelligence. [21] Where, then, is the great evil and the great good among men? Just where the difference is. And if that distinctive element stands firm and fortified, and he loses neither his regard for others nor his faithfulness, nor intelligence, then the man too is preserved. But if any of these qualities are lost or taken by storm, then the man himself is lost.

[22] All great things depend on this. Did Paris come to his fall when the Greeks attacked, and were ravaging Troy, and his brothers were dying? [23] No, for no one suffers for another's misdeed; that was the destruction of storks' nests. His fall came when he lost the

man who was reverent of others, faithful, respectful of the laws of hospitality, and decent. [24] And when did Achilles fall? When Patroclus died? Far from it. Rather, when he grew angry, when he lamented the loss of a mere woman, when he forgot he was there not to get mistresses, but to make war. [25] These are the ways human beings are undone; this is the siege, this the razing of the city, when his right judgements are demolished, when they are destroyed.

[26] 'When women and children are enslaved, and when men themselves are slaughtered—are not all these things evil?' [27] How is it you add this opinion? Inform me too. 'No, but how is it that you are saying that they are not evils?' [28] Let us turn to our standards, produce your preconceptions. And this is why I cannot be sufficiently astonished at what goes on. When we wish to judge about weights, we do not judge at random; or about straight and crooked, we do not judge at random. [29] In short, whenever we need to know the truth of the case, none of us will act at random. [30] Yet where it is a case of the first and only cause of acting rightly or wrongly, of prosperity or adversity, of failure or success, there alone we act randomly and recklessly. There I have nothing like a balance or measure, but some sense impression appears, and immediately I act upon it. [31] Am I better than Agamemnon and Achilles, in that they do and suffer such wrongs because they follow their impressions, while I am not content to follow my own? [32] And what tragedy has any other source than this? What is the *Atreus* of Euripides? An appearance. The *Oedipus* of Sophocles? An appearance. The *Phoenix*? An appearance. *Hippolytus*? An appearance. [33] What kind of man, then, neglects this matter? What are those men called who follow every appearance? 'Madmen.' But do we do anything different?

CHAPTER 29

On Steadfastness

[1] The essence of the good is a certain kind of moral character; the essence of the bad is a certain kind of moral character. [2] What, then, are externals? Materials for the moral character, by engaging

with which it obtains its proper good or evil. [3] How will it obtain the good? If it does not admire the materials. For opinions about the materials, if the opinions are right, make the moral character good; but perverse and distorted opinions make it bad. [4] God has fixed this law, and says, 'If you want something good, get it from yourself.' You say, 'No, but from another.' Do not do so; get it from yourself. [5] Therefore, when the tyrant threatens and calls me, I say, 'Whom does he threaten?' If he says, 'I will put you in chains,' I say, 'He threatens my hands and feet.' [6] If he says, 'I will cut off your head,' I say, 'He threatens my head.' If he says, 'I will throw you into prison,' I say, 'He threatens my whole body.' And if he threatens exile, the same. [7] 'Does he threaten you, then, not at all?' If I feel that these things are nothing to me, then no. [8] But if I fear any of them, then it is me that he threatens. So whom do I fear? The master of what? Things under my control? There is no such person. Things not under my control? And what are these things to me?

[9] 'Do you philosophers, then, teach contempt of kings?' Of course not. Who among us teaches us to claim against them the things over which they have authority? [10] Take my poor body, take my property, take my reputation, take those who are about me. If I provoke anyone to claim these things, indeed let him accuse me. [11] 'Yes, but I want to control your opinions also.' And who has given you this authority? How can you conquer another's opinion? [12] 'I will bring fear to bear, and so conquer it,' he says. Are you unaware that it conquers itself, and is not conquered by another? Nothing can conquer the moral character, except itself. [13] For this reason the law of god is most powerful and most just: Let the stronger always prevail over the weaker. [14] 'Ten are stronger than one.' For what? For putting in chains, for killing, for dragging off wherever they choose, for depriving one of property. The ten therefore conquer the one in that in which they are stronger. [15] So in what are they weaker? If one has correct opinions, but the others do not. Well, can they prevail in this? How? If we were weighed in the scales, must not the heavier drag the other down?

[16] 'To think that Socrates should have suffered such things at the hands of the Athenians!' Slave, why do you say 'Socrates'? Speak of the thing as it is: that the poor body of Socrates should have been carried off and dragged to prison by stronger men, and that any one should have given hemlock to the poor body of Socrates, and that it

should expire. [17] Do these things seem strange to you, do they seem unjust, do you blame god on their account? Did Socrates then have nothing to make up for them? [18] Where was the essence of his good? To whom should we pay attention, you or him? And what does he say? 'Anytus and Meletus can kill me, but they cannot harm me.' And again: 'If it pleases god, then so be it.' [19] But show me the man who has inferior opinions who prevails over one who is superior in his opinions. You cannot—not even close. For this is the law of nature and of god: Let the superior always prevail over the inferior. In what? In that in which it is superior. [20] One body is stronger than another; many are stronger than one; the thief is stronger than one who is not a thief. [21] This is also the reason why I lost my lamp, because the thief was superior to me in his ability to stay awake. But the man bought the lamp at this price: for a lamp he became a thief, for a lamp he became untrustworthy, for a lamp he became like a wild beast. He thought that he came out ahead.

[22] Fine. But a man has seized me by the cloak, and is dragging me to the public square. Others cry out, 'Philosopher, what has been the use of your opinions? Look, you are being hauled off to prison, you are about to be beheaded.' [23] And what kind of *Introduction* could I have conned, so that, if a stronger man seizes my cloak, I would not be dragged off; that if ten men lay hold of me and cast me into prison, I would not be cast in? [24] Did I learn nothing else, then? I learned to see that everything that happens, if it is independent of my moral character, is nothing to me. [25] Haven't you been benefited in this respect? Why, then, do you seek advantage in anything other than that in which you have learned that the advantage resides? [26] Then, sitting in prison, I say, 'The man who cries out in this way neither hears what words mean, nor understands what is said, nor does he care at all to know what philosophers say or do. Leave him be.'

[27] But now he says to the prisoner, 'Come out from your prison.' If you have no further need of me in prison, I come out. If you have need of me, I will enter it again. [28] 'How long will you act thus?' For as long as reason chooses to be with the body. But when reason does not choose this, take it, and farewell. [29] Only we must not do it irrationally, or thoughtlessly, or for any slight pretext. For again, god does not wish it, and he has need of such a universe, and such inhabitants in the world. But if he sounds the signal for retreat, as

he did for Socrates, we must obey the one who gives the signal, as if he were a general.

[30] Well, then, should we say such things to the multitude? [31] What is the point? Isn't it enough for a man to be persuaded himself? When children come clapping their hands and shouting, 'Today is the good Saturnalia,' do we say, 'The Saturnalia is not good?' By no means, we clap our hands too. [32] And you then, when you can't change a person's mind, know that he is a child, and clap your hands with him. And if you don't want to do this, then keep quiet.

[33] It is important to bear this in mind, and when called to any such difficulty, to know that the time is come to show whether we have been educated. [34] For a young man from school who runs into a difficulty is like a person who has practised solving syllogisms, and if someone proposes to him an easy one, says, 'Propose to me one that is cunningly involved, instead, so that I can get a little practice.' Athletes are also dissatisfied with lightweight young men. [35] 'He cannot lift me,' he says. 'This one, on the other hand, is a strapping young man.' No, but when the time comes, we have to weep and say, 'I wanted to keep on learning.' Keep learning what? If you did not learn these things in order to show them in practice, for what did you learn them?

[36] I think that there is someone among you sitting here who is in travail, and saying to himself, 'Why doesn't a difficulty come to me like the one that has come to this man? That I should be wasting my life in a corner, when I might be crowned at Olympia! When will someone announce to me such a contest?' This should be the attitude that all of you adopt. [37] But among the gladiators of Caesar there are some who are irritated because no one brings them forward and matches them in combat, though they implore god, and entreat their supervisors, that they may fight one on one. And will none of you show a like spirit?

[38] I would like to sail for this very purpose, and see what my athlete is doing, how he is practising the material. [39] 'I do not want such material,' one says. Is it in your power to take whatever material you want? There has been given to you such a body, such parents, such brothers, such a country, such a position in your country. Then you come to me and say, 'Change the material for me.' Don't you have resources, then, to use whatever has been given you? [40] 'It is yours to set the task, mine to practise it well.'

But no. You say, 'Don't propose to me this hypothetical argument, but this one; don't impose this consequence upon me, but this one.' [41] The time will soon come when tragic actors imagine that they are the masks and boots and long robe. Man, you have these things as subject-matter and material. [42] Say something so that we may know whether you are a tragic actor or comic relief; for both have the other things in common. [43] For this reason, if someone takes away their boots and mask, and brings them on-stage a mere shadow of themselves, is the tragic actor lost, or does he remain? If he has a voice, he remains.

[44] Another example. 'Take a governorship.' I take it, and when I take it, I show how a man behaves when he is educated. [45] 'Put off the senatorial robe, take up beggar's rags, and come forth in such a guise.' What then? Has it not been given me to display a fine voice? [46] How, then, do you appear now? As a witness called by god. [47] 'Come forward, you, and bear witness for me. For you are worthy to be brought forward as a witness. Is anything outside the moral character good or bad? Do I do any man harm? Have I put the advantage of each man in control of anyone but himself? What witness do you bear for god?' [48] 'I am in dire straits, sir, and unfortunate; no one cares for me, no one gives me anything, everyone slanders and derides me.' [49] Is this the witness you are going to bear, and disgrace god's summons, when he has honoured you to such a degree, and thought you worthy to be brought on-stage to bear such testimony?

[50] But the one in authority has declared, 'I pronounce you impious and irreligious.' What has happened to you? 'I have been judged impious and irreligious.' [51] Nothing else? 'Nothing else.' But if the same person had passed judgement on a conditional, and declared, 'The proposition that "If it is day, it is light" I declare to be false,' what has happened to the conditional? Who is judged in this case, who condemned—the conditional, or the man misled by it? [52] Who, then, is this man who has power to make a judgement about you? Does he know anything about what is pious or impious? Has he studied it? Or learned it? Where? And with whom? [53] And yet a musician pays no attention to the man who declares that the lowest note on the lyre is the highest, nor a geometer, if someone declares that the lines extending from the centre of a circle to the circumference are not equal. [54] And shall one who is truly educated pay any attention to the uneducated man when he makes some

judgement about what is pious and impious, what is just and unjust? Oh, the great wrong done to the educated! Did you learn these things here?

[55] Don't you prefer to leave the petty arguments about such matters to others, to lazy fellows, so that they can sit in a corner and receive their sorry pay, or complain that no one gives them a thing? And won't you come forward and make use of what you have learned? [56] For it is not petty arguments that are wanted now; the writings of the Stoics are full of them. What then is wanting? Someone to apply them, someone to bear witness to his words by his acts. [57] Assume, I, entreat you, this character, that we may no longer use old examples in our schools, but may have some examples from our own time.

[58] To whom, then, does the consideration of these matters belong? To one who has leisure. For man is a contemplative animal. [59] But it is shameful to contemplate these things like runaway slaves. We should rather sit without distraction, and listen now to the tragic actor, now to the lute-player—not as slaves do. No sooner does one look up and praise the actor than the slave glances anxiously around. Then if someone pronounces their master's name, they are disturbed and agitated. [60] It is shameful for philosophers to contemplate the works of nature this way. For what is a master? Man is not the master of man, but death, life, pleasure, and pain are. [61] Then bring Caesar before me without these things, and you will see how I am serene. But when he comes with these things thundering and lightning, and I am afraid, what else have I done than recognize my master like the runaway slave? [62] But while I have a reprieve from these things, as the runaway slave attends to the performance, so do I. I bathe, I drink, I sing, but all the while in fear and trembling. [63] But if I free myself from the masters— that is to say, from the things that make the masters formidable— what further trouble do I have, what further master?

[64] 'Well, then, should we announce this to everyone?' No, but we should accommodate ourselves to the ignorant and say, 'This man recommends for me what he imagines is good for him. I forgive him.' [65] For even Socrates forgave the gaoler who was weeping when he was about to drink the poison, and said, 'How generous of him to lament over us!' [66] Does he therefore say to him, 'That's why we dismissed the women'? No, he says this to his intimates, to those who can understand it. But the other man he accommodates as he would a child.

CHAPTER 30

What We Should Have Ready in Circumstances

[1] Whenever you come before one of the great ones, remember that another looks down from above at what goes on, and it is more important to please him. [2] He, then, asks you, 'What did you call exile, gaol, chains, death, and ill repute in your school?' 'I called them indifferent.' [3] 'And what do you call them now? Have they changed at all?' 'No.' 'Have you changed?' 'No.' 'Tell me, then, what are the indifferents?' 'Things independent of moral character.' 'Tell me what follows.' 'Things independent of moral character are nothing to me.' [4] 'And tell me what you thought good things were.' 'Proper moral character and use of impressions.' 'And what is the goal of life?' 'To follow you.' [5] 'Is this what you say now?' 'I say the same things now.'

Then remember these things, and go before the great man with confidence, and you will see what it means to be a young man who has studied what he should, when he is in the presence of uneducated men. [6] Indeed, I imagine that you will feel as follows: 'Why do we prepare so long and so hard for nothing? [7] Is this what they called power? Is this the antechamber, the chamberlains, the armed guards? Is it for this that I listened to so many lectures? All this was nothing, and I had been preparing for something great.'

COMMENTARY

Titles

On the titles of the *Discourses*, see Schenkl 1916: pp. lxxxi–lxxxii. He believes they were appended by Arrian, and I think this is possible, even though I do not share his view (the common one) that Arrian also transcribed the *Discourses*. In any case, the titles are probably not the work of E. While most, like Chapter 1's are apt or at least unobjectionable, others, like those at the head of Chapters 5, 10, 13, 17, and 21 of Book I, are not well chosen. It is doubtful that E would have felt his discourses required any titles.

CHAPTER 1

Concerning What Is In Our Power and What Is Not

The formula 'what is in our power' (*to eph' hēmin*) had roots in Aristotle (*EN* 3. 1–3; *Phys.* 2. 4–6), but became prominent in the Hellenistic period, owing to the debate over free will and determinism. This was a crux for Hellenistic ethics, because of the presuppositions of both Stoic and Epicurean physics. It is the subject of Alex. *De Fato*, Cic. *De Fato*, etc. For Stoic use of the phrase cf. Plut. *St. rep.* 1056D; Alex. *De Fato* 181. 13–182. 20, etc. For Epicurus cf. DL 10. 133; LS 20C1, 8–9 (he used the variant phrases *to par' hēmas, to di' hēmôn autōn,* and *to ex hēmōn autōn* with no discernible difference in meaning). E is quoted four times by Stobaeus in an anthology of passages 'concerning what is in our power' (2. 8. 22, 23, 27, 30).

The Academic Carneades is credited with pointing out the ethical consequences of the Stoics' logical and physical determinism (Cic. *De Fato* 40). He alleged that it was incompatible with standard notions of praise and blame. Chrysippus, the 'second founder' of Stoicism, did not retreat from determinism, but is associated with a defence of moral responsibility that has earned him the distinction of being the first compatibilist. His defence was twofold. Chrysippus maintained that, while events were predetermined by an unbroken chain of cause and effect, events that would not happen were none the less possible. This helped meet the stipulation that, to be responsible for an act, we must at least have had the opportunity to act otherwise (see LS 1. 393).

Chrysippus' second point relied on the importance of *phantasia* in descriptions of human and animal behaviour by philosophers at least since Aristotle. Chrysippus denied that the cause of a reaction to a given impression was the impression itself. Impressions are links in the continuous chain of causes that Stoics identified with fate. But action depends upon assenting to them, and the mind is capable of giving or withholding that assent. This theory was elaborated in terms of different causes (Cic. *De Fato* 39–43). The relevant distinction here is that between primary and auxiliary (or antecedent) ones. Impressions are auxiliary causes, subject to fate in being both predetermined and necessary. But assent and impulse are primary causes, and are the things *eph' hēmin*: 'in our power', or 'up to us'.

So much is uncontroversial. But critics objected that if this notion of fate be accepted, 'our impressions will always be determined by what has gone before, our impulses will accord with them, and "what is in our power" will be just a name' (Plot. 3. 1. 7. 14–16; quoted by Simplicius, *In Ench.* 24c). They wondered, in other words, if fate was not operative at every stage, if giving or withholding assent, for example, was not dictated by forces outside our control (Cic. *De Fato* 40).

Not enough of Chrysippus survives to judge what his response to this would be. Hostile sources (like Plutarch and Alexander of Aphrodisias) misrepresent his views, and even sympathetic ones (like Calcidius) confuse or conflate his position with that of other philosophers. The crucial phrase *to eph' hēmin* is itself vague and part of the problem. Chrysippus could have used it without meaning by it what others did. Alexander (*De Fato* 181. 15–182. 20) complains that Chrysippus did not use it like Aristotle did, to denote deliberation and choice, but in a degraded sense to stand for what is merely 'voluntary' (*hekousion*), and happens 'through us'. This impression derives in part from Chrysippus' analogy of human behaviour to inanimate things like a cylinder (Gellius 7. 2. 11–13), a celebrated comparison that was perhaps too successful in capturing the imagination. But one point of the analogy was to suggest that, just as it is the nature of a cylinder to roll, so it is man's nature (and fate) to exercise the uniquely human faculties of rational impulse and assent, which in Stoic psychology substitute for deliberation and choice. Other critics, with perhaps more cogency, maintained that Chrysippus' *to eph' hēmin* did not amount to 'complete autonomy' (*to autexousion*) or 'freedom' (*eleutheria*) (Alex. *De Fato* 182. 20–6; Nemesius *NH* 34. 46–9). They applied, in particular, the test of a person's ability to choose between opposing actions (Alex. *De Fato* 196. 22–197. 2; Cic. *ND* 3. 92). Sources do not say much about the Stoic analysis of choice, but the capacity of a person to choose either of two contrary acts is something that Chrysippus expressly denied (Alex. *De Fato* 181. 13–182. 20).

The opinion of many critics, then and now, is that Chrysippus intended only to reconcile belief in determinism with some meaningful sense in which we can be called the cause of our actions. He was, on this view, a soft determinist. For him *to eph' hēmin* denoted the concept of responsibility or imputability—not unqualified free will (see LS 1. 394; Sharples 1991: 6–15). Yet Cicero, a relatively reliable witness, concluded that Chrysippus 'inclined toward those who want the movements of the mind to be free from necessity' (*De Fato* 39). Augustine (*CD* 5. 10) apparently agreed. Chrysippus did, after all, speak of freedom in one particular sense, that of the sage (DL 7. 121; Cic. *PS* 33–5). And, as Long has written, the sage is just man '*in propria persona*, man as he should be if his nature is sound' (Long 1970b: 264).

A standard objection to fatalism in ancient sources is that it renders pointless encouragement, discouragement, admonishment, and the like (LS 20C2; Alex. *De Fato* 196. 24–197. 3). Whatever the force of that criticism as it applies to Chrysippus, it is surely relevant in E's case to note that exhortation and admonishment are his stock-in-trade. The prominence he gives to the theme of freedom is also significant. It seems that he interpreted Chrysippus in a libertarian manner, perhaps rightly. In any case, he sticks closely to the terms of his solution. Although he avoids the word 'fate' (preferring 'providence' instead), E often says that what is 'up to us' is 'the correct use of impressions'; see **§7** below. At **§12** he equates this with desire and impulse, elsewhere with other kinds of impulse and with assent (1. 17. 22–4, 2. 8. 29, 3. 9. 18, 4. 1. 69–71). So it is clear that he maintains the Chrysippean distinction between impressions, on the one hand, and our response to them, on the other.

One way he differs is in perspective. So far as the extant testimonies go, Chrysippus seems to have confined himself to a third-person account of human behaviour. The *Discourses*, by contrast, are dominated by second-person address. This helps confirm the intuition of personal liberty that philosophers since Epicurus had appealed to (LS 20C4, 8). As Sharples (1986: 277) observes: 'Soft-determinist accounts of choice which may be plausible in the third person are less so in the second or first.' The subjective experience of freedom encourages us to regard ourselves not just as puppets of impressions, but as masters of them in so far as we refer them to objective standards. Annas (1992: 81) remarks that E 'lays constant stress on our ability to accept or reject appearances'. This emphasis caught the attention of later writers engaged by the debate: Aulus Gellius (19. 1. 14–21) and Augustine (*CD* 9. 4) both quote E extensively on this point.

The present essay is an exercise in self-definition, since the search for 'what is in our power' is also a search for the self, for what we are. It articulates some of E's most characteristic themes. It is appropriately placed at the head of the corpus, and abstracted in chapter 1 of the *Enchiridion*. Analysis:

§§1–6 Reason has architectonic power to examine itself as well as everything else.

§§7–17 Because reason has reflexive capacity, it ought to focus on itself, not on externals like the body, which is not in our control.

§§18–32 This principle illustrated by reference to role models who had the right idea about our control over impressions and lack of control over the body.

§§1–6 E's argument in this opening section derives force from the use of two polyvalent words in combination, *logikē* and *dunamis*. *Logikē* is the adjective from *logos*, a word of wide range in Greek, with special meaning for the Stoics. Besides being a principle in their physics (Plut. *St. rep.* 1050C–D), *logos* represented the faculty of reason in Stoic psychology, comprising those functions of the human soul equivalent to or coextensive with the 'commanding faculty' (*to hēgemonikon*). It governed sensation, impression, impulse, and assent (DL 7. 159). *Dunamis* covers not only arts such as grammar and music (**§2**), but also the faculties of the soul (**§§4, 12**). For the latter use, cf. Alex. *Mant.* 118. 6–9 (= *SVF* 2. 823): 'There is one *dunamis* of the soul, so that the same thing, depending on its disposition, at one time thinks, at another time grows angry, and at another time desires.' The present discourse is also a defence of the unitary view of the soul, and therefore of Stoic rationalism, since 'the power of impulse and repulsion, of desire and avoidance—in a word, the power of using impressions' (**§12**) is assumed to be a single thing, viz. the power of reason.

In context the purpose of this argument is to furnish a theoretical basis from which to challenge the assumption that we are controlled by our mental impressions (*phantasiai*), since we are just the sort of persons to have a certain kind of impression and react accordingly. E locates an Archimedean point where impressions are both produced and evaluated. The rational faculty is responsible for generating *phantasiai* and also for passing them under review; it controls impression as well as assent (cf. 1. 20. 1–11; Aet. 4. 21. 1). In virtue of this, man has a measure of autonomy. For the general theme compare 2. 23. 5–6: 'Do not be ungrateful for [other, subordinate] gifts . . . , but at the same time remember that he has given you something better than these: the faculty that can make use of them, pass judgement upon them, estimate the value of each.'

At 1. 17. 1–3 E shows awareness of a problem inherent in the idea: 'Since reason articulates and processes everything else, and itself should not remain unarticulated, what will it be articulated by? Obviously, it must be by itself, or by something else. Now, that will be reason, or something greater than reason, which is impossible. If it is reason, what, in turn, will articulate it? If itself, well, the other reason can do the same. If we require another reason to perform the service, the process will be endless and unceasing.' The implication is that reason must be capable of self-analysis. Stoics in general defended the validity of a criterion of knowledge against the Sceptics, who argued that the idea entails a logical regress: 'When we [Sceptics] pose the argument, "If a criterion exists it is either judged or unjudged," and draw one or other of two conclusions— either the infinite regress or the absurdity of the statement that a thing is its own criterion—[the Stoics], in opposition, declare that it is not absurd to admit that a thing is its own criterion; for a straight edge can test both itself and other things, and a balance weighs both its own equality and that of other things, and light clearly reveals not only other things but even itself. Hence the criterion too can be a criterion both of other things and itself' (SE *M* 7. 441–2). Cf. Cic. *Ac.* 2. 91: 'What will the philosopher judge? What conjunctive and disjunctive argument is valid, what is ambiguously stated, what follows from what, and what is inconsistent. If reason judges these and similar things, it judges itself.' The Stoics met the Sceptics head on, affirming the possibility of a reflexive, supervisory power. This is what E predicates of reason. (For *logos* as a criterion see LS 2. 243.)

Another distinctive excellence of reason lies in its ability to confer value. Like earlier philosophers, E assumes that arts like music and grammar are value-neutral. In Plato's *Laches*, for example, it is argued that the art of medicine *qua* medicine is indiscriminate in its pursuit of healing; the decision whether to treat a particular patient belongs to another art (195c). The search for this superordinate art or faculty goes forward in the *Charmides* (164 ff.) and *Euthydemus* (291d–e), but fails in part because of Plato's adherence to the craft analogy. But *dunamis* covers more than arts and crafts; and because E conceives the problem in broad terms, he is able to identify the desired power with the rational faculty. The Stoics realized that reason was value-neutral; Chrysippus said it was as liable to abuse as any capacity (Plut. *St. rep.* 1037B). But because reason can be used to discover and condemn such abuses, it is able to police itself.

[In the translation of §3 I have, with Souilhé retained *hoti* ('that'), the reading of S, and the alteration of *graptōn* to *grammatōn*.]

The argument in §§7–11 about what is 'not up to us' proceeds *a majori ad minus*, by consideration, not only of our limits, but of god's. As noted by Long (1996a: 302–4), E contradicts old Stoic doctrine about the capacity of god, identified with the principle of cause, to 'shape matter and direct it however he wants' (Sen. *Ep.* 65. 2). This doctrine originally complemented Stoic belief in prime matter, which, while devoid of quality *per se*, was supposed to be receptive of any form (Cic. *Ac.* 1. 27; *ND* 3. 92; see Hahm 1977: 29–34). The tendency of later Stoics to regard matter as an obstacle to god's omnipotence reflects the influence of contemporary Platonism. Long cites Hierocles *apud* Stob. 1. 182. 10–12; cf. also Sen. *Ep.* 58. 27; *Prov.* 5. 8–9. Plato's influence is certainly evident in the present passage. It recasts the essay's basic distinction between 'what is up to us' and what is not in terms of a dualism of mind and body. Common ground is marked especially in bringing this dualism to bear on the concept of freedom. It recalls the account in the *Timaeus* (41b sq.) of man's creation, and the installation of divine mind in a body 'by necessity'. Other Platonic sources affirming the freedom of the mind relative to the body include *Laws* 875c–d; Plut. *Parsne an facultas* 5; [Plut.] *De Fato* 574A; Calcidius 180b–181; Plot. 3. 1. 8. (Cf. Sen. *Ben.* 3. 20. 1 and *Ep.* 65. 16, passages which I think also introduce Platonic ideas into Stoicism, despite the attempt of Inwood (1993) to represent them as exclusively Stoic.) In a figurative context like the present, dramatizing a fictional conversation between god and man about creation, E might well evoke the *Timaeus* (largely figurative itself, on the majority view), and borrow some of its ideas. Dillon (1993: 137) cites a lexical similarity between E and the Middle Platonist Alcinous on a related topic, the descent of the soul (based on *Tim.* 41d–e).

This section represents the body as the particle of matter in which 'we' (i.e. our reason) is installed. Since E's attitude toward the body is complex, it should be discussed further. Rutherford (1989: 242) remarks that 'Epictetus certainly ranks the body as inferior to the governing mind or spirit, but it is rare for him to pour scorn on it *per se*: he usually condemns only those who are too attached to it.' Attachment is precisely what he deprecates here, to the body as well as to other 'externals'. But he does not sanction its neglect. On our obligations to the body cf. 4. 11, extolling Socrates as a paradigm of personal hygiene (cf. Xen. *Mem.* 1. 2. 4, 3. 12). Simplicius also characterizes E's attitude as Socratic, adverting to the doctrine of Plato's *First Alcibiades* that the body is the instrument of the soul, and on that account is not to be despised but cared for (Simpl. *In Ench.* 2a–3b; cf. Pl. *1 Alc.* 129a–130e).

That this is roughly the right tradition to invoke emerges from 2. 23. 32–5: '[They are wrong] who assert that there is no difference between beauty and ugliness. Could a man be affected in the same way by the sight of Thersites and Achilles? Or Helen and some ordinary woman? . . . The important thing is this: to give every faculty its due, and observe the value of each; but to learn the highest of all things [reason], and devote ourselves to this, treating the rest as of secondary value, though without neglecting them, so far as that is possible. For we must take care of our eyes too, yet not as the highest thing, but for the sake of the highest; because the latter will not attain its natural perfection except it use the eyes with reason.' From this we infer the real, if subordinate, value of the body, and the role of the senses in gaining knowledge. E's position is in agreement with Stoic empiricism, but clashes with Plato's a priori epistemology: regard for the senses also tends to dignify the body.

Stoic physics in any case limited the extent to which its view of the body could be assimilated to Plato's. Eschatology of the sort one finds in the *Phaedo* or *Republic* 10, with all that implies for the soul's independence, is alien to the Stoa. There is no transcendence in either a metaphysical or a personal sense. 'What there was of fire in you shall pass into fire, earth shall pass into earth, air into air, water into water. There is no Hades, no Acheron, no Cocytus, no Phlegethon' (3. 13. 15; see commentary ad 1. 9. 10–17). As Simplicius writes, 'One might well admire this quality of his discourses, their ability to render happy those who obey them and put them into practice, without having to promise rewards for virtue after death' (*In Ench.* 3a). For E, fulfilment as a human being comes in the embodied state or not at all. Bonhöffer calls attention to passages in which E calls life a festival, game or banquet, to document his positive view of the body and bodily existence (1890: 33–40).

According to another school of thought, however, E depreciates the body because the body, and bodily actions, are not 'up to us'. Cf. Botros 1985: 286: 'Epictetus (rather like Wittgenstein in the *Tractatus* and like modern libertarians) applied the term [*eph' hēmīn*] only to activity that we could never conceivably be hindered from performing, and since even simple bodily movements (not to mention complicated action sequences) could not pass this stringent test, willing alone remained a candidate for this description.' For similar views see Inwood 1985: 53 (citing 'Epictetus' constant assertion that human impulses are unhinderable while our bodily actions are not'), and Bobzien 1996: 10–11.

While there are passages that could support this interpretation (e.g. 4. 1. 72–3), I don't think it can finally be sustained in light of the prominence E gives to the doctrine of social duties. Duties (or 'proper functions', *kathēkonta*) in respect of family, friends, city, etc. were central to Stoic ethics (cf. LS 57D). E makes them the second stage in his philosophical curriculum (3. 2. 4; the subject is treated at length in 2. 10). And he is emphatic about man's need to perform them: 'Am I saying that man is an animal made for inactivity (*aprakton*)? Not at all!' (1. 10. 7). Stoics defined themselves in contrast to rival schools by their commitment to social and political action: see comment on 1. 10. 7–12. The relevant distinction to bear in mind is that, for a Stoic, the moral value of an act inheres in the effort, not the outcome—a point actually intended to forestall and eliminate excuses for inaction. This becomes clear in E's advice to perform his duty by his estranged brother and visit him: 'Am I telling you, "Go like a man who is certain to get what he wants," and not simply, "Go in order to do what becomes you"?

"Why then go at all?" So as to have gone, so as to have performed the function of the citizen that you are, of a brother, of a friend' (3. 24. 46–7). Action can be frustrated and fail to produce the result intended; to that extent freedom of action is reduced. But that social relations entail certain actions proves they are feasible up to a point: 'ought' implies 'can'. To renounce bodily action altogether is to accept the Lazy Argument (Cic. *De Fato* 28–30), or to fail to distinguish target from end (cf. Cic. *Fin.* 3. 22).

In **§12** 'the power of making correct use of impressions' (§7) is glossed as 'the power of impulse and repulsion, of desire and avoidance'. It was earlier (§§4–5) identified with reason. That impulse, desire, and reason are 'in our power' is orthodox Stoic doctrine (Alex. *De Fato* 183. 22–4). That they should be identified particularly with 'the power of using impressions' is E's own contribution, though reflecting the prominence of *phantasia* in Stoic psychology generally (cf. DL 7. 49). With this phrase E focuses attention on what precisely can be done and what is 'in our power'. He is careful to specify 'correct use', since mere use of impressions, without reason, also characterizes the beasts (cf. SE *M* 8. 275–6).

The need of man to test impressions is the dominant theme in E's philosophy: 'The first and most important duty of the philosopher is test and distinguish impressions and to admit none that is untested' (1. 20. 7). Passages like the following are frequent: 'Do not be swept off your feet, I urge you, by the vividness of an impression, but say, "Wait a moment, impression; let me see who you are and what you are an impression of; allow me to put you to the test"' (2. 18. 24; cf. 2. 22. 5, 3. 2. 8, 3. 12. 15, 3. 24. 108, 4. 3. 7; *Ench.* 18, 20, 34, etc.). E calls unprocessed impressions *tracheiai* ('raw': *Ench.* 1. 5), and writes: 'Make it your practice at the outset to say to every raw impression, "You are an impression and not at all what you appear." Then examine and test it by the rules that you have.' Simplicius ad loc. provides a list of such rules: 'Ask whether it refers to a spiritual good, a good of the flesh, or a mere external good. Next ask whether its reference is to benefit or merely pleasure; then whether it is practicable or impracticable' (*In Ench.* 44a). The answer to these questions determines whether to give an impression one's assent. Two errors are possible: assent to what is false and rash assent to what is unclear (Plut. *St. rep.* 1056F).

Origen, who knew E well and mentions him six times by name, seems to draw on him directly when treating of the use of impressions in the context of fate and free will: cf. *SVF* 988–90 with Inwood 1985: 84 and Hahm 1991: 42–5.

The description in §12 of reason as 'a part (*meros*) of god' recurs at 1. 17. 27 and 2. 8. 10–11; cf. Cic. *ND* 2. 147–9; Sen. *Ep.* 31. 11, etc. It was also a Platonic commonplace; cf. Plut. *De Sera num.* 559D and *Plat. quaest.* 1001C. In this section E advises his readers to 'care for' (*epimeleisthai*) the element that they share with god. This recalls the Socratic command to 'Know yourself, for once we know ourselves, we may learn how to care (*epimeleisthai*) for ourselves' (Pl. *1 Alc.* 124a–b).

[The *de* after *euchomai* in §13 is apparently superfluous, which has given rise to various emendations (*ge*, *dē*, etc.). But it can stand. See Denniston 1966: 171–2 for its use in dialogue, real or (as here) imagined, to introduce the answer to a second question.]

§§18–32 The last third of the discourse illustrates the main point through the use of historical examples. In line with Aristotle's prescription (*Rhet.* 1394a10–18) and his practice elsewhere (e.g. 1. 2, 1. 9. 27–34, and 1. 19), E uses anecdotal material to bring discussion to a close. This section demonstrates what is 'in our power' when confronted with fate in the form of external force. The figures cited were all members of the Pisonian conspiracy against Nero. Since the body is not completely 'in our power', all suffered exile or death. But knowledge of what actually was in their power enabled them to maintain their dignity and emerge with their freedom of action intact. The passage reflects the preoccupation of Roman Stoicism with moral *exempla*, personal role models. Cf. Sen. *Ep.* 6. 5: 'the journey [of the philosopher] is long if one follows precepts, short and efficient through *exempla*'; on this subject see Schofield 1986: 51–2.

Plautius Lateranus was consul designate in AD 65, but joined the Pisonian conspiracy in that year and was executed (Tac. *Ann.* 15. 51. 3, 15. 67). The point of the anecdote in §19 lies not only in his willing acceptance of death for his opposition to tyranny, but in his doing so, in a sense, twice. He submitted to beheading a second time after the axe slipped. Cf. Sen. *Prov.* 2. 12: 'To confront death requires not so great a soul as to confront it again.' Such poise as Lateranus showed illustrates in context the theme of control over one's impressions. He 'shrank back', but only 'a little'. In other words, he could not help having a fearful impression, but he stifled the impulse to flee and accomplished his resolve. Relevant here is what E and other Stoics had to say about *propatheiai*, 'swift and unconsidered motions that forestall the action of the intellect' (fr. 9).

Such instinctive reactions to impressions of danger, bad news, etc., are not 'up to us'. But it is 'up to us' to withhold assent and not yield to them. 'Chrysippus said that the good man is not always courageous or the base man cowardly, the necessary condition being that when there are certain impressions the former abides by his resolutions and the latter retreats' (Plut. *St. rep.* 1046F). So Lateranus immediately restored his neck to the block, and did not let his incipient fear prevail. Sen. *Ep.* 82 discusses the topic of *propatheiai* at length, particularly anxiety in the face of death, which he distinguishes from actual fear, settled belief in imminent evil, which death is not: 'Death is no evil, for it is not shameful' (E 1. 24. 6). On *propatheiai* cf. also 3. 24. 108; Sen. *Ep.* 11, 57. 3–5; *De Ira* 1. 16. 7, 2. 1–4; Gellius 12. 5. 11–12. See Cherniss 1976: 521; Abel 1983; Inwood 1993: 164–83; LS 2. 417.

The point of the anecdote involving Epaphroditus in **§20** is obscure, and the difficulty is compounded by trouble with the text. If Lateranus is still the subject, perhaps his action here can be connected with the petition to Nero that was to have served as the conspirators' original pretext for approaching and then assassinating him (so Griffin 1984: 166–7). The idea is interesting, but speculative. Epaphroditus was a freedman of Nero (cf. also 1. 19. 19, 1. 26. 11), and after AD 62 his secretary in charge of answering petitions. According to ancient tradition, he had been E's master.

[As Lateranus is well known, Schweighaüser proposed to delete the indefinite pronoun *tis* after his name in **§19**; better, I think, to go further and omit the whole phrase *tis en tēi Rōmēi* as an intrusive gloss, the solution proposed by Upton. The anecdote in **§20** should probably be connected with the one preceding, as the phrase 'and also before that' (*kai eti proteron*) suggests. The ending on the participle 'approaching' (*proselthont-*) is illegible in S. It seems best to restore -*ta*, and assume that Lateranus remains the subject. We then need to delete the following *tis*, or, as Schenkl proposed, change it to *tōi*. If Schenkl's suggestion is accepted, *kuriōi* must be deleted, or [*tōi*] *kuriōi* changed to *tōi apeleutherōi*, the reading of a second hand in S. Both changes have been assumed in the translation here.]

§22 depends on a contrast between an act and the manner in which it is performed, the 'what' as opposed to the 'how'. Cf. Sen. *Ep.* 95. 40, discussing the efficacy of ethical maxims: 'Precepts will help you do what should be done; but they will not help you do it in the right way; and, if they fail in that, they do not conduce to virtue. . . . Credit lies not in the deed itself, but in the way it is done.' Cf. *Prov.* 2. 4: 'Not what you endure, but how you endure, is important.' Things contrary to nature, such as death and exile, were expressly 'dispreferred' and 'not-to-be-taken' (cf. Stob. 2. 83. 10–2. 84). But if forced upon one, they offered scope for particular virtues like fortitude. Cf. 4. 1. 127: 'How, then, does a person suffer no harm if he be flogged, chained, or beheaded? Is it not thus: if he endures it with a noble spirit, he also comes away with increased profit and advantage?' Seneca's *De Providentia* develops the point using many *exempla* (cf. esp. 3. 4–14). For other passages in E that turn on the same 'what–how' distinction see 1. 2. 21, 2. 16. 15–17, 3. 9. 2, 3. 10. 8–9.

'Moral choice' in **§23** is Greek *prohairesis*. E was the first philosopher since Aristotle to make this term a key part of his ethics. I have argued elsewhere (Dobbin 1991) that his use derives from Aristotle, but indirectly by way of the Hellenistic debate over fate and free will, into which Aristotelian terms and ideas were introduced from the time his works were rediscovered. It cannot be understood with reference to Stoic precedent. At Stob. 2. 87 *prohairesis* is classified as a species of practical impulse, and defined as 'a choice prior to a choice (*hairesis pro haireseōs*)'. This is far too restricted a definition to explain E's use; E applies it not only to all types of impulse, but to assent and desire as well (cf. 1. 17. 21–4). The subject of this discourse is what is 'in our power'. And starting with Aristotle, *prohairesis* was closely linked to that phrase: '*prohairesis* in general seems to concern the things in our power' (*EN* 1111b30; cf. Alex. *De Fato* 180. 3–10; [Plut.] *De Fato* 571D; E 1. 22. 10, 2. 5. 4, 2. 13. 10). As *prohairesis* was, along with luck, nature, and necessity, one of Aristotle's four principles of movement, it was often juxtaposed to these, especially the last (*Met.* 1015a27; *EN* 3. 5; Alex. *De Fato* 211. 3–4; SE *M* 9. 112, etc.). Thus it became an apt term to invoke when contrasting 'what is in our power' with necessity or fate. E could count on readers' familiarity with the word and its associations in suddenly introducing it. One of E's most characteristic claims about *prohairesis* is implicit here, that it is free and unhinderable (cf. also 1. 17. 21, 1. 18. 17). Bonhöffer (1890: 259) writes that 'Epictetus with this term usually designates the entire psychological constitution of man, especially when focused on the idea of freedom'. It represents, in a word, the principle of autonomy, what is 'in our power'. And this can be nothing other than the faculty of using impressions, an equivalence spelled out at 1. 30. 4: '[What is the good?] Proper *prohairesis* and use of impressions';

cf. 1. 8. 6, 2. 22. 29, 3. 22. 103. It is clear that *to eph' hēmin* is thereby defined in the manner of the earlier Stoics, in referring impressions to reason.

' "But I will fetter you." What do you mean, man? My leg you will fetter, but not even Zeus can conquer my moral choice.' For the trope in §23 cf. DL 9. 59: 'Beat the sack containing Anaxarchus; Anaxarchus you do not beat'; *4 Macc.* 9. 7; Philo, *Prob.* 109. Cf. 1. 18. 17: 'The tyrant will chain . . . your leg . . . What will he neither chain nor chop off? Your moral choice.' For the thought, cf. also Socrates at *Apol.* 30c, which E cites repeatedly, and Vlastos (1991: 219) calls his 'favourite text': 'Anytus and Meletus can kill me, but they cannot harm me' (1. 29. 18, 2. 2. 15, 2. 23. 21). The body is subject to constraint; moral choice is invulnerable.

'These are the things you ought to practise if you study philosophy.' In context, this phrase in §25 seems indebted to Plato's description of philosophy as 'the practice of death' (*Phd.* 64a; see Chroust 1972: 18–19). Cf. 4. 1. 172: 'Will you not, as Plato says, study not merely to die, but to be tortured, or exiled, and in a word, to give up everything that is not your own?' There is no Platonic suggestion, however, that we should shed the body and 'flee from this earth as quickly as possible' (*Tht.* 176b). E's point is made more explicitly by Marcus at 2. 17: '[Philosophy is] above all waiting for death with a good grace, as being but a setting free of the elements of which every living thing is composed.'

'Choice' in §27 is *eklogē*, a term of art in Stoic ethics, which defined the end (*telos*) as 'rational selection [*eklogē*] of the primary things in accordance with nature' (Plut. *Comm. not.* 1071A). This doctrine is elsewhere qualified, or refined, by indicating that there is a 'preferential reason' for selecting the primary things in accordance with nature when circumstances permit (cf. Cic. *Fin.* 3. 20). At 2. 6. 9 E quotes Chrysippus as saying, 'As long as the future is unclear to me, I always hold to those things which are better adapted to obtaining the things in accordance with nature; for god himself has made me disposed to select (*eklektikon*) them.' The present passage about Thrasea is interesting as posing the question of how to choose between acknowledged evils. If we apply the doctrine in his case, we infer that, since the future is uncertain, he ought to choose the lesser of the two, and rest content with banishment. It may be that Musonius tried to stem excessive vainglory and the pursuit of martyrdom for its own sake. Thrasea did commit suicide; but while E, in line with most Stoics, approved of suicide in cases of extreme duress, he discourages it otherwise (1. 9. 10–17). On the injunction to be content with what it is given, compare 4. 3. 11, 4. 4. 29, 4. 10. 3, fr. 2.

Rufus (**§27**) is Musonius Rufus, E's teacher, on whom see also 1. 7. 32, 1. 9. 29, 3. 6. 10, 3. 23. 29. Thrasea Paetus, consul *suffectus* in 56, was one of the best-known heroes of the senatorial opposition to the principate, or to what the principate had become: cf. Marc. 1. 14; Juv. 5. 36. Brunt (1975: 8) identifies him as 'the centre of a circle, including Helvidius Priscus and Arulenus Rusticus, which offered the most intractable opposition to certain emperors, opposition which was certainly ascribed to Stoic teaching'. Thrasea wrote a biography of the younger Cato (Plut. *Cato Minor* 25, 36). He committed suicide when the conspiracy was discovered. Musonius was eventually exiled. Scholars debate how much their opposition owed to Stoic principles versus other, less abstract motives, like resentment at the loss of senatorial privilege. For a survey of views see Brunt 1975; Griffin 1984: 171–5. Agrippinus (**§28**) is mentioned again at 1. 2. 12 and in frs. 21–2. His equanimity in the face of exile or death contrasts with the attitude of Thrasea, with whom he is implicitly compared. Q. Paconius Agrippinus was a senator, and another prominent Stoic put on trial with Thrasea. For their part in the Pisonian conspiracy see Griffin 1976: 362–6 and 1984: 171–5; Griffin tends to downplay what it owed to their Stoic affiliation.

'I don't stand in my own way.' The thought seems to be that Agrippinus does not hurt his cause so far as lies in his power. Cf. Sen. *Ep.* 94. 28: 'Fortune favours the brave, but the coward stands in his own way (*sibi obstat*).' For the redescription of death, or loss of any kind, as 'returning what is another's', cf. 2. 16. 28, 4. 1. 102, 172; Sen. *Prov.* 5. 5.

CHAPTER 2

How a Man May Preserve his Proper Character in Every Circumstance

This chapter focuses interestingly on personality as a factor in ethics. The Stoics defined the end, the universal goal, as 'living in agreement with nature' (DL 7. 87). Chrysippus said that the 'nature consequential upon which one ought to live is . . . both the common and, particularly, the human' (DL 7. 89). That is, humans ought to conduct themselves, not only in accord with the law of universal nature, but also with regard for their nature as rational beings.

E expands the concept of the end to include the distinctive natures of individual persons. Similarity to the earlier Stoic Panaetius on this point has long been noted: see Bonhöffer 1894: 10–11; Brunt 1975: 32–5; Alesse 1994: 269–78. Panaetius was apparently the first to extend the concept of nature to include the personal traits and talents of individuals. Cf. Cic. *Off.* 1. 107: 'It should also be understood that nature has endowed us with two roles, as it were. One of these is universal, from the fact that we all share in reason and that quality that raises us above the beasts; this is the source of all rectitude and propriety, and the basis of the rational discovery of our proper functions. The second role is the one which has been assigned specifically to individuals. For just as there are great bodily differences among people, so there are still greater differences in their mental capacities.'

This passage is from Cicero's treatise *De Officiis*. At 3. 7 Cicero admits his dependence on Panaetius' work *On Proper Function* (*Peri tou Kathēkontos*; it can also be translated 'On Duty'). Panaetius was head of the Stoic school in Athens from about 129 BC until his death in 109. His book is now lost, but E would have had access to it, as Aulus Gellius (13. 28) did nearly a century later. E's affinity with Panaetius' thought is evident elsewhere. Long and Sedley note that his 'analysis of proper functions by reference to titles [at 2. 10, 3. 2. 4, 4. 12. 16, etc.] makes use of a functionalism . . . very similar to Panaetius' delineation of roles'. On Panaetius' attention to individuality in his ethics, see discussions by Brunt (1975: esp. 13–14), De Lacy (1977), Gill (1988) and Alesse (1994: 23–39). There is some precedent in Aristotle's advice at *EN* 2. 9 to adjust effort to hit the mean relative to one's personal nature.

A problem in Stoic ethics was who should receive ethical instruction, and how specific it should be; see LS 1. 429. In suggesting that proper functions vary among people, Panaetius might appear to be promoting a relative morality. But his philosophy did not give licence to individuals to cultivate their idiosyncrasies *ad libitum*. He insisted that talent adapt itself to first principles. 'We must act in such a way as not to oppose the universal laws of human nature, but while preserving those, to follow the bent of our own particular nature' (Cic. *Off.* 1. 110). Personality was Panaetius' second *prosōpon* ('role'). The first was human nature *simpliciter*, which suggests that, in determining duties, the claims of rationality and social instinct took precedence. E agrees. In §25 below, after hearing of an act of courage, the interlocutor asks, 'How did he do this, as an athlete or as a philosopher? E's reply, 'As a man', suggests that his ideal of behaviour is grounded in human nature primarily. Likewise 2. 10, which treats of proper function, begins: 'Consider who you are; to start with, a man, that is, one who has nothing more sovereign than moral character, but keeps everything subordinate to it' (§1). Only after honouring human nature does E turn his attention to specific roles, like husband and father—then the demands of individual nature.

Regard for personality is nevertheless an important element in the ethics of both E and Panaetius, one that imparts a particular interest and attraction. For attention to it elsewhere, cf. *Ench.* 37: 'If you undertake a role that is beyond your capacity, you both disgrace yourself in that one and forfeit the one you might have fulfilled.' Cf. also 3. 21, on the role of teacher: 'Perhaps not even wisdom is all that is needed for the care of the young. One ought to have a special fitness for the task, and a particular physique' (§18). 3. 22, on the calling of a Cynic philosopher, develops at length the theme of personal vocation, based on intuition of a special capacity. Awareness of one's particular faults also comes into play; cf. 3. 12. 7: 'I am inclined to pleasure; I will go to the opposite extreme, and that beyond the mean, so as to train myself.' This latter passage seems particularly indebted to Aristotle; cf. *EN* 1109b1–13 on amending flawed character as one would straighten a bent stick, in order to reach the mean. In the present discourse E reserves a place in his ethics for outstanding virtue, and a name for it: 'the purple in the robe'.

The discourse may be analysed as follows:

§§1–4 Proper function is universally determined by the standard of what is reasonable in a given circumstance, not by pleasure or anything else.

§§5–11 But what is considered reasonable varies not only according to circumstance, but from person to person; and the person himself alone can decide what is reasonable.

§§12–29 This principle illustrated with reference to historical figures who made decisions wherein the standard of what was reasonable for them overrode considerations that weigh most with the mass of people, like life, pleasure, security, etc.

§§30–2 The question posed of who these people are who place such a premium in their deliberations on self-worth.

§§33–7 E admits that they are exceptions whom most of us cannot emulate. Yet their example shows what is possible when the factor of self-worth comes into play; and helps inspire actions that, if not as bold, at least partake of some of the same independence.

The structure of this essay is broadly similar to that of Chapter 1, in that the exposition of the main points in the first half yields in the second to illustration through personal example. The use of moral *exempla* complements E's emphasis on the unique or exceptional in human nature.

'Reasonable' in §§1–5 is Greek *eulogos*. The adjective figured in Stoic definitions of proper function, something which, when done, has 'a reasonable justification' (Stob. 2. 85. 14; DL 7. 107; cf. *ratio probabilis* at Cic. *Fin.* 3. 58). Panaetius apparently used *eulogos* in his own definition, to judge from Cicero's imitation: 'You should do nothing for which you cannot give a reasonable (*probabile*) justification: that is practically a definition of proper function' (Cic. *Off.* 1. 101; cf. 1. 8). So E says that a proper function is one done 'reasonably' (*eulogistōs*: 3. 2. 2). Establishing the context for his statements explains E's purpose in attending to moral personality: it helps to define proper function. In particular, it helps in the selection or non-selection of the primary things in accordance with nature. This refines a cardinal point of Stoic ethics that figures in one definition of the moral end (*telos*): 'rational selection (*eklogē*) of the primary things in accordance with nature' (Plut. *Comm. not.* 1071A).

The Stoic theory of value began by acknowledging the distinction between things in accordance with, and contrary to, nature, a distinction E upholds in §10: 'I will tell you that getting food is preferable to being deprived of it, and being whipped is worse than not being whipped.' But choice is not determined solely by the value of externals; circumstances can militate against the selection of a thing with preferential value. So suicide could be judged 'reasonable' under certain conditions, as E goes on to suggest. Diogenes of Babylon redefined man's ethical end as 'acting reasonably (*eulogistein*) in the selection and non-selection of things in accordance with nature' (Stob. 2. 76. 9–15; on the evolution of the Stoic formula for the end, see Long 1967). E's emphasis in this passage on the criterion of 'the reasonable' reflects a similar preoccupation. Besides 'circumstance', he introduces self-worth as a factor in determining proper function.

As indicated above, the attention to individual character in the essay reflects the influence of Panaetius. Earlier Stoics had treated the subject of duty or proper function (*kathēkon* in Greek, *officium* in Latin) with increasing sophistication, as it relates not only to men generally, but to such roles as father, brother, master, and slave (DL 7. 108–9). Panaetius got more personal still, elaborating the duties incumbent on individuals. The word used in Cicero's *De Officiis* to designate personality and various social roles is *persona*. This is a translation of Greek *prosōpon*, the word E uses in §§7, 14, 28, 30 (where I have translated it 'character'), and at 2. 10. 7–8, with the same range of reference. It was borrowed from the theatre, where it meant a mask, a role, or the actor playing that role.

Whipping in §2 refers to the ritual whipping of Spartan youths in the cult of Artemis Orthia; cf. SE *PH* 3. 208; Simpl. *In Ench.* 90b. With §3, 'Whenever one feels that it is reasonable, he goes and hangs himself', cf. Plut. *Comm. not.* 1060C–D: 'Stoics say that nature endows us with repugnance toward [things contrary to nature] and congeniality toward [things in accordance with nature] . . . congeniality and repugnance so intense, in fact, as to make suicide and the renunciation of life a reasonable (*eulogōs*) course for those who miss the one and fall into the other.' Other references to suicide as a 'reasonable exit' (*eulogos exagōgē*) can be found at DL 7. 130; Alex. *Mant.* 159. 20, 168. 2. Important modern discussions of the Stoic teaching on suicide include Bonhöffer 1894: 29–39; Rist 1969: ch. 13; Griffin 1976: 367–88; and Griffin 1986.

With §6, concerning the need 'to bring our preconception of the reasonable and unreasonable into conformity with nature', cf. 1. 22. 9: 'What . . . does it mean to get an education? It means learning to apply natural preconceptions to particular cases in accordance with nature.' See comment ad loc. The argument in these opening sections (§§1–11) resembles a kind found in Sceptic sources. Cf. SE *PH* 1. 79–81, on the Pyrrhonists' second mode of suspending judgement, based on the differences among races and individuals; 3. 208, citing the ritual whipping sanctioned by Spartans in their cult of Artemis; and 1. 135–6, on the relativity of how things appear to different people. E is elsewhere found drawing on Sceptic arguments: cf. 1. 18. 1–2 and 1. 22, with comment. The example of the chamberpot in §8 is paralleled in Plut. *Apoph. Lac.* 234C and Sen. *Ep.* 77. 14–15, where death is preferred to such a demeaning role.

'Preferable' in **§15** is *hairetōteron*, from *hairetos*, another technical term in Stoic ethics: cf. DL 7. 101; Stob. 2. 78. 7. The question posed here, whether pleasure or pain is preferable, is rhetorical. E endorses the view that the primary things in accordance with nature have preferential value. But he implies that the person asking the question cannot escape responsibility for his decision based on this consideration alone. Cf. Sen. *Ep.* 66. 19: 'The reply which I make, is that there is a great difference between pleasure and pain. Asked to choose, I will take the former and avoid the latter. The former is according to nature, the latter is contrary to it. So long as they are judged by this standard, there is a great difference. But when it is a question of the virtue involved, it is the same in either case, whether it comes through pleasure or pain.' In Stoic eyes, virtue is the only good; externals, at best, have selective value. The present passage assumes this point, and adds another: we must weigh the value we place on our own self-worth. It may dictate that we accept pain in certain circumstances.

The image of 'the purple' in **§18** derives from the *toga praetexta*, the outer garment at Rome worn by the higher magistrates. E uses it to symbolize a moral aristocracy. He applies it particularly to those whose greatness of spirit is reflected in contempt for externals. Cf. 3. 1. 23: 'Do not say to the exceptional individual, "Who then are you?" He will get a voice from somewhere and reply, "I am the same sort of things as purple in a mantle . . . Do not blame my nature if it has made me superior to the rest."' Such a person performs acts of moral supererogation. These are not strictly required of him; and assuming the role of hero or saint may earn him not the respect, but the envy or suspicion, of others. Thus the indignant question, and the other's defensive response in **§18**. 'Why, then, do you say to me, "Be like the rest"?' The attitude of Agrippinus may be paraphrased thus: 'I cannot do what you are doing because my self-esteem forbids it. But this is not to condemn your decision: you are doing what is right by your own lights.' Thus the outlook E espouses is not, at bottom, judgemental. As Brunt (1975: 15) remarks, another man, such as Florus is represented here, is 'not bound to the same intransigence'. (On Agrippinus see note ad 1. 1. 28.) Aristotle reserved a place in his ethics for this sort of presumption: 'In all the actions that men are praised for, the good man is seen to assign himself the greatest share in what is noble' (*EN* 1169a34–b2). On extraordinary virtue in Aristotle, and its place in ancient ethics generally, see Hardie 1980: 401–4; Annas 1993: 115–20. E intends something similar with his 'purple stripe'. But the purple adds lustre to the whole, including the white threads that compose most of the garment. So it is not just a question of personal pride, E also appeals to the corporate spirit. The bravery of one person does credit to the rest.

§§19–24 is discussed by Brunt (1975: 31), who writes: 'Helvidius had assumed a role, conscious of what his personality required, had prepared himself to play it, and was resolved to play it to the last. And his conception of that role was determined by constitutional principles, to which indeed most men now rendered only lip service. His stand was unsuccessful. To a Stoic that was of no consequence.' Helvidius Priscus was son-in-law of Thrasea Paetus (on whom see comment on 1. 1. 26). He was praetor in 70. Tacitus (*Hist.* 4. 5–8) reports that he was a Stoic hostile to Vespasian. The emperor had him executed around 75 (Cassius Dio 66. 12). Juvenal (5. 36–7) represents him and his father-in-law as drinking to the assassins of Julius Caesar on their birthdays, thereby signalling their Republican sympathies. The Senate remained the great council of state during the principate, at least in theory. Vespasian was respectful of its prerogatives. But Helvidius, for his part, ran afoul of the emperor by challenging the legitimacy of the principate. In view of the fact that the principate survived, while Helvidius was killed, one might well ask (§22), 'What good did he accomplish, who was but a single man?' E says that he served as a *paradeigma* (*exemplum*, 'role model') to the rest. His decision to honour his role put the emperor in a bind, where he either had to relent or resort to force, thereby exposing the autocratic basis of his power. Helvidius' sacrifice ultimately advanced his cause. For this reason I do not agree with Brunt when he states simply: 'His stand was unsuccessful.' MacMullen (1966: 55) comes nearer the truth: 'Vespasian regretted [Helvidius'] fate . . . , foreseeing the embarrassing consequences to the Flavian house.'

§21 'It is yours to put me to death, mine to die without flinching; yours to exile me, mine to depart without complaining.' This sentiment depends in part on the distinction between the matter of an action and its manner, the 'what' as opposed to the 'how'; see comment on 1. 1. 22.

§26 'How did he do this?'—i.e. what role dictated death as a proper function in such conditions? The reply, 'As a man', indicates that the most important role is what Panaetius called the first *prosōpon*, human nature *simpliciter*. All other roles are variations of that, and subordinate. Thus, attention to individual character does not come at the cost of moral relativism or fragmentation. The athlete's willing acceptance of death engages some of the same issues discussed above in connection with suicide. There is the option of living, but at too high a price. Respect for one's own identity gives contour to moral choice.

In §29 E imagines himself addressed, in terms similar to those addressed to the athlete; only here it is his beard that is at stake. For the identification of the beard with the philosopher, cf. 2. 23. 21, 3. 1. 24, 4. 8. 12; Muson. fr. 21. Demanding that he shave can be understood either on the supposition that a full beard was an affront to Roman manners (in accordance with which men generally went clean-shaven), or that philosophers were viewed with suspicion by men in authority, especially by the emperor (see Zanker 1995: 198–266).

3. 1. 22–3 recapitulates the same themes as §§30–2, with some of the same imagery; cf. also 3. 22. 6–8; Lucr. 5. 1033–40; Marc. 11. 18. 1; and Cic. *Fin*. 3. 66: 'Just as bulls have a natural instinct to fight with all their strength and force in defending their calves against lions, so men of exceptional gifts and capacity for service, like Hercules and Liber, feel a natural impulse to be defenders of the human race.' Our passage draws on the theory of *oikeiōsis* ('appropriation'), especially as regards instinct in animals and its manifestation in man; cf. DL 7. 85–6, and see comment ad 1. 19. 15 below. The Stoic theory presupposed 'awareness' (*sunaisthēsis* in §30) of its constitution as the condition of a creature's 'appropriation' to it. In this passage we find an instance of appropriation theory applied to personality and the choice of an appropriate profession. For the thought in §33, together with the use of the marketing analogy, cf. Sen. *Ep*. 42. 6–7: 'Some objects are superfluous, others not worth the price we pay for them. But we do not see this clearly, and we regard things as free gifts when they actually cost us very dear.'

The accent on progress in §§33–7, even without prospect of reaching the summit, is characteristic of later Stoicism; see comment ad 1. 4 below. The question in §34, why all men do not attain to the greatness of their true nature, faces up to a problem for Stoicism. If virtue is the perfection of reason, why aren't all men over the age of 14 (when reason develops) virtuous? Or, as critics of the Stoics often put it (e.g. Plut. *St. rep*. 1048E), why are there so few, or even no, sages? This passage illustrates the fact that nature in Stoic ethics served a normative as well as a descriptive function (see LS 1. 352). E implies that it is our nature always to strive after the perfection of our character, though he concedes to the evidence of experience that some advance further than others.

§36: 'Epictetus will not be better than Socrates.' This wry bit of self-reference is typical of E; it is meant to combat complacency. It certainly does not give licence to moral laxness or relaxation, as the sequel shows. Cf. *Ench.* 51. 3: 'Even if you are not yet a Socrates, still you ought to live as one who wishes to be Socrates.'

§37: 'For I will not be Milo either, and nevertheless I do not neglect my body.' On E's attitude to the body, see comment on 1. 1. 10–13. This passage confirms that he thought it worthy of regard. In this passage the comparison of spiritual goods with bodily and material ones is based on the traditional Greek tripartite division of goods. As a Stoic, however, E avoids calling them 'good' (see comment on §15 above).

CHAPTER 3

From the Thesis that God is the Father of Mankind, How May One Proceed to the Consequences?

This discourse is thematically close to 1. 9. As there, we have impressed upon us our share in reason by virtue of our divine heritage. The discourse basically explores the dualism of mind and body by invoking other dualities: god/beast, immortal/mortal, virtue/vice. The expression has a Platonic flavour in parts (see Jagu 1946: 123–5).

The epithet 'father of both gods and men' in §1 is Homer's designation of Zeus; cf. *Il.* 1. 544, etc. It is repeated by E again at 1. 19. 12. The kinship of god and man was an axiom of Graeco-Roman religion; cf. Pl. *Prot.* 322a, etc. Philosophers often gave it a personal turn. Stoics said that man has a portion of the divine within him, and identified this with reason. Aratus 4–5 (quoted in Acts 17: 28) is a classic statement of the idea. In his *Hymn to Zeus* (LS 54I1) Cleanthes writes: '[W]e are your offspring, and alone of all mortal creatures that are alive and tread the earth we bear a likeness to god.' At 1. 13. 3, E tells a master that his slave is 'your own brother, who has Zeus as his ancestor, and is a son born of the same seed as yourself'; cf. DL 7. 147; Cic. *Laws* 1. 24–5; Sen. *Prov.* 1. 5. On the whole subject see Bonhöffer 1890: 76–80.

'Primary' (creatures of god) translates *prohēgoumenos*. At 1. 9. 4–5, E says that 'from god have descended the seeds of being . . . [and] chiefly (*prohēgoumenōs*) to rational beings, since they alone are equipped by nature to have communion in the society of god, being entwined with him through reason.' Cf. 2. 10. 3: 'You are a citizen of the world, and one of the parts not destined for service, but one of primary (*prohēgoumenon*) importance.' Stoics defined the universe as a state created for the enjoyment of gods and men (DL 7. 137–8). By virtue of their mutual share in reason, they sit atop the *scala naturae*; all plants and other animals exist for their sake. Origen (at *SVF* 2. 1156–7) offers a parallel to this passage, and, as often with Origen, it seems to derive from E directly (especially from 1. 9. 4).

'God is father of both gods and men.' The apparent illogic of E's statement in §1 can be rationalized on the supposition that 'god' refers to Zeus specifically, as at Muson. 86. 19–87. 1: 'Zeus, the common father of all, both gods and men.' E's phrase reflects henotheistic attitudes in Stoicism and Greek thought overall. Compare Xen. fr. 23 DK: 'God is one, greatest among gods and men.' For the comparison of god with Caesar *a fortiori*, cf. 1. 9. 7, 1. 14. 15, 3. 13. 9–14.

['Whole-heartedly believe' is Greek *sympathō*. 'Hoc est, ex animo ita sentire' (Wolf). The verb is not often found with such a cognitive meaning, but here seems to function as a strengthened form of *paschō* ('feel'), which E does use in the cognitive sense; cf. 1. 2. 3, 1. 18. 1, 1. 28. 3, etc.]

For E's use of the phrase 'But as it is' (*nun de* in §3), see note ad 1. 16. 6. For his attitude to the body, see comment ad 1. 1. 14–17. In general, he favoured its subordination to the spirit, not mortification. In this he agreed with Seneca at *Ep.* 5. 2. For a useful comparison with Marcus, more ascetic in his attitude, see Rutherford 1989: 241–4. 'Mortal' is Greek *nekran*; cf. 1. 9. 19, 1. 19. 9, 3. 22. 41; and see comment on 1. 19. 9. For Platonic statements of the distinction between soul and body, and the related claim that the former is the true self, cf. Pl. *Phd.* 115c–e; *Laws* 959a–b. E's expression certainly owes something to that tradition, but it was a tradition that shaped Stoic thought generally, as Nussbaum (1994: 326) remarks.

As in other passages exhorting man to assimilate himself to god or to the divine half of his nature, the consequences are potentially twofold. It could mean pursue the life of reason and contemplation (so Aristotle at *EN* 1177b19–26), or exercise the virtues (cf. Plato, *Tht.* 176b; *Rep.* 613a–b). The sequel suggests that E has the latter in mind. In the Platonic tradition the two were not rigidly distinguished, however: cf. Alcin. *Epit.* 28 with Dillon ad loc. Stoics also regarded virtue as the perfection of reason (DL 7. 94). For the thought compare *Ench.* 41.

§4 is an expression of psychological determinism, and central to E's philosophy; see introductory comment ad 1. 28, and compare 2. 26. 3–7. 'Fidelity' is Greek *pistis*. 'Man is born to fidelity, and the man who undermines this undermines man's characteristic quality' (2. 4. 1). The concept owed much to the Roman virtue of *fides*. E often links it with the virtue of respect (*aidōs*), as here: cf. 1. 28. 23, 2. 4. 2, 2. 10. 22–3, 3. 7. 36, 4. 13. 15; *Ench.* 24. 3. *Aidōs* was included among the Stoics' 'good feelings' (*eupatheiai*): DL 7. 115. It was regarded as a kind of proto-virtue; cf. Cic. *Fin.* 4. 18 (where it is translated *verecundia*): 'Since man is the only animal endowed with a sense of respect . . . , and with a concern to avoid any conduct unbecoming, from this seed given by nature develop judiciousness, modesty, justice and moral virtue generally.' On *aidōs* see further Billerbeck 1978: 67–8.

For the thought and figurative expression in **§§7–9**, cf. 2. 9. 1–6, 2. 10. 2, 4. 1. 127, 4. 5. 37. Sextus (*PH* 1. 69) calls Chrysippus 'the sworn enemy of irrational animals'. Animal metaphors, applied in a derogatory sense, are also common in Seneca (*De Ira* 2. 8; *Ep.* 55. 5) and Marcus (5. 33; 9. 37, 39; 11. 15). Cf. Pliny, *NH* 2. 26: 'Man was not born god's next of kin to approximate the beasts in vileness.'

CHAPTER 4

On Progress

Prokopē ('progress') was a controversial subject in the Stoa, owing to their penchant for extremes in the delineation of virtue: what some have called the Stoic either/or. They denied existence of a state intermediate between virtue and vice, and maintained that

anyone not virtuous was on that account wicked. As Long and
Sedley (1. 386) characterize their position, 'Since virtue and vice
are related as contradictories, no intermediate, transitional state is
possible.' Cf. Plut. *Prof. in virt.* 75C: 'So in philosophy we should
assume neither progress nor any perception of progress, if the soul
discards and purges itself of none of its stupidity, but deals in
absolute badness right up to its acquisition of the absolute and
perfect good'; Plut. *Comm. not.* 1063A–B: 'Just as in the sea the
man an arm's length from the surface is drowning no less than the
one who has sunk five hundred fathoms, so even those who are getting close to virtue are no less in a state of vice than those who are
far from it. And just as the blind are blind even if they are going to
recover their sight a little later, so those progressing remain foolish
and vicious right up to their attainment of virtue.'

The point is related to the problem of the sage: Stoics allowed
that he was virtually unattested (SE *M* 7. 432; Sen. *Ep.* 42. 1). Hence
all humanity were perfect fools, since the Stoic position ensured
there was no *tertium quid*. Critics found this all-or-nothing position
repugnant; cf. Plut. *Comm. not.* 1062E–1063B; *Prof. in virt.* 75F–
76E; Alcin. *Epit.* 30. 2. Pressure arose to admit degrees of virtue
and vice. But even older Stoics seem to have done as much, at least
in principle: the person approaching virtue, like the man nearing
the surface of the ocean, was that much closer to being saved.

Later Stoics tend to spell out that implication. From the doctrinal
standpoint the discrepancies are trivial, but probably arose from the
exigency of moral training: something E engaged in on a daily basis.
Zeno *et al.* could insist on the rigid distinction between virtue and
vice in their treatises, but so hard a doctrine was discouraging in
practice. So there was a perceived need for, and tangible evidence
of, some modification here, or at least a shift in emphasis. Seneca at
Ep. 75. 8–18 distinguishes three stages of progress, and recognizes
different values among all three. He writes: 'Are there no degrees
of wisdom? Is there a sheer drop-off below wisdom itself? In my
opinion, no. For although the person making progress is still num-
bered among the foolish, yet he is removed from them by a long
interval. Even people making progress can be divided into widely
spaced groups' (§8). E devised something similar with his three
topoi, alluded to in this discourse, and discussed below.

References to progress attest to Stoic advocacy of the idea throughout their history, however it was construed; cf. DL 7. 91; Plut.

Comm. not. 1067F–1068A; Cic. *Ac.* 1. 20; E 3. 6. 4, 3. 13. 22, 4. 2. 4;
Ench. 51. 2; Sen. *Ep.* 5. 1, 71. 30, 109. 15; *VB* 16. 3, 24. 4, etc. In
the later Stoa, however, the paradoxical formulations are dropped,
and the new attention to degrees of virtue enabled progressives to
chart their moral development in successive stages. On the subject
of progress see further Bonhöffer 1894: 144–53; Luschnatt 1958
(although his discussion is marred by a weak grasp of Stoic psychology); Inwood 1985: 182–215; LS 1. 385, and 1. 427 on later changes;
Annas 1993: 405–6.

   Much of the present discourse is concerned with distinguishing
real moral progress from delusive progress that consists in memor-
izing ethical treatises. The structure is as follows:
§§1–4 A brief statement of what true moral progress consists in.
§§5–17 Using the criterion of 'serenity', E distinguishes genuine
moral progress from specious progress that consists in becoming an
expert on the views of Chrysippus *et al.*
§§18–27 Substantial progress again, as in §§1–4, explained, but at
greater length, and in slightly different terms, as detachment from
externals.
§§28–32 A coda in which Chrysippus is extolled as the one who has
discovered and revealed the nature of true progress, and therefore
the key to serenity.

The philosophers in **§1** are the Stoics. Compare SE *M* 11. 30: 'Some
put it this way: "Good is that which contributes to happiness."
Others say, "that which helps to fulfil happiness". And happiness,
as Zeno and Cleanthes and Chrysippus have defined it, is "a good
flow of life".' Cf. also *M* 11. 110: 'Let us consider if it is possible to
live at once with a good flow of life, and happily. Now [the Stoics]
assert that this, and nothing else, is actually the case; for according
to them the man who acquires the good and avoids the bad is happy.'
'Good flow of life' translates *euroia biou*. E uses the abbreviated
form *to euroun*. For the concept compare DL 7. 88, where it is
identified with, or said to be constitutive of, happiness, and see
Irwin 1986: 224–8. On 'desire' and 'avoidance' (*orexis* and *ekklisis*)
see note ad 1. 1. 10–13. On 'impassivity', or 'absence of passion'
(*apatheia*), cf. DL 7. 117: 'the wise man is impassive'; Anon., *In Arist.
Eth. Nic.* 128. 5 (= *SVF* 3. 201): 'the virtues reside in impassivity.'
   Rejection of the passions was one of the most distinctive elements
of Stoic ethics, but controversial; for discussion see Dillon 1983;

Frede 1986; Engberg-Pedersen 1990: ch. 8; Nussbaum 1994: 359–401. Among other objections, critics charged that impassivity was actually incompatible with virtue, because there had to be desire for virtue if virtue were to be acquired, and desire was an emotion: cf. Stob. 2. 6. 6; Galen *PHP* 4. 5. 26–7 (= Posid. F 164. 12–22 EK); Plut. *Prof. in virt.* 77C. But Stoics did not oppose all emotions, and disparaged complete impassivity. They said that there were 'good emotions' (*eupatheiai*: DL 7. 115). And in addition to calling the wise man impassive, they said that 'in another sense the term "impassive" is applied to the bad man' (DL 7. 117; cf. E 3. 2. 4: 'I ought not to be impassive like a statue').

Against this background it is easier to understand E's advice in §1 to remove desire or else defer it 'to another time'. This is part of his doctrine of three topics (*topoi*), further discussed below in connection with §§5–11. This particular point troubled Simplicius. He calls it inconsistent with E's advice elsewhere to pursue virtue enthusiastically (a variant on the traditional objection to Stoic *apatheia*). He asks, 'How is it possible for man to live without desire?' (*In Ench.* 48b–c). His puzzlement is understandable in light of the expansive Aristotelian conception of *orexis* and the belief that moral education concerns its training, both ideas he subscribes to (*In Ench.* 19b–21b). Philosophy is etymologically the 'love of wisdom'. One definition of philosophy in the Hellenistic period was 'the desire (*orexis*) for wisdom' (cf. Alcin. *Epit.* 1. 1 with Dillon ad loc.; Chroust 1972: 24–5). It goes back to Plato (*Rep.* 475b–c; *Symp.* 218a, etc.), but also owes something to Aristotle's statement that 'all men by nature desire (*oregontai*) to know' (*Met.* 980a1). As heir to both these traditions, Simplicius found the notion of philosophy without desire inconceivable. In the end, though, he comes to terms with it by focusing on the advice to defer it 'to another time' (*In Ench.* 49b–50a). He interprets the doctrine as enjoining a temporary suspension of desire in order to stifle vicious desires and prepare for new, enlightened ones.

This is basically right. In Stoic psychology, as Billerbeck (1978: 61) points out, desire was a *vox media*. It could be good or bad. (There is some confusion in the testimony about this, but see Nussbaum 1994: 399 n. 77 for an explanation.) If good, or 'reasonable', it was equivalent to 'wishing' (*boulēsis*) a good emotion. If bad, it was equivalent to 'appetite' (*epithumia*: DL 7. 113, 116; Cic. *Ac.* 2. 135). At 3. 13. 21 E says to 'refrain sometimes from desire altogether, that at a later time you may exercise desire reasonably (*eulogōs*)'. This is evidently the 'reasonable desire' of which the Stoa approved. But first one has to get rid of 'appetite', bad, irrational desire. And so E recommends temporarily suspending desire altogether. The special reason for this is that the consequence of frustrated desire is drastic. Cf. 3. 2. 3: 'A passion only arises when desire fails to attain its object, or avoidance falls into what it doesn't want. This is the *topos* which introduces us to . . . passions which make it impossible even to listen to reason.' For the purpose of education, moral and otherwise, E believed it was necessary to suppress or forestall the bad emotions. Only after they are removed can education, which proceeds through reason, begin. Once passions are forestalled, desire in the good sense can be directed toward wisdom, or virtue. (For philosophy as progress toward virtue, cf. 1. 26. 15, 2. 11. 1, 3. 12. 12; Sen. *Ep.* 89. 8). Aristotle's statement of the same problem at *EN* 1095a1–11 is a famous passage, the substance of which I suspect was known to E, and influenced him here.

'Promise' in §3 is Greek *epangelia*. The sense of the word hovers somewhere between 'promise' and 'meaning'; it refers to the assumptions that inform our everyday use of a word. For its use by E see Long 1983: 188. Bonhöffer (1890: 199) rightly says that it functions sometimes as a synonym of 'preconception' in E's distinctive sense (on which see 1. 22). Cf. 3. 22. 39: 'Turn your attention to yourself; consider the preconceptions you have. What do you imagine the good to be? A good flow of life, happiness, freedom from restraint.' Cf. also 3. 23. 9; *Ench.* 2. 1. In §§5–17 E contrasts progress toward real virtue, or wisdom, with unprofitable progress in other directions. That is the point of the generalization in §4.

With §§5–9 compare *Ench.* 49: 'When a person gives himself airs because he can understand and interpret the works of Chrysippus, say to yourself, "If Chrysippus had not written so obscurely, this man would have nothing to give himself airs about."' Chrysippus was unfortunate in his style (cf. 1. 17. 16; DL 7. 180, 10. 27; Hülser fr. 601E, with comment). His writings consequently had a forbidding reputation.

E maps the actual course of progress on to three *topoi*, or 'topics'. This aspect of his philosophy is more fully laid out elsewhere, especially in 3. 2. It illustrates the more sophisticated and detailed pedagogical schemes that emerged in later Stoicism in response to a felt need. In conceiving of progress in three stages, it resembles the course outlined by Seneca at *Ep.* 75. 8–18. As indicated, E's first *topos* concerns desire and avoidance (*orexis* and *ekklisis*). From 3. 2. 2 it emerges that the second relates to impulse (*hormē*) and repulsion (*aphormē*), 'and, in a word, proper function (or "duty": *kathēkon*)'. Older Stoics made impulse the topic of first importance in their ethical theory (DL 7. 84). This may appear to conflict with E's decision to put it second. But E's three topics are structured for educational rather than theoretical ends, and in any case desire and avoidance, the first topic, serve rather a propaedeutic function in the whole programme. To suspend desire is really a preliminary step intended to forestall harmful emotions like fear and grief (the ones mentioned here), so that education can go forward.

The third topic, according to 3. 2. 2, concerns 'infallibility and discretion, and, in general, assent (*sunkatathesis*)'. The goal here is to avoid precipitate and weak assent, so as to be secure in one's impressions. Inasmuch as this describes the mental prowess of the sage (LS 41G–H), it is clear that progress still supports the existence of an ideal, as Bonhöffer (1894: 148) notes. E helpfully points out that this topic 'only applies to those who are already making progress' (3. 2. 5). 'Infallibility' (*anexapatēsia*) and 'discretion' (*aneikaiotēs*) were dialectic virtues ascribed to the sage in the old Stoa: DL 7. 46, 122; see Long 1978: 108–9. As Long and Sedley (1. 259) write, 'By allowing all normal people to have some cognitions, albeit weakly held in most cases, the Stoics provided a basis for "progress" exactly analogous to their doctrine of "proper functions." What perfects these latter is not a change in their objective content, but the expert understanding, consistency and moral integrity of their agent. So too with the conversion of cognitions into scientific knowledge.' Progress, in other words, could be viewed under two aspects, and both are relevant for the transition from E's second *topos* to his third. E makes plain that one graduates to this stage last, and only after much preparation; if you aspire to be faultless in your cognitions when you are still 'trembling and moaning', i.e. prey to emotion, you are two steps ahead of yourself. E sometimes associates the third *topos* with the study of logic: cf. 3. 2. 6 (and possibly *Ench.* 52. 2 (so Pohlenz 1964: ii. 162), though this actually seems to assume a different programme).

If we set aside the first *topos*, suspension of desire, E's scheme approximates to Panaetius' twofold division of soul into impulse and reason (Cic. *Off.* 1. 132 = Panaetius fr. 88 van Straaten; see

Alesse 1994: 50–4, 195–6). The influence of Panaetius on the second *topos*, impulse and proper function, has long been recognized
(cf. LS 59P and Q with comment at 1. 368; Alesse 1994: 267–78).
Panaetius had a particular interest in educating progressives (cf.
Sen. *Ep.* 116. 5 = fr. 114, part). If he influenced the third as well
as the second of E's *topoi*, he was only transmitting a venerable
distinction between the soul's practical and speculative sides; it
is foreshadowed in Plato, but became formalized in Aristotle; see
Cherniss 1976 *ad* Plut. *De An. procr.* 1025D–E. E makes a partial
and tentative attempt to co-ordinate this division with the traditional Stoic division of philosophy into physics, ethics, and logic.
Thus he associates the third *topos* with logic (and calls it *theōria*,
'theory', at 1. 26. 3). But I think it is vain to look for a complete
correlation, *pace* Bonhöffer 1890: 22–8. Nor can I see that E's plan
conforms to the division of ethical topics sketched by Seneca at
Ep. 89. 14, as Long and Sedley (1. 346) would have it, or to the
tripartite schemes of Philo and Eudorus (at Stob. 2. 39–45). The
effect of ranking the subjects serially is to privilege proper function
over logic. Panaetius, in a parallel move, put action before theory,
and associated the latter with abstruse subjects like 'dialectics': Cic.
Off. 1. 19 (= fr. 104, part; cf. 1. 153, and see Sandbach 1975: 124).
But E (like Panaetius) evidently does not discount logic altogether.
It is, after all, one of his three *topoi*. And putting it last confers a
certain distinction on it, as being the summit of a person's education.

For other references in E to his three topics cf. 1. 17. 20–6, 2. 17.
14–18, 3. 9. 18, 3. 12. 7–17, 4. 4. 13–18. For additional discussion
see Bonhöffer 1890: 22–8, 1894: 46–9, 58–60; Pohlenz 1964: i.
328–9; Hijmans 1959: 38–40; Billerbeck 1978: 60–2; P. Hadot 1978;
Inwood 1985: 115–26; LS 1. 346, 2. 342; Reale 1989: 78–80.

§10 'Why do you distract him from the consciousness of his own
faults?' Cf. 2. 11. 1: '[T]he beginning of philosophy is consciousness
of one's own shortcomings.' This acts as a motive to change. 'Consciousness' in **§10** is Greek *sunaisthēsis*. This term figured import-
antly in Stoic accounts of appropriation (*oikeiōsis*); cf. Hierocles 3.
56, 4. 58 and Stob. 2. 47. 13, indicating that consciousness of one's
nature comes by instinct. The present passage, though, suggests that
awareness of one's moral shortcomings normally requires some outside prompting. For the thought and vocabulary cf. 2. 21. 10.

[In **§10** the interlocutor should be limited to one question (as he
usually is), 'Why do you mock him?' The next series of questions

belong to E. This arrangement is also adopted by Schenkl and Souilhé.]

'Attention' in §11 is *prothesis*, on which see Inwood 1985: 231–2. With §§13–17 compare Sen. *Ep.* 33. 7–9: '"This is what Zeno said." But what have you to say? "This is the view of Cleanthes." But what is your own? How long will you march under another man's orders? Take command, say something memorable yourself. . . . "Zeno said this, Cleanthes said that." Put some distance between you and your books. How long will you be a student? From now on be a teacher as well.' In the same spirit Marcus (2. 3) says: 'Away with your books! Do not be drawn to them any longer, it is not allowed.' Context and comparison with §§28–32 below suggest that E does not object to theory so much as to its vain display. Theory and erudition have their place, but not as ends in themselves. §16 depends on that distinction. Books are not ends, but means to an end. Commentators on books are means to a means to an end, putting their diminished value in perspective. The argument is similar to 1. 17. 13–19. Cf. also 2. 9. 13–15, 4. 4. 11–18, *Ench.* 10, 49; Muson. 21. 17–23. 3.

It is notable that E rarely purports to comment on older Stoics in the extant diatribes. As Seneca famously said (*Ep.* 108. 23), that is not philosophy, but philology. Cf. *Ench.* 49: 'If I admire the art of interpretation, what else have I become but a grammarian instead of a philosopher?' Nussbaum (1994: 344–8), discussing this and the Seneca passage, speaks of an 'anti-authoritarian' strain in Stoicism. In so far as this suggests a hostile or subversive attitude toward older authority, I find it misleading, especially in light of the paean to Chrysippus in §§28–32 below. The relationship of later Stoics to the founders was complex, but should not be confused with what is at issue here. E simply restates a point made earlier by Aristotle: 'It is by doing good acts that the good man is produced. . . . But most men do not act on this. They take refuge in theory and suppose they are being philosophers and will become good this way, behaving like patients who listen attentively to their doctors, but carry out none of their instructions' (*EN* 1105b10–15). E, like Aristotle, saw that moral education differed from other kinds in that reading or listening to lectures is not enough, and, beyond a certain point, was useless.

'End result' in §13 is Greek *apotelesma*. E is adapting a technical term used in other Stoic sources to mean 'product' or 'effect': cf.

SE *PH* 3. 14; *M* 9. 197, 201. Marcus adapts it in a similar manner at 6. 42. Cf. also Alcin. *Epit.* 170. 1 with Dillon ad loc.

§14 '*On Impulse.*' Works with this title are attested for virtually all the old Stoics: cf. DL 7. 4 (Zeno), 7. 174 (Cleanthes), 7. 177 (Sphaerus). Von Arnim (*SVF* 3. 201. 30) cites the present passage, in conjunction with §6, to support the assumption that Chrysippus wrote one too. This reflects its importance to Stoic psychology. On the psychic functions alluded to (application, preparation, intention: *epibolē, prothesis, paraskeuē*), usually classified as species of *hormē*, see Inwood 1985: 231–4.

[The change from *prostithesai* in **§14** to *protithesai* is ascertained by comparison with *prothesis* ('attention') in **§11** above.]

In **§15** E makes the sincere suggestion that his student write a book instead of just commenting on one. But he cannot then resist observing that he will get only five denarii for the sale of each book, as that sets up another joke at the expense of the commentator, to the effect that, by rights, he is worth even less.

On *prohairesis* in **§18**, here translated 'moral character', see comment on 1. 1. 23. For the collocation of epithets 'elevated, free, unhindered', etc., cf. 1. 6. 40, and the note there. As to why a person who desires externals 'not in his power' is untrustworthy, cf. 1. 22. 14. Eating and bathing in **§20** qualified as 'intermediate functions' in Stoic ethics (cf. Stob. 2. 85. 13–86. 4; Cic. *Fin.* 3. 58). They are not good or bad *per se*, unlike honouring one's parents (which is inherently good) or dishonouring them (always bad: DL 7. 108–9). How they are judged depends on how they are performed. Cf. Sen. *Ep.* 92. 11: 'When I wear suitable clothes, or walk as I should, or eat as I ought to eat, it is not the food, or my walk, or the clothes that are good, but the choice I make in regard to them, preserving in each case a manner conformable with reason.' Eating and bathing properly means in moderation; cf. 4. 8. 13, 17; *Ench.* 33. 7. That may seem odd in the latter case, but we find moralists in the Roman Empire inveighing against over-indulgence in hot baths; see Mayor ad Juv. 1. 143.

[**§22** 'But if he is wholly intent on reading books' is the translation of Hard, which makes most sense of the Greek, and which I have therefore borrowed. Comparison with 2. 18. 1–4 (where *hexis* is used, as here), suggests that E indeed refers to the habit (*hexis*) of reading books, as opposed to applying what one reads.]

For the goal of the philosopher, or one engaged in the pursuit of wisdom, as 'learn[ing] what death is' (**§24**) see note ad 1. 1. 25. For E, and other Stoics' views of tragedy, see comment ad 1. 28. E's attitude may appear to be hostile, but, like Horace (*Epist.* 1. 2), he evidently believed that poetry was valuable for insights into how *not* to behave. As he puts it elsewhere, 'Look how tragedy arises, when chance events happen to fools' (2. 16. 31; cf. 1. 24. 16–18). Marcus at 11. 6 offers a somewhat more complex appreciation of tragedy.

§24 refers, of course, to the imprisonment of Socrates. The quotation is from Pl. *Crito* 43d, with the alteration of a single word in the received text (*estō* to *ginesthō*). It is cited again in this form at 1. 29. 18, 4. 4. 21, and *Ench.* 53. 3.

§27 'If one had to be deceived. . . . ' Schweighäuser and Oldfather suppose this refers to the deception of the audience involved in tragedy (the kind Gorgias condoned: frs. 11. 9, 23 DK), but I think it refers to the fact that in certain circumstances the Stoic wise man was licensed to deceive others for their own good. Cf. 4. 6. 33 and Plut. *St. rep.* 1057A: 'Chrysippus said that both god and the wise man implant false impressions'. The doctrine recalls, and may have been influenced by, the deception practised by the Guardians upon the inferior classes in Plato's *Republic* (389b–d, 414–15). Although in both cases it is well-intentioned, there is an element of patronizing and manipulation involved that is obnoxious to modern taste. On the topic see further Long 1971*b*: 99–101.

§28 is excerpted by von Arnim as *SVF* 3. 144, although it does not, of course, purport to be a direct quotation of Chrysippus. With **§§29–32** cf. Lucr. 5. 13–19: 'Do but compare the ancient discoveries considered godlike, made by others. Ceres is said to have introduced grain to mortals, Bacchus the juice of the vine-born grape; but life could have gone on without these things, as we hear some nations live even now. The good life, on the other hand, was impossible without a purged mind, which makes [Epicurus] seem to us with better reason a god.' Cf. also Lucr. 3. 1, for similar imagery involving light and illumination, and 6. 1–2, on the gift of agriculture, both again in the course of praising Epicurus. One difference to note between these passages and ours is that Epicurus' benefactions render him 'with better reason a god', whereas E deflects credit for Chrysippus' philosophy on to Zeus. Epicurus' followers (like

Plato's) established a cult of their founder, with annual sacrifices on his birthday. No such honour was extended to the first Stoics. Sedley (1989: 119 n. 51) wonders what accounts for the difference. Lucretius indicates that one explanation can be found in their respective theologies. Epicurean 'atheism' left room for a genuine, beneficent god, a god 'with better reason' (despite their belief that man's preconception of god does not include concern for him). Epicurus himself filled it.

The language in §29 is that of Greek honorary decrees, which commonly invoked the honoree as an *euergetēs* ('benefactor'); see Nock 1972: ii. 720–35, esp. 725–6. As he points out, it was a title also extended to the gods; cf. Plut. *St. rep.* 1051E.

This passage attests to the position that Chrysippus, Stoicism's 'second founder', had attained as its principal exponent. Plutarch, E's contemporary, also treats Chrysippus as the acknowledged authority for Stoic doctrine; see Babut 1969: 17–18; Duhot 1989: 32–3.

[In §28 von Arnim, evidently puzzled by the duplication of the preceding *esti*, proposed changing *apantai* to *hapanta* (to agree with *biblia*, 'books'), but the hyperbaton would be uncharacteristic of E. In §29 'conformable' (*akoloutha*) is Schenkl's proposal to emend an evident lacuna in the text (the *te* is idle otherwise). Schweighäuser proposed *alēthē*, and this is adopted by Souilhé, but is rather flat, and *akoloutha* has the advantage of being co-ordinate with *sumphōna* ('harmonious') and the dative *tēi phusēi*. Forms of *akolouthos* appear several times in E for certain, and demonstrate his casual use of terms borrowed from logic: cf. 1. 7. 9, 10, 17, 20, 24; 1. 26. 1–2; 4. 8. 12.]

For the trope in §31 cf. Pl. *Crito* 48b; Plut. *In Col.* 1108C.

CHAPTER 5

Against the Academics

The title, as transmitted, is open to the obvious objection that the Academics are not named, though they are elsewhere—e.g. at 1. 27. 2, 15, and 2. 20. 5. It nevertheless gives a partial idea of the content, though a better one might be 'Against the Sceptics'. At 1. 27. 2 and

15 E mentions Academics and Pyrrhonists together in a way that suggests that, fair or not, he did not distinguish them. In so far as the Academy is implicated, it is the sceptical Academy inaugurated by Arcesilaus. On the progress of its debate with the Stoics see Long 1980; Ioppolo 1986. E's attacks on the Academics evoked a hostile response from Favorinus in the form of a book now lost but mentioned by Galen at *Lib. prop.* 11 (= Mueller 2. 120), who also opposed scepticism and so came to E's defence with a book of his own—also, unfortunately, lost.

Since the arguments in this chapter could apply to Pyrrhonists as well as Academic sceptics, the title is wrong to omit them. It is also misleading in that the chapter transcends philosophical polemic, as Schweighäuser (ii. 69) pointed out. The reason why Academics (and Pyrrhonists) are not named is that E intends his remarks to apply more generally. He inveighs against a foolish consistency and adhesion to principle wherever it is found. The opening two sections, for example, seem aimed at cases of obstinacy among E's students. As the psychological analysis of stubbornness in a bad sense, this discourse covers some of the same ground as 2. 15. Analysis:

§§1–5 As reason is the vehicle of all communication, it is impossible to reason with someone who perverts his reason from its natural operation. This can result not only from the failure of reason, but from another part of the psychology—the sense of shame, when it is atrophied.

§§6–10 Examples given of such shameless insensibility, and shown to be more culpable than failures of reason.

The *a fortiori* argument in §§1–5 contrasting body and soul resembles 1. 4. 30–2 in extending an idea from a literal to a metaphorical sense. Most of us, unreasonably, fear the deadening of the body, but not the deadening of the soul. In §5 the latter condition is explained, and a further distinction is drawn. Of psychic deadening there can be two kinds: one, where a person simply cannot understand the course of argument, and so cannot be persuaded; a second, where the same thing stems from a contentious spirit. The former is deplored, the latter commonly, and wrongly, admired as a show of resolution. 2. 15 develops the idea at greater length, and compare Cic. *Ac.* 2. 9: 'For some reason most men prefer to be wrong and to defend tooth and nail the position that they have espoused, rather than lay aside obstinacy and seek for the doctrine

that is most consistent.' This hardihood E denies is true strength of
character, here, and again in **§10** below.

For the image of petrifaction in **§2** used in connection with the
Sceptics cf. Cic. *Ad Fam.* 9. 8. 1; Plut. *In Col.* 1122B–C. '[C]aught
in an argument' is Greek *apachtheis*, from *apagô*. The translation
depends in part on comparison with 1. 7. 25; 3. 2. 17; and DL 7. 47,
where the meaning emerges more clearly from the context.

[S is damaged in the area of **§§1–2**. The translation is based on
the text supplied by a second hand.]

The word for 'belligerent stance' in **§3** is *paratetagmenos*. Marcus
uses forms of the same verb, *paratassō*, at 8. 48 and 11. 3, when
contrasting judgements made on reasonable grounds, with those
made from a determination to be different. 'Self-evident truths' is
ta enargē. For E's use of the term compare 1. 27. 6, 2. 20. 1, 3. 3. 4,
4. 1. 136. It is cognate with *enargeia*, a word first used in a technical
sense by Epicurus to denote what is immediately apparent to the
senses (DL 10. 48). For its use by the older Stoics see Cherniss
1976: 524 note c, 629 note b, 630 notes a, b, and d. It became the
distinguishing characteristic of the clear, convincing presentation—
what they called the *phantasia kataleptikē*; cf. Plut. *In Col.* 1122F;
SE *PH* 3. 266. It was their main weapon of defence against scepticism. E does not, however, seem to be opposing Sceptics exclusively.
His vocabulary reflects his tendency to apply technical terms in a
broad sense; compare *apotelesma* at 1. 4. 13.

§§6–7 have more obvious relevance for the Sceptics. The word
for 'apprehend' in **§6** is *katalambanō*. It is the verbal form of the
technical term for cognition, *katalēpsis*, the existence of which the
Stoics upheld, and Sceptics denied. On Sceptic *akatalēpsia*, 'inappre-
hensibility', cf. SE *PH* 1. 1–3; 200–1, etc. For dreams adduced as
a motive to scepticism, cf. Cic. *Ac.* 2. 47–8, 51–4, 88–90; SE *PH*
1. 104, 113, 219. E's position is close to that defended at Cic. *Ac.*
2. 51: 'As soon as we wake up, we dismiss such visions [as we had in
sleep], and do not hold them in the same regard as those we had
[awake].' This claim is no doubt true to experience. But Cicero's
point is that we cannot compare such impressions at any one time,
so that for the length of time we are sleeping, at least, dreams are
accounted real. At *Ac.* 2. 88 he accuses the spokesman for Antiochus
of failing to appreciate the New Academy's argument on this head.
Sextus, speaking for the Pyrrhonists, flatly denies that we can see any
difference between waking and sleeping impressions, and therefore

maintains that there is no reason for preferring one over the other; see Annas and Barnes 1985: 85–8. Stoics, in contrast, did not dignify dreams with the name 'impression' (*phantasia*), but stigmatized them as delusive 'figments' (*phantasmata*) instead; cf. DL 7. 50, and see Chilton 1971: 47–8 for discussion, in the context of analysing an Epicurean attack on the doctrine (Diogenes of Oenoanda fr. 7).

That it is futile to engage the Sceptics in debate is a common complaint. In Cicero's *Academica* the representatives of the 'Old Academy' frequently accuse them of arguing in bad faith (cf. 2. 9, 18, 26). Stoics are referred to as 'dogmatists' in ancient sources, but see Barnes 1990*b*: 2618–19 on how this should be understood. It is actually their opposite number, the Sceptics, whom E convicts of clinging to an untenable position and refusing to listen to reason, or accept the plain evidence of the senses. For him, their obstinacy betrays itself in their refusal to yield—either to a convincing presentation or to their opponents in debate.

For the thought in §§7–9 compare 4. 5. 21: 'Here is a man who does not listen to reason, who does not understand when he is confuted: he is an ass. Here is one whose sense of respect has been deadened: he is useless, a sheep, anything but a human being.' The one who sees a contradiction, but pretends he does not, is judged more harshly than one who is merely stupid. The former is a voluntary fault, the latter involuntary. Cf. 2. 21. 6: 'In the case of most errors, the main reason men are prepared to admit them is that they suppose there is an involuntary element.'

CHAPTER 6

On Providence

On the importance of providence in Stoic thought and its ubiquity in Stoic sources, cf. Plut. *St. rep.* 1050A–B: 'That universal nature and the universal reason of nature are destiny and providence and Zeus is not unknown even to the Antipodes, as the Stoics bruit this everywhere.' E esteemed the subject above all others: 'The philosophers say that the first thing we must learn is this, that god exists and provides for the universe' (2. 14. 11). As providence assumes a

theistic context, it was part of Stoic theology, which was divided
into four parts: 'First, they prove that gods exist; then they explain
their nature; next, they show that the world is governed by them;
and lastly, that they take thought for human affairs' (Cic. *ND* 2. 3).
The subject of providence relates to the latter two: divine government of the world and concern for mankind. Cf. Seneca at *Prov.* 1.
1–5 for a survey *in praeteritio* of things a comprehensive treatment
of the subject should include, but he partly omits. This discourse
does not pretend to exhaust all aspects either; E offers further variations on the theme in 1. 16, 2. 14, 3. 17, and fr. 13.

In the history of Western thought, Stoics and Church Fathers
(relying mainly on the Stoics) did most to develop the topic, but
it had a long history. Of particular note are two passages in
Xenophon's *Memorabilia* (1. 4. 3–19, 4. 3. 3–9, see Theiler 1924:
104; Pohlenz 1964: i. 99, ii. 56). We find E rehearsing some of the
same arguments for teleology in nature as Socrates uses there. Cicero
in his *On the Nature of the Gods* also draws on Xenophon; at *ND*
1. 31, 2. 18, and 3. 27 his work is cited by name. Plato, too, in the
Timaeus and *Laws* 10, gave the subject much of its subsequent
direction. For a complete survey of antecedents see Pease 1941;
Pohlenz 1964: i. 98–101, ii. 55–8; Solmsen 1963.

What is distinctive in Stoicism is, first, the emphasis put on god's
concern for mankind (but see Sedley 1991 for the rudiments in
Aristotle). To support their view, Stoics systematically applied to the
world the principle of means serving ends that informs most arguments from design. So in the present discourse E not only adduces
the eye as proof of providence, but claims that the animal kingdom
collectively can be viewed as an instrument to serve man's ends.
Then, Stoics identified nature with god and assigned it all the attri-
butes of reason, thus transforming their teleology into a doctrine
of providence.

The present discourse assumes these points. It may be analysed
thus:
§§1–11 An argument from, or more properly to, design, illustrating
what has traditionally been called 'natural theology'. E focuses on
the co-adaptation of things in nature, and on the workings of the
mind.
§§12–22 A protreptic section, based on the powers of the mind and
the place this makes for man in the natural order. The inference from
effects to causes that underlies arguments from design is possible for

man alone, hence nature is constructed for his appreciation. This section draws on distinctively Stoic arguments for providence, to the effect that man is chiefly benefited. Now, anthropocentrism invites counter-arguments, and these the Stoics received in full measure, from Epicurus (Plut. *St. rep.* 1051D–E; *Comm. not.* 1075E) and the Sceptics (SE *PH* 1. 32, 3. 9–12; LS 54R). Anticipating these objections (which he places in the mouth of an imaginary interlocutor), E appends a form of theodicy.

§§23–43 Transition to the theodicy section by a notable use of the analogy of life to the Olympic games. The explanation of evil E offers assumes two things: (1) We are armed with faculties to face all evils. (2) Evils alone suffice to stimulate these faculties: Heracles would not have been Heracles otherwise.

Additional testimony for Stoic views on providence includes Cleanthes, *Hymn to Zeus* (*SVF* 1. 537 = LS 54I); Sen. *Prov.*; *NQ* 1; Cic. *ND* 2. 87–153; Philo, *Prov.*; Plut. *St. rep.* chs. 31–8; *Comm. not.* chs. 13–20; SE *M* 9. 75–122; Cleomedes, *Met.* 1; *SVF* 2. 1106–26; and scattered later sources cited in Pease 1941. For modern discussions, besides the literature already cited, see Goldschmidt 1953: 79–111; Long 1968*b*; Mansfeld 1979; Schofield 1983. §§1–11 of this discourse is excerpted as Stob. 1. 1. 33.

The translation assumes that we retain in **§1** the reading of S, the principal MS. Koraes proposed emending *hekastōi* to *hekastou*, which would alter the sense of the passage to 'a comprehensive view *of each thing* that happens'. I do not think this helps much, and Stellwag's *hekastote* ('each time') is no better. The problem is that reference to 'a comprehensive view of the things that happen to each person' hints at a form of theodicy. Stoics often distinguished between the good of the world and the good of individuals, to the effect that god consults the former primarily, sometimes to the prejudice of the latter: cf. Plut. *St. rep.* 1050A and E; Sen. *Prov.* 3. 1; Philo, *Prov.* 2. 55, etc. But E does not use that argument. The sequel shows that he intends a different point, one concerning the co-ordination of things in nature. Theodicy, however, is essayed in §§26–43, so it is possible that the opening sentence anticipates that section. Moreover, we have in §2 a reference to the 'usefulness of what has happened', a phrase that figured in Stoic explanations of evil, and which recurs below in §36. But if the reference is not to the end of the discourse but to the immediate sequel, it is possible that E confuses two ideas standard in arguments for providence, but different in kind: one about the fate of individuals in the economy of the whole, another about the 'interweaving' of nature, how its parts cohere and complement each other. Marcus combines the ideas at 2. 3 and 3. 11; cf. also Plot. 3. 2. 15 (basically Stoic).

[The text of §1 is lacunose but emended by a second hand in S, as at 1. 5. 1–2. This does not affect *hekastōi*, which is disputed on internal grounds.]

The form and some of the details of the arguments from design of the senses in §§3–6 go back to Socrates: cf. Xen. *Mem.* 1. 4. 5, 4. 3. 3, 11. This section also recalls Pl. *Rep.* 507c–508a: 'Have you ever observed how the creator of the senses has lavished by far the greatest expenditure on the faculty of seeing and being seen? . . . Though vision may be in the eyes and its possessor try to use it, and though colour may be present, yet without the presence of a third thing specifically and naturally adapted to the purpose, you are aware that vision will see nothing and the colours will remain invisible . . . , the thing you call light.'

Biological parts and their adaptation to their function are the most common form of evidence in natural teleology, beginning with Xenophon. Of all Aristotle's works, teleology is most pronounced in his *On the Parts of Animals* (esp. 639b14–22; see Ross 1964: 124). Ancient physicians often invoked the principle in their discussion of organs; cf. Galen, *De Nat. fac.* 1. 35, 2. 91, 132; *Meth. med.* 2. 6. 7; *De Usu part.* 3. 760–89; see Hankinson 1989. Stoics maintained that tradition, as the present discourse shows. Cf. also SE *PH* 1. 98: 'Nature has made the senses commensurate with their objects.' Annas and Barnes (1985: 74–5) reasonably hypothesize that Sextus is referring to the Stoic view, in which case E's argument was typical of his school. Cf. esp. Cic. *ND* 2. 140, 142, 145, expatiating on the powers of the eye in the course of praising man's senses generally. The focus continues in modern briefs for providence or teleology. William Paley in his *Natural Theology*, chapter 3, likens the eye to a telescope, and calls it 'nature's best cure for atheism'. Cleanthes, spokesman for what is essentially the Stoic view in Hume's *Dialogues Concerning Natural Religion*, exhorts us to anatomize the eye, and consider its 'curious adjustment' to its purpose and conditions (ed. N. K. Smith, pp. 154, 185). E offers a more sophisticated version of the argument, in that he suggests that not only are the eyes adapted to their environment, but their environment is adapted to them. We have, then, an instance of co-adaptation, or 'eutaxiological argument', here and in §8 below.

§7 is a classic formulation of the design argument, combining an analogy to artefacts with an inference a posteriori to a craftsman of the world at large. For Stoic parallels cf. Cic. *ND* 2. 87–8; SE *M* 9. 99–100. Nature itself is presumed to be artificial, a system or machine contrived by an agent who is identified, *ex hypothesi*, with god. The simile of sword and scabbard (§6) derives from Chrysippus: 'For as Chrysippus cleverly put it, just as a shield-case is made for the sake of a shield and a scabbard for the sake of a sword, so everything else but the world was created for the sake of something else: grain and fruits for the sake of animals, animals for the sake of man' (Cic. *ND* 2. 37).

The atomists, chiefly Epicurus, should be understood as unnamed proponents of the view in §7 that nature operates at random (*eikēi*); cf. *eikēi* at Dio Chrys. 12. 37 of Epicurus; Plot. 3. 2. 16. 20. For the Epicurean appeal to natural selection in order to refute the view of the biological organs set forth here, cf. Lucr. 4. 823–57; LS 13J.

With §9 cf. Cic. *ND* 2. 128: 'Why speak of the amount of rational design displayed in animals to secure the eternal preservation of their kind? To begin with, some are male and some female, a device of nature to perpetuate the species. Then parts of their bodies are most skilfully contrived to serve the purposes of procreation and of conception, and both male and female possess marvellous desires for sex.' In both these passages two things are distinguished: the physical organs, adapted for procreation, and the psychological desire that impels their use. The more factors involved, the less likely that they cohere by chance. And just as his discussion of vision involved not only the eye, but colour and light, so E here recognizes a third factor, the 'power' (*dunamis*) that uses the genitals. He is perhaps thinking of the mechanism that prepares the genitals, especially of the male, for sex, a process not well understood and so wondered at: cf. [Arist.] *Probl.* 879a15–22. An earlier version of the basic argument is credited to Socrates at Xen. *Mem.* 1. 4. 7.

Epicureans acknowledged the principle of co-ordination in nature; cf. Lucr. 5. 849–54: 'We see that living things need many things in conjunction, that they may forge the cycle of generations by propagating. . . . That male be joined to female, they must have the means to share mutual pleasures.' Again, they tried to discount the theistic implications by appeal to natural selection (ibid. 837 ff.). But that does not do complete justice to the force of the argument from co-adaptation, where 'the means to share mutual pleasure', i.e. the penis and vagina, must appear simultaneously.

The text in **§10** is corrupt in several places. The translation assumes the text of Oldfather. E's list of five mental functions traces a process of increasing abstraction. It is similar to other Stoic accounts: cf. 1. 14. 7–8; DL 7. 52–3; SE *M* 8. 58–60; Cic. *Fin.* 3. 33. Descriptions of human reason had an honoured place in arguments for providence, as they were used to infer the existence of an even greater reason that created it: cf. Cic. *ND* 2. 18 and 3. 27 (alluding in turn to Xen. *Mem.* 1. 4. 8); *TD* 1. 70; SE *M* 9. 95–103. E does not spell out that inference, but perhaps implies it. The first verb describes the initial step in any empiricist epistemology such as the Stoic (or Epicurean: cf. DL 10. 32–3): 'we . . . have their forms imprinted upon us' is Greek *tupoumetha*. Cf. Plut. *Comm. not.* 1084F: 'Impression is a printing (*tupōsis*) in the soul.' This derives from Plato's description of mental images as resembling the impression of a seal in wax (*Tht.* 191d). For controversy within the Stoa as to how literally it should be taken, see Annas 1992: 73–5.

To 'make a selection' (*eklambanomen*) from among impressions could mean to withhold assent from some, as Stoics, E especially, often urge: cf. SE *M* 7. 416; E 2. 18. 23–6, 3. 12. 15, etc. But since he does not use the verb this way elsewhere, E may instead be referring here to the almost unconscious act of screening the impressions that constantly flood in on us. Cf. Cic. *Ac.* 2. 30: 'The mind seizes some impressions in order to make immediate use of them, others, which are the source of memory, it stores away so to speak, while all the rest it arranges by their likenesses, and thereby conceptions of things are produced.' To 'subtract and add' (*aphairoumen kai prostithemen*) impressions probably refers to the way in which we form such concepts as that of a pygmy (by 'subtracting' from man) or a giant (by 'adding'); cf. DL 7. 53.

'Make these sorts of combinations' is *suntithemen*, a verbal form of the abstract noun *sunthesis*, which is classed among the mental functions contributing to concept formation; cf. SE *M* 9. 395; DL 7. 52–3: 'By combination [we think of things like the] Hippocentaur.' It may also refer to the art of inference, if von Arnim is right in supposing that it is rendered by *conjunctio* at Cic. *ND* 2. 147 and *Fin.* 3. 33. To 'pass from certain things' is *metabainomen*, and refers to the process of analogy described at DL 7. 53: 'Furthermore, there are notions which imply a sort of transition (*metabasis*) to the realm of the imperceptible, such as space and the meaning of terms.' Cf. also SE *M* 9. 394–5, where combination (*sunthesis*) is classed as a species of 'transitional' (*kata metabasin*) impression. Cf. *M* 8. 276: 'It is not by the merely simple impression that [man] differs [from other animals], for they too receive impressions, but by impressions produced by transition and combination (*metabatikē kai sunthetikē*).' By virtue of these two mental functions, man has a conception of incorporeals, including *lekta* and such things as space and time, as well as things that do not exist, like giants and Hippocentaurs. (For the ontology cf. SE *M* 10. 218.) On this whole section cf. 1. 14. 7–8. Many of the same mental operations are rehearsed at Cic. *Off.* 1. 11.

[The change from *epipiptones* to *hupopiptontes* in §10 is supported by comparison with SE *M* 8. 60 and 9. 395. Schweighäuser's *peripiptontes* is also possible (cf. SE *M* 9. 397), but involves greater alteration of the text.]

'[W]hat causes' (each of these things) in §11 is Greek *to poioun*, one of two principles in Stoic physics, the other being matter, *to paschon*: cf. LS 44B–C. Stoics typically conceived of god in terms of the former. Cf. SE *M* 9. 11: 'When the Stoics declare that there are two principles, god and unqualified matter, they suppose that god acts and that matter is passive.' '[R]andomly and haphazardly' is *eikēi kai apo t' automatou*, again, as in §7, a reference to Epicurus; cf. Plot. 3. 2. 1. 1; Cic. *ND* 2. 44.

In going out of his way in §12 to concede that man has many things in common with other animals, E highlights continuity among the various orders of nature, continuity that Stoics described technically in terms of different pneuma tension (LS 47N–Q). The Stoic hierarchy of natural objects, like Aristotle's, was organized on the principle that the higher levels on the scale include the characteristics of the lower ones. But each has its own excellence and corresponding office, and reason sets man apart (cf. Cic. *ND* 2. 33–4). 'Ends' in §15 is *erga*; this is a version of the *ergon* argument familiar from Plato (*Rep.* 352e–354a) and Aristotle (*EN* 1097b28–1098a17). Asked why man should use his impressions with a difference, E's reply is: Because he can. Hence the transition in this passage from exposition to paraenesis.

Stoics applied the *scala naturae* idea in a new way, owing to their focus on the teleology of the whole. Lower orders of nature exist for the sake of the higher, and the whole for the sake of beings that can use the others correctly owing to their endowment of reason. Plants and animals are means, people and god are ends (cf. 2. 10. 3; Cic. *ND* 2. 133). Aristotle hints at this view (*Pol.* 1256b15–20; *Phys.* 194a35), but Stoics integrated it with other aspects of their philosophy. That is evident from what E says here about the use of impressions, and what Stoics in general said about value and indifference, where reason is the deciding factor. See note ad 1. 1. 7–9, and cf. 2. 8. 6, 2. 14. 15.

'Nature and constitution' in **§15** is Greek *phusis kai kataskeuē*; 'understanding' in §14 is *parakolouthēsis*, a difficult word to translate, but resembling what we mean by 'self-consciousness'. It is based on the word *akolouthō*, meaning 'to follow'. For the complex of ideas here, cf. SE *M* 8. 276 (quoted in part earlier): 'It is not by the merely simple impression that [man] differs [from other animals], for they too receive impressions, but by impressions produced by transition and combination. This amounts to human beings possessing the conception of "following" (*akolouthia*) and directly grasping, on account of following, the idea of sign. For a sign is itself of this sort: "If this, then that." Therefore the existence of signs follows from a human being's nature and constitution (*phusis kai kataskeuē*).' The beasts, in other words, use their impressions, as man does; but man also 'follows' his use and monitors it; he is conscious of his actions. On the present passage see Long 1996*b*: 116–17.

With **§19** compare Cic. *ND* 2. 37: 'Grain and fruits are produced by the earth for the sake of animals, animals for the sake of man: the horse for the sake of riding, the ox for ploughing, the dog for hunting and keeping guard; but man himself came into existence for the purpose of contemplating and imitating the world.' That the lower animals were created to serve man's various needs is argued in detail at Cic. *ND* 2. 158–61; other references are collected at *SVF* 2. 1152–67. As our passage suggests, animals usually appear in arguments for providence as part of the anthropocentric thesis. For similar views cf. Xen. *Mem.* 4. 3. 10; Arist. *Pol.* 1256b15–22 (an anomalous passage for Aristotle, we should note).

That man has come into the world 'to be a spectator of [god] and of his works' (**§19**) follows from the nature of his intellect: he is uniquely qualified to appreciate the world's (and his own) construction. As Cicero puts it (*ND* 2. 115): 'Creation not only postulates intelligence, it is impossible to understand creation without intelligence of the highest order.' Cf. SE *M* 7. 93 (= Posid. F 85 EK): 'Just as light is apprehended by luciform vision, and sound by aeriform hearing, so also the nature of all things ought to be apprehended by its kindred reason.' 'Not merely a spectator, but an interpreter too': E suggests that, in addition to contemplating nature, we ought to do what he himself is doing, initiate others into the world's wonders and (starting in **§26**) justify the ways of god to man.

'[C]ontemplation' in **§21** is Greek *theōria*. According to DL 7. 130, Stoics valued a life composed of both *theōria* and *praxis* (action). In their accounts of Peripatetic ethics, Arius Didymus (*apud* Stob. 2. 143. 24 ff.) and Aetius (874F–875A) ascribe the same view to Aristotle. Not too much importance can be attached to such bits of doxography, but together with the present passage they do call into question the difference in attitude many scholars assume between Stoics, on the one hand, and Plato and Aristotle, on the other. See Annas 1992: 86: '[Stoics] reject, in their ethics, the Platonic view that philosophy is a peculiarly abstract kind of thinking like mathematics, and do not think that the only appropriate life for a philosopher is the "contemplative" life so valued by Plato and Aristotle, the life devoted to abstract study.' It is true that Chrysippus disparaged the life devoted solely to contemplation (Plut. *St. rep.* 1033C–D). And Stoics did not recognize a class of abstract reasoning on the order of Plato's contemplation of the Forms. But they stoutly defended physics as a subject of study: cf. Cic. *ND* 2. 37, 40, 153, 155; Sen. *De Otio*; *NQ praef.* 11–12; E fr. 1; Marc. 10. 11, etc. We should not overlook the part that they assigned the contemplation of nature in the complete life. The contrast with Plato and Aristotle is overdrawn in any case, because it ignores the complexity of their own views. The philosopher in Plato must participate in politics (*Rep.* 500d), and Aristotle held that the exercise of virtue was a component of happiness (see Irwin 1988: 616 n. 24)—a view reflected in the doxographers. On the background to the question see Cherniss 1976: 247 note f; Dillon 1993: 56–7.

On the work of Pheidias mentioned in **§23**, cf. 2. 8. 18–20. The colossal chryselephantine statue of Zeus at Olympia constructed in the late fifth century BC was one of the Seven Wonders of the Ancient World. By some it was even accounted a contribution to theology, since it realized a new and exalted conception of the deity (Quintil. 12. 10. 9; Dio Chrys. 12. 45). E's point is that there are 'sermons in stones', and one need not travel to Olympia to appreciate god's greatness.

[The translation of **§24** assumes the reading *all' este ēdē kai paresti tois ergois*. It requires that we understand Zeus as the subject of the second verb (*paresti*), based on the reference to his statue in §23. This is admittedly difficult, but in view of the fact that E has argued for some such view as this reading implies in the preceding sections, and says essentially the same thing at 1. 14. 9, I think it is possible. Oldfather also takes Zeus to be the subject of *paresti*.]

On the need to discover 'who you are, or for what you have been born' (**§25**), cf. 1. 10. 10: 'Please learn from Chrysippus what the administration of the universe is, and what place the rational animal has within it. Consider, too who you are.' The traditional Greek injunction to 'Know yourself' commended itself to Stoics particularly; cf. Julian 185D–186A: 'That the Stoics held the maxim to "Know yourself" to be the heart of their philosophy you may gather not only from the works they composed on this very subject, but even more from what they made the end and aim of their teaching. For this end is life in agreement with nature, and it is impossible to agree with nature unless one knows who, and of what nature, you are.'

In **§§23–7** E exploits the analogy of life to the Olympic games that goes back to Pythagoras; cf. Cic. *TD* 5. 9; DL 8. 8; see Gottschalk 1980: 23–36. He develops it more explicitly, but in an identical context, at 2. 14. 23–9; cf. 4. 1. 103–10. The application he puts it to serves to refresh a traditional trope. It eases transition to the problem of evil in a providentially ordered universe. As often, E's thought is best appreciated by reconstructing a polemical context, and as usual, it is the job of the interlocutor to supply it. Stoic versions of theodicy were formulated especially in response to Epicurean and Sceptic attacks on their doctrine of providence. For varieties of Stoic theodicy cf. LS 54Q–U and the classification at LS 1. 332.

To their vigorous defence of providence later Stoics still admitted qualifications. They sometimes allowed that matter acted as a distinct cause in creating the world, and constrained god's purpose; cf. Sen. *Ep.* 58. 27; *Prov.* 5. 8–9; *NQ* 6. 3; Marc. 10. 33. 3; see comment ad 1. 1. 7–11. Hence (**§30**) the flesh is weak, and noses tend to run. E's example is trivial, so that his interlocutor gives the impression of petulance. But Chrysippus (according to Gellius 7. 1.

1–13), 'takes seriously the question "whether human illnesses come about in accordance with nature"—whether, that is, nature herself or providence, which created the structure of our world and the human race, also created the illnesses, infirmities, and diseases of the body which men suffer from. In his opinion, it was not nature's principal intention to make men liable to disease. . . . But while she was bringing about many great works and perfecting their fitness and utility, many disadvantages accrued that were inseparable from her actual products.'

While E assumes this point, he offers in **§30** a form of argument that became popular in later Stoicism: there are resources, moral (e.g. magnanimity) or physical (e.g. hands), to compensate for such disadvantages. Cf. *Ench.* 10: 'In the case of everything that befalls you, remember to turn to yourself and see what faculty you have to deal with it'; Sen. *Prov.* 6. 6: 'You say that many things dreadful and hard to bear befall us. Yes, because I, god, could not withdraw you from their path, I have armed your minds to withstand them all.' Cf. also E 2. 16. 13–14; 4. 11. 9; *Ench.* 10; Marc. 9. 11, 9. 42. 1–2. To that, E's interlocutor objects that it violates the principle of economy for there to be runny noses in the first place. Stoics, after all, had endorsed the view that 'nature does nothing in vain' (Alex. *De Fato* 179. 26). Like Chrysippus, E admits a residue of evil in the world, but seeks to neutralize it by reference to the means given us by god to deal with it. The argument in the next section (**§32–6**) is more ambitious, in that it attempts to alchemize evil into good.

'Useful' in **§36** is Greek *euchrēstos*. The adjective appears in Plut. *Comm. not.* 1066B–C and 1068A, likewise in the context of a Stoic defence of providence (where evil, *kakia*, is called 'useful'). Chrysippus applied the variant (and more tentative) phrase, 'not useless', in the same way. In the second book of his *On Nature*, he said that 'the occurrence of evil was not useless (*ouk achrēstos*) in relation to the whole, for otherwise good would not exist either' (Plut. *St. rep.* 1050F; cf. *Comm. not.* 1065A–D, 1068A; Plot. 3. 2. 5. 8). At Plut. *St. rep.* 1044D bedbugs are declared useful for waking man up and mice for forcing him to be neat. So E says that savage men and animals were 'useful' in producing a Heracles. Porphyry, *De Abst.* 3. 20. 1, and Philo, *Prov.* 2. 56, assert that the existence of lions, leopards, bears, etc. is no argument against the thesis that nature maximizes mankind's interest, since they provide man with opportunities for the exercise of virtue, or just exercise (the hunt).

This is a version of the Stoic explanation of evils as 'blessings in disguise'. For the Epicurean and Sceptic use of wild animals to refute Stoic providence, cf. Lucr. 5. 201, 218–20; Cic. *Ac.* 2. 120. It became such a standard counter-example that Plotinus shows impatience and dismisses it out of hand (3. 2. 9. 37–9).

A part of E reacted against the idea that we should be completely dependent on god's providence. We should rather be like god, as Heracles ascended to divine status by helping mankind and rising to the challenge posed by first-order evils. This explanation of evil, as providing 'circumstances and occasions' (§34) for the display of virtue, found particular favour with Seneca; it underlies most of his work *On Providence*. Cf. 4. 6: 'Disaster is virtue's opportunity.' Magnanimity, one of the virtues named above, is often praised by Seneca in this connection; cf. *Ep.* 111. 2, 120. 11; *Cons. sap.* 11; *Clem.* 1. 5. 3–5.

Heracles (§32–6) was by this time well established as a Stoic, and especially a Cynic, hero: cf. 2. 16. 44, 3. 22. 57; Cic. *Fin.* 2. 118, 3. 66; Dio Chrys. 1. 58–84 (offering a variant on the Choice of Heracles at Xen. *Mem.* 2. 1. 21–34); 8. 28–36; see Galinsky 1990: 293–4, where the present passage is discussed. But §§35–6 reflects a difference in outlook between Stoics and Cynics. Cynics glorified *ponos* (labour, trouble) as an end in itself. E (like Seneca) flirted with Cynic *askēsis*. But here he denies that trouble should be courted for its own sake. The Stoic value system, unlike the Cynic, did not turn the conventional one completely on its head. The trend of argument, particularly when illustrated with reference to Heracles, brings E to the brink of what we may for the sake of convenience call the 'Cynic attitude'. But here he distinguishes: evils should be accepted if they cannot be avoided, and should even be looked upon as an opportunity when they do appear. But, as he writes elsewhere (2. 6. 9), 'as long as the consequences are unclear to me, I always incline toward the things better suited to secure for me the things in accordance with nature'—i.e. goods in the conventional sense. Simplicius (*In Ench.* 91a–b) offers a variant of the same argument.

The conclusion (§§37–43) pulls together various threads of thought. Most of it speaks for itself. With the argument from consequences in §39 cf. 2. 22. 17. The epithets 'free from restraint, compulsion and hindrance' (*akōluton, ananangkaston, aparapodiston*) in §40 are regularly applied by E to the faculty of *prohairesis*. As Long says (1971a: 190), they 'command the reader's attention by repetition'.

They amount to a strong claim for human freedom within the frame-work of Stoic fate, but note E's brand of compatibilism: our will is free only because god willed it so, 'as befitted . . . a true father'.

CHAPTER 7

On the Utility of Changing Arguments, Hypothetical Arguments, and the Like

This essay argues for the position that logic, or dialectic, has a bearing on morals. E's views on logic are complex, but, as a master rhetorician, he framed different lessons for different audiences and occasions. Sometimes he encourages its study (here and at 1. 17. 10–12, 2. 25), other times he discourages it (as at 2. 2. 6, 2. 23. 41; *Ench.* 52). Either way, logic and the question of its relevance loom large in his teaching. The conventional view that there is little logic in E is only partly true. He does not engage in logical exposition directly—not, at least, in the extant diatribes. But 1. 26. 13 suggests that training in logic was a part of his school's curriculum. And, again, he often addresses the problem of why, and how, it should be practised.

The present essay defends the study of logic. E's strategy is not to demonstrate its range, as in 1. 17 and 2. 25, where he invokes the expansive Stoic conception of logic, which included rhetoric and epistemology as well as syllogistic (cf. DL 7. 41). That is one approach, but here we find the opposite: he demonstrates the range, not of logic, but of ethics, by arguing that it includes competence in logic. He does this mainly by appeal to an ethical ideal in the person of the good man, and to our antecedent expectation that logical ability will be among his accomplishments.

On E's attitude to logic, besides Barnes 1997, see Bonhöffer 1894: 122–7; Long 1978: esp. 119–21; Nussbaum 1994: 348–51. Analysis of the discourse:

§§1–4 It is clear that logic has relevance for daily life, because we assume that the good man will engage in dialectic when challenged to—hence the need for logical training to emulate him.

§§5–12 Training in logic is training in the essential functions and operations of reason: it is indispensable. It demands conscious training in order to distinguish what is true, false, and unclear, and to manage logical inference.

§§13–29 But inference is not a straightforward business. The hypothesis can change in various ways. That is clear in the case of changing and hypothetical arguments. Their complexity makes the necessity of specialized training in logic even more apparent.

§§30–3 Granted that logic is the structure of reason itself, is logical error really as culpable as moral error? This doubt rests on a false antithesis; logical errors translate directly into moral ones.

'[M]atter' in §2 is Greek *hulē*. E often says that the 'matter', or situation with which we are confronted, is indifferent, neither good nor bad; it is how one conducts oneself in it that is good or bad. Cf. 2. 5. 15–23, esp. 15–16: 'This is what you find in the case of skilful ball-players; none of them is concerned with the ball as something good or bad; but about throwing and catching it. Accordingly, form and skill relate to that.' E invokes that principle in §§1–4 to argue that the duty incumbent upon the virtuous man when a logical puzzle is posed is not to act randomly, but expertly, as defined by the rules of logic. The phrase 'carelessly or at random' in §3 (cf. §§21, 27, and 33) is a virtual synonym for acting contrary to proper function. E puts logic on a level with other activity, or, more accurately, puts occasions for the exercise of logic on a level with other occasions. He does not argue here that logic has any particular claim on our attention because it is continually required of rational beings —the argument he advances at 1. 17. 4–6 and 2. 25.

In §3 E constructs a dilemma in order to argue that the virtuous man will be capable of handling question and answer. Originally this was a Platonic conception of logic, as 'the education that enables one to ask and answer questions intelligently' (*Rep.* 534d; see Robinson 1953: 75–84). In the Stoa, as Long and Sedley (1. 218) point out, 'this dialectical aspect was never lost sight of. Arguments are standardly "asked", not just stated, and although the texts only rarely set out the premises in interrogative form, the reader is expected to take them that way.' Cf. DL 7. 42: 'By dialectic the Stoics understand the science of correctly discussing subjects by question and answer'; DL 7. 47–8; SE *PH* 2. 231; Alex. *In Arist. Top.* 3. 8, 5. 7–10 (= Hülser fr. 58); Sen. *Ep.* 48. 10; §§4 and 33 below; see further Long 1978: 103–4; LS 1. 189. In other Stoic definitions of dialectic, however, the question-and-answer aspect is not in evidence: cf. DL 7. 62. E's decision to highlight it may have a special point. He concentrates here on arguments with a 'dialectic' colouring, such that their practice assumes the form of a dialogue or debate. Because he typically conceives of ethical action in terms of engagement with others (cf. 2. 10), it supports his thesis in this discourse to represent logic this way.

Question and answer was thus a format in which any sort of argument could be presented. But E's expression in **§1** and at 3. 2. 6 and 3. 21. 10 implies that there existed arguments in interrogative form that were co-ordinate with changing and hypothetical arguments. This would not have been a format, then, but an independent schema. The problem is that there is no other evidence for this type of argument. If such existed, we must imagine for ourselves how it worked, because E's references are too summary. Changing and hypothetical arguments, which were recognized schemata, are enlarged upon below in §§13–21 and 22–9, respectively.

[My translation assumes the change proposed by Schenkl of *mē* to *ē* ('Or') at the beginning of **§4**.]

The purpose of **§§5–12** is to show that the workings of reason are complex and require special study, study that amounts to a science of its own, viz., logic. 'Purport to do' in **§§5** and **9** is Greek *parangelletai*; the word reflects E's functionalist view of nature. Like all natural faculties, reason is assumed to have a certain range of activities providentially assigned to it, which are its duty to discharge. With the list of reason's functions in **§5** cf. 1. 28. 2, 3. 3. 2. This was a standard description of dialectic within the Stoa; cf. SE *PH* 2. 94: 'Dialectic is the science of things true, false, and neither.' It refers to the testing of the truth or falsity not only of propositions, but also of impressions and arguments. For the analogy in **§§5–7** to testing coins for their authenticity, cf. 1. 20. 7–11, 2. 3. 2– 5, 3. 3. 3–13; Plut. *Comm. not.* 1063E; see comment ad 1. 28. 28–30.

§10 is concerned with learning in what cases Q follows from the single premiss P, and in what cases Q follows from the set of premisses P_1, P_2, P_3, etc. But, as Barnes (1997: 140) points out, ancient logic knew nothing of valid single-premissed arguments—with a single exception devised by Antipater (cf. SE *PH* 2. 167; *M* 8. 443; Hülser frs. 1050–7). Barnes suggests that perhaps logicians in E's day 'on at least one point preferred Antipater to Chrysippus'.

With **§11** compare *SVF* 2. 19. 31, where the goal of dialectic is defined as 'knowledge of demonstrative procedures'. For dialectic as useful especially for detecting sophisms cf. Xen. *Mem.* 4. 6. 1, where Socrates proclaims the necessity of learning dialectic on the

grounds that others do, others who can take advantage of the un-
tutored with specious argument. This defensive justification of the
science was absorbed into Stoicism. Cf. SE *PH* 2. 229: 'It is no
doubt not out of place to spend a little time discussing sophisms,
since those who extol dialectic [i.e. the Stoics] say that it is indispensable for their solution.' That logic is 'necessary' (**§12**) was a
standard Stoic claim, made on this and other grounds; cf. E 2. 25;
DL 7. 46–7; Plut. *St. rep.* 1046A.

§§13–21 is excerpted as LS 37J, part; **§§19–23** = Hülser fr. 1121.
The whole passage concerns the changing arguments (*metapiptontes
logoi*) alluded to in §1. E refers to them in passing again at 2. 23. 41,
3. 2. 17, 3. 21. 10, 3. 24. 80, 4. 12. On this class of argument cf. also
SE *PH* 2. 231, 234; *M* 8. 103; Dionysius of Halicarnassus, *De
Compos. verb.* 22. 11–17 (= Hülser fr. 1024); Simpl. *In Arist. Phys.*
1299. 36–1300. 10 (= LS 37K); Alex. *De Fato* 177. 21; DL 7. 76,
195–6; see Frede 1974: 44–8; Bobzien 1986: 21–3; Barnes 1997:
99–125. Changing arguments typically had a temporal indexical,
and their truth-value depended on the time of the utterance. Thus
'It is raining today' expresses the same *axioma* whenever it's uttered,
but its truth-value changes with the weather. E does not furnish an
example, but the analogy to a debt and the conditions of its remaining binding suggests that he likewise has in mind statements with a
temporal component, such that the premisses involve the notion of
truth-at-a-time (DL 7. 65; SE *M* 8. 103). Changing arguments were
evidently liable to trip one up, perhaps by design. For this reason E
recommends being on particular guard against them.

[**§18** is added to the text *exempli gratia* to eke out the argument.
All editors assume something like it. Upton produced some Greek
from his codex at this point to mend the lacuna, but it too is evidently mere guess-work.]

Hypothetical arguments, referred to in passing in §1, are the subject of **§§22–5**. They employed third-person imperatives of the form,
'Let it be the case that . . .' Cf. 1. 25. 11–12: '[A]s we behave in . . .
hypothetical arguments, so should we behave in life. "Let it be
night." So be it. "Well, then, is it day?" No, for I accepted the hypothesis that it is night' (cf. 3. 22. 68). Cf. 1. 26. 1: 'When a person
was reading the hypothetical arguments, E said, "This also is a hypothetical law, that we must accept what follows from the hypothesis."'

§23 suggests that someone may choose to reject a hypothesis. As
we saw in the case of changing arguments, a criterion of certain

Stoic arguments was not only coherence but truth. It is possible that hypotheses could be rejected on the grounds that their truth-conditions did not apply; hypotheticals such as 'Let it be night', *vel sim*. In addition, 1. 25. 11–13 might suggest that hypotheses could be posited on the strength of previous ones. A hypothesis might therefore be rejected as inconsistent with a previous one. Although collateral Stoic evidence is lacking, such a procedure is outlined by Aristotle at *An. pr.* 41a37–b1. For Chrysippus' attention to hypothetical arguments cf. DL 7. 196. For Stoic reliance on hypothesis in general, with Sceptic criticism, cf. SE *PH* 1. 168; *M* 3. 1–17, and see Barnes 1990c: 210–12.

§25 indicates that a hypothesis of something possible can entail an impossible conclusion; cf. 2. 19. 3. Alex. *In Arist. An. pr.* 177. 25–178. 1 (= LS 38F) indicates that Chrysippus maintained that the proposition 'this one is dead' follows from the proposition 'Dion is dead', but is 'impossible' with reference to Dion when Dion is dead. This is related to changing arguments (cf. esp. Simpl. *In Arist. Phys.* 1299. 36–1300. 10 (= LS 37K)). The difference is that 'this man' has not changed its reference, but has, according to Chrysippus, become meaningless, since it no longer has a referent at all. In Stoic terms such statements were not false but 'impossible'. See further Barnes 1997: 97–8.

'Examination' (*exetasis*) in §25 refers, I think, to the scrutiny not of the subject-matter or of argument, but of persons. E has in mind testing a person's logical prowess through a battery of questions. Seneca refers to this procedure (disapprovingly) at *Ep.* 48. 10.

In §§26–9 E reprises the appeal to moral authority or generic moral *exemplum* that informed the opening section (§§1–4). Here E invokes the preconception (*prolēpsis* in §29) of the good man to support his claim that proficiency in logic is desirable. This was a characteristically Stoic form of argument; cf. the reference to 'the preconception of a philosopher' and 'the preconception of a Cynic' at 4. 8. 6 and 3. 22. 1. Bonhöffer (1890: 197–8) suggests that this type of preconception was transitional between those derived a priori and those derived empirically. His equivocation just shows that these Kantian categories should not be pressed too hard. The epithet 'good' (*spoudaios* in §§3 and 29) was an alternative designation of the Stoic sage (DL 7. 118). As Stoics allowed that the sage was as rare as the phoenix, few could have known of him by experience. E is relying on centuries of Stoic theorizing about the sage in appealing to this 'preconception'. They said that 'without dialectic the sage cannot be flawless in reason . . . , nor put questions and answers scientifically' (DL 7. 47; cf. Alex. *In Arist. Top.* 1. 8–14 (= LS 31D)). In E's diatribes the sage functions as an ideal to be emulated, even if his degree of perfection was judged ultimately out of reach; see comment ad 1. 2. 36.

'[B]ecomes superfluous' in **§29** is Greek *parelkei*. On this term (and cognate noun *parolkē*) see Barnes 1980: 166, citing SE *PH* 2. 156–67.

The concluding section **§§30–3** reinforces the point that logic has moral significance, by arguing the inverse of what went before: as success in the sphere of logic is proper to the good man, so failure in this sphere is a type of moral failing. Cf. Cic. *Fin.* 3. 72: 'To the other virtues they also add dialectic and natural science: they call both virtues, the first because it establishes principles which guard against assenting to what is false, or ever being tricked by a deceptive plausibility, and enables us to uphold and defend what we have learned about good and evil. For the Stoics think that without this skill anyone can be tempted away from truth and fall into error. So, if in all matters rashness and ignorance count as vice, then the skill which removes them is justly called a virtue.' Atherton (1993: 54) observes that 'dialectic's significance is ultimately explained by the fact that it is assent which governs a human's being life for good and ill. . . . Assent to certain impressions constitutes an "impulse" in the human soul to perform some action. . . . Many of the actions performable by human agents have moral value.' It is significant that E's third *topos* constitutes both logic and assent (cf. 3. 2. 2), which tends to confirm the connection. Stoics did not regard mistakes in logic as innocent or venial: 'Falsehood produces a disturbance in the mind, from which arise many passions and causes of instability' (DL 7. 110).

Killing one's father and burning the Capitol (**§§31–2**) are instanced elsewhere as particularly heinous crimes; cf. Cic. *PS* 24 for the former, *De Amic.* 37 and Plut. *Tiberius Gracchus* 20. 4 for the latter. The Capitol really did burn down in AD 69 and 80, which may have prompted the comparison. Rufus is Musonius Rufus; see comment on 1. 1. 27.

In implicating himself in his students' mistakes in **§32**, E shows himself a shrewd teacher. Self-criticism helps disarm resistance toward someone who presumes to dictate to others how to behave.

CHAPTER 8

That Capacities are Treacherous for the Uneducated

This chapter demonstrates E's complex attitude toward the subject of logic. The juxtaposition of this essay with 1. 7 throws this ambivalence into high relief. In this one E focuses particularly on the rhetorical side of logic; it should be compared with 2. 23, 'On the Faculty of Expression'. It may be summarized as follows:

§§1–3 Because the number of possible permutations of an argument is large, it would seem that the prospective philosopher should make a special study of the subject.

§§4–10 But in fact training in logic, and rhetoric in particular, is dangerous, because it fosters a superior attitude in new recruits, which inhibits progress toward virtue.

§§11–16 That Plato was a master stylist is no argument to the contrary, since Plato did not write well *qua* philosopher. The ability to express oneself well should not be despised, but should not be confused with the true aim of philosophy, a virtuous character.

In **§1** 'terms that are equivalent' renders Greek *ta isodunamounta*. Cf. DL 7. 101: '[Stoics] hold that "the good" is equivalent (*isodunamein*) to "the beautiful".' In other words, the sets of things denominated by either term are coextensive. Stoics favoured identity statements of this kind: 'All good is expedient, necessary, useful, serviceable, beautiful, advantageous, choiceworthy and just' (DL 7. 98; cf. Clem. *Protr.* 1. 54. 18–55.4 (= LS 60Q)). Barnes (1997: 31–2) first recognized that **§2** is not an argument, but a pair of sentences that, though formulated differently, are logically equivalent. They may be symbolized, respectively, as:

$$\text{If P and not Q, then R}$$

and

$$\text{Not ((P and not Q) and not R)}$$

For the varied use of *isodunamein* among philosophers of the early Empire, to apply not only to synonyms, but also to logically identical statements, see further Barnes 1993a: 46 n. 64.

The definition of an enthymeme as 'an incomplete syllogism' in §3 is also found in some texts of Aristotle at *An. pr.* 70a10. But Burnyeat (1994) argues that the reading is not only unsound, but that this definition of 'enthymeme' actually originated with the Stoics. It was read back into the text and interpretation of Aristotle by ancient commentators who were influenced by the Stoic tradition of the word. Evidence suggests that it applied particularly to truncated, rhetorical versions of the third of Chrysippus' five indemonstrable arguments. This took the form: 'Not both P and Q; P; therefore not Q.' Cicero gives three instances (*Top.* 55):

(1) Fear this, and do not fear that.
(2) Do you condemn the woman whom you accuse of nothing; and at the same time assert that punishment is due the woman whom you consider deserving of a reward?
(3) What you know is of no advantage; is what you do not know a disadvantage?

All three examples conceal the first premiss of the third indemonstrable, i.e. the contrariety 'Not both P and Q'. But they are 'incomplete', because the conclusion is not expressly drawn. Evidently the enthymeme was suited to exhortation, rhetorical questions, and rhetorical contexts generally.

Stoics standardly divided logic into two halves: rhetoric and dialectic (DL 7. 41; see LS 1.188–9). Their overall contribution to ancient rhetorical theory was slight, compared to what they accomplished in dialectic, however, and their few remaining statements about rhetoric are conventional for the most part. Cicero at *Fin.* 4. 7 delivers a harsh judgement on Chrysippus' one book on the subject. Atherton (1988) collects the testimony relating to Stoic rhetoric, and tries to make a virtue of this relative neglect. Perhaps their most significant contribution to the field lay simply in their taking rhetoric seriously, treating it not as a travesty of philosophy, like Plato, but as a legitimate expression of the *logos* principle— more in the spirit of Aristotle.

Beginning with §4 the argument takes an abrupt turn. I assign §4 to an imaginary interlocutor, because this device regularly motivates such shifts. In this case we can imagine the interlocutor to be one of E's students, asking why more time is not devoted to logic if what was said in §§1–3 is true. From E's reply, we infer that it is only with reluctance that he slights it. In §§5–10 he gives his reasons.

First, he explains that it detracts from time spent directly on progress toward moral virtue (*kalokagathia* in **§5**). This is a point he makes elsewhere (3. 2. 6, 3. 24. 78; *Ench.* 59. 2). It is not strictly compatible with his advice that 'one must advance toward the ethical goal through *logos* and its instruction' (2. 23. 40). But the contradiction is discussed below, and in any case is less glaring when the rhetorical half of logic is the focus of discussion, as here.

In **§§6–10** E adds that logic is objectionable because it nurtures presumption (*oiēsis*) in its students; cf. 1. 26. 9. But it was E's contention that philosophy, in the moral sense, begins by shedding presumption: 'What is the first business of one who pursues philosophy? To abolish presumption' (2. 17. 1; cf. 3. 14. 8, 3. 23. 16; DL 7. 23, 4. 50). Why was facility in logic such a snare? **§10** implies that a young man no sooner becomes an adept in logic than he can no longer be told anything—on this or any subject. Pride in his skill prevents him from realizing that he is deficient in other respects, and he becomes deaf to moral admonition. E evidently speaks from experience. The central role that the Stoics assigned *logos* in all departments of life—and, therefore, the importance they assigned logic—evidently caused practical problems for him. He endorsed this position in theory, but viewed with alarm the sophomoric impulse to make a fetish of logical puzzles like 'The Liar', and to adopt a superior attitude that was inimical to the ultimate goal of becoming good. He therefore had to limit his students' access to logic. This can help explain the inconsistency of his statements on this head.

§§7–8 seem to allude to the view, going back to Plato (*Grg.* 456c–457c), that rhetoric is a morally neutral 'power' or faculty—a *dunamis tōn enantiōn*, in Aristotle's terms. E's own point is that this power is dangerous for 'the uneducated'—meaning, I take it, the morally uneducated—because it distracts them with what he elsewhere calls its 'Siren song' (2. 23. 41), and makes them arrogant. That is why E slights it in his teaching, especially (like most Stoics) on the rhetorical side. **§9** seems to touch on an additional difficulty: i.e. that rhetoric is the only possible means to impress upon an insolent student the error of his ways. But being already accomplished in its use, the student can counter those appeals. He can produce a self-refutation argument whose substance is that you cannot consistently use rhetoric (although you cannot practically use anything else) to persuade someone of the unimportance of rhetoric.

In §§11–16 E responds to the suggestion, again assigned to an interlocutor, that rhetorical eloquence or a graceful style is a necessary ornament of philosophy. The interlocutor cites Plato, but E distinguishes: Plato's style is an attractive feature of his philosophizing, but not an essential one. Plato did not write well *qua* philosopher; his eloquence was a feature he shared with Hippocrates, a physician, not with Chrysippus, a philosopher. That Chrysippus had a notoriously crabbed style is probably relevant here; see note ad 1. 4. 5–9. Stoics did not despise eloquence. Of all the philosophical schools, in fact, they 'alone called eloquence a virtue and a form of wisdom' (Cic. *Orat.* 3. 65). But they promoted a simple and direct style of discourse with little embellishment, which required little time or effort to learn; cf. DL 7. 59, and see Atherton 1988: 400–5; 1993: 87–92. For the thought of this section compare *Ench.* 44.

Fronto (*De Eloq.* 2. 16) urged Marcus to imitate Plato's style in his own writing. He was plainly at odds with E here. But even E is not dismissive of the virtues of style, as §15 shows. Cf. 2. 23. 46: 'When I say these things to some people, they think I am disparaging the study of rhetoric or theorems. It is not this that I disparage, but the ceaseless concern with those things and resting one's hopes on them.' With §§15–16 compare also 2. 23. 25–7: 'There is a certain value in the power of eloquence, but it is not as great as that of the moral character. When I say this, let no one suppose that I am urging you to neglect speech, any more than I bid you neglect your eyes. . . . But if you ask me, "What is the most important thing of all?," what shall I say? That it is the power of eloquence? I cannot. It is rather that of moral character, provided that it is *right* moral character.' E's attitude is thus complex but consistent overall. Individual passages relating to the study of logic (logic in the broad, Stoic sense) are inconsistent with one another, it is true, but E pitched his lesson to whatever set of students he was addressing (itself a rhetorical strategy). Since at least some of them were evidently dazzled by eloquence, he had to cure them of their infatuation, and sometimes promote moral virtue with as little reference to rhetoric as possible. On E and rhetoric, see further Brancacci 1985: 28–32.

§14 is E being self-deprecating and ironic in his usual way in implying that he is not a philosopher; cf. 1. 9. 10–19, and 2. 19. 23–4 (where he implies that he does not know any Stoics).

CHAPTER 9

How from the Fact that We are Akin to God Should One Proceed to the Consequences?

For most of its length this essay explores in familiar ways the theme of the autonomy of the moral self, its independence from externals. In §§10–17 a new motif is introduced, concerning the impiety of suicide and the need to 'wait upon god'. This line of thought derives from Socrates in the *Phaedo*. It is introduced here to forestall the drastic conclusions that youthful idealism might be inclined to draw from the opposition of internal and external values that E draws in the first nine sections, and often elsewhere.

The essay as a whole is thematically close to 1. 3. It may be summarized thus:

§§1–9 A statement of man's kinship with the gods, emphasizing the corollary idea of the universe as a city composed of gods and men.

§§10–17 The distinction between our local habitation and our citizenship in the world at large, recast in Platonic terms as a dualism of the *Dieser-* and *Jenerwelt*. E discourages the impulse to abandon one for the other, borrowing an argument from the *Phaedo* about the duty to persist in whatever station god assigns us.

§§18–26 Holding aloof from externals alone secures freedom from outside force; Socrates is cited as a model of the attitude E wishes to instil. By remaining faithful to his station in this life, he showed his affinity to god—not by leaving it to find god elsewhere.

§§27–34 Anecdotes demonstrating the kind of indifference to externals, and therefore to the temporal authorities that control them, that one is capable of when inspired by the example of Socrates, and in turn by the more abstract ideal of kinship with god.

§§1–7 expounds and draws implications from Cynic–Stoic cosmopolitanism. Cf. Sen. *De Otio* 4. 1: 'There are two communities: one, which is truly great and truly common, embracing gods and men, in which we look neither to this corner nor that, but measure the boundaries by the sun; and another, which we have been assigned by the accident of our birth.' Cf. E 2. 10. 3; Sen. *Ep.* 28. 4;

Helv. 9. 7; *Marc.* 4. 4. This thought was a source of consolation in the literature on exile: cf. Plut. *De Exilio* 600D–601B and Muson. 42. 1–2 (both again citing Socrates); Cic. *PS* 2. 18. For its attribution to Socrates, cf. also Cic. *TD* 5. 108: 'When Socrates was asked what nationality he claimed to be, he used to answer, "Of the world".' This is not only anachronistic, but belied by the exclusive attachment to Athens which Socrates professes in the *Crito* (52a–53a; cf. *Tht.* 143d). Moles (1995: 132) says that the attribution of cosmopolitan sentiment to him 'is naturally explained as retrojection of Diogenic material upon the "father" of the Cynic–Stoic "succession".' For the ascription of the sentiment to Diogenes cf. 3. 24. 66; DL 6. 63; E may be thinking of him in **§§1** and **3** in connection with Corinth. On Cynic–Stoic cosmopolitanism generally, see Baldry 1965: 151–66; Schofield 1991: 57–92, 141–5. On the kinship of god and man, and the associated, distinctively Stoic idea that the world is a city composed of both, cf. *SVF* 3. 333–48, and see comment ad 1. 3. 1–2. The argument here is similar to the last passage, especially in drawing a comparison between kinship with god and kinship with Caesar. Origen at *SVF* 2. 1156–7 offers another close parallel, which seems to borrow directly from **§§4–5**.

§§4–5 depends on the distinctively Stoic idea of god as generative reason, *spermatikos logos*. Cf. DL 7. 136: 'God is the generative reason of the universe.' Zeno argued a posteriori from the existence of the rational creature man to the rationality of the universe: 'That which projects the seed of the rational is itself rational. But the universe projects the seed of the rational. Therefore the universe is rational' (SE *M* 9. 101). Primary fire and generative reason were supposed to contain in themselves the germ of all earthly life and reason: cf. Cic. *ND* 2. 28, 58. As E implies, human reason derives from the generative reason, i.e. from Zeus, and this is the basis of our association with him.

In **§§8–9** E uses a two-pronged argument *a minori ad maius*, to urge that the philosopher, who is conscious of his kinship with god, should be more confident than beasts or slaves that his needs will be met. This section is Cynic in spirit: using beasts as the criterion of what is natural in terms of essential needs was a characteristically Cynic move: cf. DL 6. 22. For the comparison with runaway slaves cf. DL 6. 55: 'When told to go in pursuit of his runaway slave, Diogenes replied, "It would be strange if Manes can live without Diogenes, but Diogenes cannot live without Manes."'

The argument in **§§10–17** derives from Plato's *Phaedo* 61b–62e, where Socrates says that suicide is a crime against god, unless he sends a signal in the form of 'some necessity' (62c) to abandon this life for the next. The motive to suicide that E considers, contempt for the body and for life on earth, informs the view of philosophy in the *Phaedo* as 'a practice for death' (64a, 67e, 80e). Suicide, however, is forbidden. The ban was originally Pythagorean (*Phd.* 61e; Cic. *Cato* 73), but is affirmed in the *Phaedo*, and repeated by later writers, undoubtedly under Plato's influence. Besides E here, cf. Cic. *Rep.* 6. 15; *TD* 1. 74; Sen. *Ep.* 24. 22–5.

Although Plato discourages suicide, a loathing for life and for the body is a characteristically Platonic attitude. It is found among later Stoics; cf. 1. 1. 11, 1. 13. 5; fr. 23; Marc. 6. 28, 7. 35 (quoting Plato), 8. 37; Sen. *Ep.* 23. 6, 65. 18–22, etc. The characterization of the body as 'chains' on the soul (**§§11** and **14**) also borrows from Plato; cf. *Phd.* 67d, 82e; *Grg.* 492d. It too became common; cf. Cic. *Rep.* 6. 14; *TD* 1. 75; Sen. *Ep.* 65. 21; see Powell 1988 ad Cic. *Sen.* 81. That man has a kinship with god is a view Stoics shared with Plato: see comment ad 1. 3. 1–2. But that we descend from a divine state when we are embodied, and (if we are good) return to one after death, was an idea more elaborated in the Platonic tradition: cf. *Phdr.* 248c–249d; *Tim.* 41d–42b; Cic. *TD* 1. 43; see Boyancé 1936: 129–33. Stoics were comparatively tentative in their eschatology; see comment ad 1. 1. 14–17. Again, however, there was a trend in Stoicism from Posidonius on to admit Platonic ideas on this head (which were largely popular ideas anyway). Cf. Sen. *Cons. Marc.* 24. 5: 'What we see wrapped around us, bones, sinews and skin, the face and hands that serve as our human vesture—these are chains and shadows over the soul. By these things the soul is crushed and strangled and stained, kept from what is truly its own, and cast into error. It always strains against this weight of flesh to avoid being dragged back and sunk; it strives to rise to that place from which it is descended.' Cf. Sen. *Ep.* 79. 12; 102; *De Otio* 5. 5; Manil. 4. 887; Velleius 2. 123. 2 with Woodman ad loc.

What we find in the present passage, and often in Marcus, is an effort to support such ideas with reference to the distinctively Stoic idea of 'generative reason'. Cf. Marc. 4. 14: 'You have subsisted as a part of the whole. You will disappear into that which engendered you, or rather ascend into the generative reason by a process of change'; cf. also 4. 21. 1, 6. 24, 7. 10, 10. 7. 2. Implicit in such passages is the belief that reason, the true man, returns to its kind, just as the elements of which the body is composed return to theirs; cf. Cic. *Sen.* 80 with Powell 1988 ad loc. Other Stoic authorities speak of the soul returning to the realm of *ether*, the element out of which it is fashioned—and predicate immortality, or some limited term of survival, on that basis; cf. SE *M* 9. 73; Cic. *TD* 1. 42–3; Sen. *Ep.* 79. 12.

Having considered the background to the ideas expressed in **§§11–15**, it is time to consider their context. Most are ascribed to a suppositious pupil. For Bonhöffer (1890: 35–6, 52–3, 65–6) this meant that they do not represent E's views at all. I am not so sure, since in **§11** E speaks *in propria persona*, and does not directly challenge the ideas in the subsequent sections, only discourages the impulse to suicide that could result. It is true, and a point in Bonhöffer's favour, that nowhere else does he expound such eschatology, on his own account or otherwise. At 3. 13. 14 he says that after death we return to what is akin (*sungenēs*) to us (as in **§11** here). He then identifies this with 'the elements'—but without mentioning the soul, or drawing any implications for immortality. 4. 7. 15 is even more circumspect. Overall, however, I am inclined to think that in this passage E does for once adopt Platonic ideas concerning the afterlife. The passage certainly reflects Plato's influence in other respects. And such influence would be consistent with a contemporary trend in Stoicism. The passage in general is a notable example of philosophical eclecticism: Cynic cosmopolitanism, the Stoic idea of 'generative reason', Platonic dualism and eschatology. On **§§10–17** see also Hoven 1971: 135–7 (although he has little to add). For the phraseology in **§17**, 'Stay, do not depart on unreasonable grounds', compare the discussion of suicide at 1. 2. 1–11, and see comment ad loc.

§23 is a paraphrase of Pl. *Apol.* 29c, **§§24–5** a paraphrase of *Apol.* 28d–e; cf. 30c1. E seems to imply that Socrates showed himself a true kinsman of the gods in adhering to the post which god assigned him. How this would make him a true kinsman of the gods, however, is not immediately clear; 'servant' might seem a better description. The argument is elliptical. When Stoics spoke of man's kinship with the gods, they had in mind their mutual share in reason; see comment ad 1. 3. 1–2. E implies that in remaining faithful to his philosophical mission Socrates honoured reason above his body and this life. It is in pursuing the life of reason, philosophy, even at the risk of death, that Socrates showed his kinship with the gods. This does not conflict with what was said earlier. It is true that Socrates' death is presented in the *Phaedo* and in other ancient sources as a form of suicide, since he did not try to escape it (see Gallop 1975: 85). But he only accepted it as a consequence of his commitment to his duty in this life, the philosophical one. His life became meaningless when this role was denied him.

With §§22–6, and §16 above, cf. 3. 24. 99: 'Whatever station and post you assign me, I will die ten thousand times over, as Socrates says, before I abandon it.' These passages, together with 1. 29. 29 and Marc. 7. 45, indicate that the characteristically Stoic comparison of life to a term of military service under god was Socratic in inspiration. Cf. also 1. 14. 15, 3. 22. 69, 3. 24. 31–4, 112; *Ench.* 22; Sen. *Ben.* 5. 2. 4; Marc. 2. 17. 1, 11. 9, etc.; see Rutherford 1989: 61 n. 42, 148, 240–1. In this essay the idea of remaining at one's post seems to be associated with the prohibition against suicide, as at Cic. *Rep.* 6. 14. 4; cf. Sen. *Ep.* 65. 18; Marc. 3. 5.

The use of 'bellies' (§26) as an insult directed against people enslaved to their appetites goes back to Hesiod (*Theog.* 26); 'genitals' evidently refers to those enslaved to sexual desire. For E's distinctive use of 'corpse' in reference to the body see comment ad 1. 19. 7–10. He applies it here to those who identify exclusively with the body, the outer man, subject not only to desires, but to the will of others who have power over it. By including himself in the general condemnation in §19 and assuming some of the blame for his students' characters, E forestalls the resentment such fault-finding naturally incurs.

§§27–34: for E's use of anecdote toward the end of a discourse, see comment ad 1. 1. 18–32. He had a friend who evidently was once influential in Rome but subsequently had fallen on hard times. Whether due to forced or self-imposed exile, he was now living in the provinces ('here' in §27 must be Nicopolis). In the view of the many (*hoi polloi* in §27), these were evil circumstances; and E either shared that point of view at this stage in his life, or assumed it temporarily for his friend's sake. He wrote a letter for him. But piqued by the letter's anxious tone, the friend rejected his help. E evidently still had much to learn, and the man in straitened circumstances was best placed to teach him. E's friend's absence from Rome was in fact no evil, for reasons given earlier: as a citizen of the world, he ought to be at home anywhere. And money and power, of course, were not absolute goods for a Stoic; cf. DL 7. 101–3.

The second anecdote (§§29–30) is rather obscure, but is evidently meant to reinforce the first, which assists in its interpretation. It is clear that E tells both at his own expense, in keeping with the wry tone of §19 and most of his references to himself. Musonius Rufus, E's teacher when he was still a slave (see note ad 1. 2. 27), would test his reaction to a threat on the part of his master. E's sententious reply (a single word in the Greek: *anthrōpina*) reflects a conventional way of looking at misfortune: timid, resigned, and submissive in the face of fate as the letter for his friend was submissive (on *anthrōpina* see Headlam ad Herondas 5. 22). E is looking for a little life from his students, and in his characteristic way admits that he once fell short in this regard. Rufus' sarcastic response may be paraphrased thus: 'Why should I ever ask your master for something, when it is clear that I can miraculously get the same thing from you, who are only his slave?' But what Rufus gets is not in fact to his liking, being the sort of guarded attitude he expects from one in thrall to wealth and power like E's master, not from a pretender to philosophy like E himself. (The idea of getting something from another, in both §§31 and 32, does not, I think, signal any significant connection in thought.)

E's mature thoughts on goods and evils and indifferents are outlined in the final sections, §§31–4. They evidently took time to develop. Compare 1. 30. 2–3 for the right attitude, and for the thought, cf. 1. 28. 10, 3. 19. 1, 4. 8. 25; *Ench.* 48. 1.

CHAPTER 10

To Those who have Applied Themselves to Advancement at Rome

The title is misleading, because the discourse is *about* those who busy themselves with affairs in the capital, but is addressed *to* E's own students of philosophy, in whom he tries to excite a like enthusiasm for their subject. The discourse is a good example of E's pedagogical style, especially in its subtle use of psychology. The argument proceeds through a series of comparisons, based on different dualities: philosophy/business; Nicopolis/Rome; action/contemplation; youth/old age. The main thesis is that philosophy is not as idle or opposed to action as is commonly supposed. Philosophy's young recruits should rescue its reputation by showing just how active and productive it can be. Summary:

§§1–6 An anecdote about a personal acquaintance of E who chose the exciting life of business in Rome and the court over philosophy.

§§ 7–12 Philosophy itself, however, is not leisurely and inactive. It is action of a higher order.

§§12–13 Rather than old men who usually teach philosophy and with whom the discipline is identified, youth should take the lead in its practice.

The point of the story in **§§2–6** is to dramatize the competing values of Rome, on the one hand, and philosophy, on the other. E had left Rome behind, literally and figuratively. His friend had reasons to reject it too: his advanced age, when one usually contemplates retirement instead of a new career; past misfortune in Rome leading to exile; and his (superficial) conversion to philosophy under E's influence (note that *ataraxia* ('tranquillity' in **§2**) was a key term of Hellenistic ethics, Stoic as well as Epicurean and Sceptic). In this man's case, worldly values easily win out. The tone of the passage, however, and the subsequent argument indicate that E does not condemn his friend completely. He admires his zeal, while suggesting that it could be bestowed on a worthier object.

[The closing phrase in **§4** translates literally as 'suppose what you please'. This is obscure. Souilhé translates it 'I will give you whatever you desire', but E does not elsewhere uses the verb *hupolambanein* in the rare sense of 'take' or 'seize'. My translation is based on that of Oldfather and Hard.]

The argument in **§§7–12** depends on a distinction. In criticizing his friend, E does not mean to criticize business or the life of action. Philosophy, contrary to what most people believe, is not opposed to action. Philosophers simply uphold a kind of activity different from what engages most of the world, a kind that, properly understood, is actually more productive. E suggests in **§§7–8** that the reason for this misconception is that philosophy is popularly identified with old men like himself, for whom any kind of exertion is unwelcome.

Of course this is facetious. The issue concerns the character of philosophy, not its practitioners. Philosophers since Pythagoras had extolled, and been identified with, the life of contemplation (see note ad 1. 6. 18–22). But E argues that the traditional opposition between action and contemplation rests on a false antithesis: contemplation is actually the highest form of activity. This neat resolution of an old debate essentially develops an idea out of Aristotle (*Pol.* 1325b16–23) by way of Chrysippus (who calls philosophy 'an activity [*ergon*, as in §1 here] worthy of the greatest effort' at *St. rep.* 1033B) and Antiochus of Ascalon (Cic. *Fin.* 5. 58; *Ac.* 2. 108). On the whole topic see Müller 1968. Seneca pursues a similar line in *Ep.* 8; cf. *De Otio* 5. 8–6. 5. Both are motivated to this defence in part because of their school's commitment to an active life (DL 7. 123).

With the wry self-reference in **§§7–8**, compare the earnest injunction of Marcus at 5. 1 to rise early, a passage that in other respects seems to reflect the influence of this one. **§8** provides a brief look at the daily workings of E's school. Study apparently included reading and commenting on philosophical texts; responsibility was shared among E and his students. For contemporary descriptions of such a curriculum cf. Fronto, *De Eloq.* 5. 4; Gellius 17. 20; Lucian, *Hermotimus*. On the prominence of commentary in the philosophy of this period, see Barnes 1993; Lakmann 1995: 216–20. 1. 26 and 2. 21. 11 also shed light on the discipline of E's school.

For the weighty issues reviewed in **§10** with which philosophy is supposed to busy itself, see comment ad 1. 6. 25, and cf. Sen. *Ep.* 82. 5–6: 'Gird yourself about with philosophy. . . . This means knowledge of self and of nature. The soul should know where it is going and from where it has come, what is its good and what is its evil, what it seeks and what it avoids, and what is the nature of reason.'

In the closing sections, **§§12–13**, E suggests that, since philosophy concerns itself with such vital matters, it is best adapted to the vigour of youth. Young men, rather than old, are its proper champions, and should, in turn, infect their teachers with their enthusiasm. E subtly flatters his students while appearing to criticize them. His talent as a teacher is evident even as he makes light of it.

CHAPTER 11

Of Family Affection

E's diatribes are schematic quasi-dialogues for the most part. The interlocutor is a mere device, limited to a few lines. The context of the discourse is rarely referred to, or if it is, normally only at the start; cf. 1. 13. 1, 1. 14. 1, 1. 26. 1, 2. 14. 1, etc. What is unique in the present discourse is that the dialogue form, from which the diatribe developed, is restored in full. The interlocutor is no stick figure, but a real person in a real situation. We don't have a name, but he represents a familiar type, the anxious *paterfamilias*. And he continues to put and answer questions throughout the discourse, not just at the beginning. This is as close as E ever got to writing a dialogue on the model of the Socratic dialogues. The expression also bespeaks a debt to Plato, as noted at points below.

The discourse dramatizes a problem that can arise from an over-estimate of the value of externals, in this case the health and continued life of the man's daughter. The result of his misjudgement is passion, leading him to desert his daughter and, paradoxically, to lose any chance of rendering her useful service of a kind that would promote her health or well-being. His failure in virtue, in other words, results in a failure to promote her primary natural goods.

The structure of the discourse is as follows:

§§1–15 A man claims he acted rightly in leaving the side of his sick daughter, pleading that this is commonly done. E challenges his assumption, using it as a basis for asserting the need to establish a criterion of what is right and wrong.

§§16–26 E sets forth a hypothesis as a means to discovering whether the man's act was, as he claims, right and natural.

§§27–40 As a further refutation of the man's claim that he could not control himself in acting as he did, E argues that all our actions are determined by our judgements, and these are under our control.

The Socratic *elenchus* (examination) begins in **§5** with E asking the man if he acted rightly (*orthōs*) in abandoning his sick daughter. In response the man claims that he acted *phusikōs* (naturally). This seems related to a common use of nature (*phusis*) in ancient Greek, to denote what is beyond man's control, what is 'independent of human effort or volition' (Bury 1894: 300, giving references to Plato). But in Stoicism nature was also the standard of correctness. Cf. DL 7. 87: 'Zeno in his book *On the Nature of Man* was the first to say that living in agreement with nature is the end, which is living in accordance with virtue. For nature leads us toward virtue.' E accordingly concedes to the man that if he acted naturally, then he acted rightly. In §§6–7, however, he proceeds to rebut the man's assumption that everything that happens, or is done, is on that account natural. What E says can be squared with Stoic doctrine, though it skirts a complex issue.

Stoics said that disease ('tumours' in §7), drought, famine, and other first-order evils, as well as the second-order evil of wrongdoing, were actually contrary to the nature of individuals. They nevertheless maintained that they were consistent with universal nature: 'Since the organization of the universe as a whole proceeds in this way, it is necessarily in conformity with this organization that we are in whatever state we may be, including whether contrary to our individual nature we are ill or maimed' (Plut. *St. rep.* 1050A). As for wrongdoing, Chrysippus maintained that virtue could not exist without it (Gellius 7.1). E himself writes that god 'ordained that there be summer and winter, abundance and dearth, virtue and vice, and all such opposites for the harmony of the whole' (1. 12. 16; cf. 2. 5. 24–9, 2. 6. 9, 2. 10. 4–6). So, in implying that disease and wrongdoing are not in accord with nature, E must mean individual nature. Either that or he is just speaking popularly, in keeping with the informal character of the essay. On the larger issue see Long 1974: 179–84.

Domestic duties loom large in E's diatribes. According to Barth and Blanke (1994: 463), among pagan authors 'Epictetus has been considered the classic source' for practical instruction relating to the reciprocal duties of parents, children, masters and slaves. E devotes much of his second *topos* to this. Cf. 3. 2. 4: 'The second *topos* concerns duty; for I should not be unfeeling like a statue, but should maintain my relations, both natural and acquired, as a pious man, a son, a brother, a father, and a citizen.' Cf. 2. 17. 31–2, 3. 7. 25–6, and the whole of 2. 10. Interest in these is also evident in Sen. *Ep.*

94, which attests to a current, if controversial, interest among other Stoics (see Kidd 1978; LS 1. 429).

With **§§9–15** cf. 1. 22. 4 and 1. 28. 28–30, with comment ad loc. For the sequence of thought cf. Pl. *Euthphr.* 7b–d, except that E argues not from analogy, but *a minori ad maius*, as at 1. 18. 6. 'So Epictetus asked' in **§3**, and 'And Epictetus said' in **§9** are simply *Kai hos* in the original, a Platonic formula and a use of the pronoun *hos* not otherwise attested in E. It reflects the essay's stylistic, as well as thematic, debt to the Socratic dialogues. **§§9–11** is very similar to Muson. 34. 2–11. The suggestion in **§9** that the senses function as a criterion of truth is orthodox Stoic doctrine (DL 7. 54), but treated here as common opinion.

In **§8** the man could not meet E's repeated challenge, to prove that his act was natural. He offered a counter-challenge. In **§§16–26** E suggests a means to meet it. This conforms to a pattern in Socratic dialogues; see Guthrie iv. 122. It resembles especially *Meno* 86e–87b in proposing a hypothesis: we cannot decide whether your act was in accordance with nature. But we agree that what is affectionate and what is reasonable are in accordance with nature. Thus, if we can establish that your act was affectionate and reasonable, then we will know that it accords with nature.

E's reasoning in this section is worth analysing in detail: (1) That parental affection is in accordance with nature was not only formally acknowledged by the Stoics (DL 7. 120) but emphasized, to prove that consideration for others is innate (Plut. *St. rep.* 1038B). Parental affection, then, would be a species of the genus of things in accordance with nature. In calling it 'good' in **§17**, however, E appears to depart from strict Stoic usage, since Stoics were careful to reserve 'good' to virtue and virtuous actions. An act of parental affection would be a proper function, but only a right action and 'good' if done in a particular way: cf. DL 7. 108. Nor were all things in accordance with nature 'good': cf. LS 58C. But perhaps E is not concerned to maintain these distinctions, is speaking popularly, and ignores the difference between proper function (*kathēkon*) and right action (*katorthōma*), as in fact he usually does.

(2) An act of parental affection, then, is good and natural. For the purposes of argument, this is the only hypothesis E needs. But he complicates it in **§17** by introducing another factor, 'the rational' (*to eulogiston*). This is treated as logically on a par with parental

affection, i.e. as another species of what is good and natural. E is setting the man up, because he is on the point of arguing that his behaviour was neither affectionate nor rational, so that he will not have a leg to stand on.

(3) In **§18** it is agreed that 'what is rational is not in conflict (*mache*) with family affection'. When applied to predicates, the only sense that 'conflict' can bear is a 'contrary of'. But E's further statement that 'if they were in conflict, one would be in accordance with nature, while the other would be contrary to nature' only holds if either term were not a species of, but coextensive with, the class of things in accordance with nature—and this he has not attempted to prove. Still, such a thesis could be defended for 'the rational' given the role it plays in Stoic definitions of proper function; see comment ad 1. 2. 1–5.

§19 contains a Platonic reminiscence in the phrase 'confidently declare' (*tharrountes apophainometha*); cf. *Euthd.* 275d; *Tht.* 157d, etc.

[The translation of **§17** assumes with Schenkl that the phrase 'in accordance with nature, and good' is repeated. This helps to clarify the structure of the argument.]

There are two problems with the argument in **§§20–6**. E has proposed a hypothesis, using 'the rational' and 'the affectionate' as means to establish that an act is 'in accordance with nature'. But what he then does is to argue that the act was neither rational nor affectionate, leaving unresolved the original question. In formal terms:

$$p \vee q \supset r \neq \sim p \cdot \sim q \supset \sim r.$$

Even if it can be shown to meet neither criterion, the man's behaviour could still be in accordance with nature if it belonged to a different subset of things in accordance with nature. The only way E's argument works is if either 'the affectionate' or 'the rational' is coextensive with the class of things in accordance with nature, or if between them they exhaust it. E has not proved either thesis, but, as indicated, 'the rational' could well be coextensive with 'what is in accordance with nature'.

In **§§21–4** E lays himself open to a more serious charge: viz. that in claiming that the man's behaviour was not consistent with family affection, he employs the same sort of argument he reproached the man for above, i.e. an appeal to the behaviour of others as a standard of correctness. The fact that this behaviour is real in the one case, hypothetical in the other, is immaterial. On its own terms E's argument is compelling, but in context it seems inconsistent.

In §20 E first addresses himself to the possibility that the man acted rationally. (He intends to argue by way of a dilemma.) He dismisses the possibility out of hand, not even bothering to secure the other's agreement. This must be because it is assumed to be self-evident that in walking out on his sick daughter the man was impelled by emotion, not reason, and because the man has not attempted to defend his action on rational grounds.

'Yes, let us consider' in §20 is *skopōmen dē*, a type of phrase familiar from Plato's Socratic dialogues; cf. *Meno* 87b, *Crat.* 401a, etc.

The sense of §§27–8 is, first, to concede that there must have been some natural basis for the man's act; but then to trivialize it, by comparing it to the fatuous behaviour of a devotee of the horse-races. In leaving the side of his sick child, the man acted on impulse; but, as E repeatedly says, it is not natural for a man to yield to any and all impressions. In the case of mankind, what accords with nature is that reason become 'the craftsman of impulse' (DL 7. 86). So, in trusting to his first impression, the man acted contrary to the nature of a human being.

The 'philosophers' in §28 are the Stoics, as they normally are in E; cf. 1. 4. 1, 1. 18. 1, 1. 25. 32, 1. 29. 9, etc. But he favours this generic designation in part to transcend a narrow sectarian appeal; the rationalist thesis which he defends here actually goes back to Socrates and Plato. In the remainder of the discourse, §§28–40, E expounds the rationalist thesis in order to attack his friend's too ready assumption that he could not help doing what he did; for rationalism implies that we always do what we think best. This does not conflict with §20, where E claimed that the man's act was not rational. E does not deny that the man used reason when he abandoned his daughter. All human impulses are rational in Stoic psychology (cf. Plut. *St. rep.* 1037F). E doubts, however, that he used it well, since his opinions had been barely scrutinized. Passages similar to §§28–33, in upholding the sovereignty of opinion (*dogma*) in determining our actions, are common in E, and include 1. 17. 26, 1. 19. 8, 2. 16. 24, 4. 5. 29, 4. 7. 1–5; *Ench.* 5; and the whole of 3. 9.

The last third of the discourse, **§§27–40**, is an argument for moral responsibility. This is a prominent theme in E (cf. 1. 1), and had special urgency owing to his school's determinism. It may be compared with Aristotle's discussion of the issue of personal responsibility at *EN* 3. 5. The rationalist explanation of Achilles' behaviour in **§31** is actually a contribution to an ancient debate, since Achilles' excessive grief over Patroclus seems to call for a special explanation. (A few critics adduced it as evidence that they were lovers.) With **§36** cf. esp. *EN* 1113b6–14, where Aristotle argues that virtuous and vicious acts must equally be 'in our power', if either is. With E's claim in **§37** that 'we, not externals, are masters of what things appear best to us', cf. the claim at *EN* 1114b2–3 that 'each man is himself somehow responsible for how things appear to him'. As this discourse shows, E has his own moral determinism. All our actions are determined in accordance with our opinions. By implying in **§§39–40** that it is never too late to learn, E indicates that it is never too late to save ourselves. This contrasts with Aristotle's view that our characters are fixed afer a certain stage. But the complicated logical analysis in this discourse makes plain, as E says in **§40**, that the process of revising our opinions 'does not happen overnight'.

CHAPTER 12

On Satisfaction

The diatribes are addressed to the individual, to orient the individual consciousness to the universe as the Stoics understood it. E's concern with the individual is reflected in his physics in the way he emphasizes god's own concern for individuals. He tries to reconcile this heartening message with the traditional Stoic view that the universe is designed primarily for the good of the whole. §§1–7 are excerpted in Stob. 1. 1. 40, in a section 'On the gods'. Analysis:

§§1–3 A survey of views about the gods and the extent to which they interest themselves in individual human beings.

§§4–9 This speculation shown to have practical benefit, in that our relation to the gods is central to ethics.

§§10–35 Freedom, for instance, is secured by appreciating the complex course of nature and aligning our will with the wishes of the gods. Our overall goal should be to adapt to circumstances as they are; our minds we can change, circumstances are less tractable. The consequences of our success or failure to do this are far-reaching.

E opens with an inventory of five shades of belief. Cicero at the opening of *On the Nature of the Gods* (1. 5) says that 'There is no subject upon which so much difference of opinion exists, not only among the unlearned but among educated persons as well.' Before attempting to identify E's five groups, we should note that there is probably a reason why his list is anonymous (except for the reference to Socrates at the end). His purpose is to indicate how divergent views about the deity could be, and what degree of error was possible. He is less interested in naming names. It is actually wrong to try and associate just one philosopher or school with each view, since on this subject there was considerable doctrinal overlap.

Concerning E's first group, the complete atheists, ancient sources regularly report the names of Diagoras of Melos, Theodorus of Cyrene, Critias of Athens, and a few others; cf. SE *PH* 3. 218; *M* 9. 50–7; Cic. *ND* 1. 2 with Pease ad loc. It is difficult to determine how reliable these lists are, since the charge of atheism was levelled rather indiscriminately. Not all were as scrupulous as E is to distinguish degrees of faith. Adherence to any of the first four views on his list, for instance, could be grounds for being called an atheist, even though only the first denies god's existence outright. Plato, however, refers to thinkers who held that gods exist only by convention, not by nature (*Laws* 889e–890a); for speculation as to who these men were, see Guthrie v. 360–2.

E is thinking primarily of the Epicureans in the second group, those 'who say that [divinity] exists, but is inactive, negligent, and takes thought (*pronoein*) for nothing'; compare the characterization of their position at 2. 20. 23. For Epicurean denial of Stoic providence (*pronoia*), cf. Epicurus, *KD* 1 (DL 10. 139): 'That which is blessed and immortal is not troubled itself, and causes trouble to no other.'

'A third group says it exists and takes thought, but only for great things in the heavens, not for anything on earth' (**§2**). The reason for the association of divinity and the heavens, one of either

identity or control, was the regularity of movement of the heavenly
bodies. The standard reason for dissociating divinity from mundane affairs was the existence of unjust suffering or good fortune.
Cf. SE *PH* 1. 32: 'Against those who try to establish that there is
providence from the orderliness of the heavenly bodies, [Sceptics]
oppose the view that often the good do badly while the bad do
well, and conclude that there is no providence.' But the deists in
E's third group distinguish, recognizing such a thing as providence,
but restricting it to the heavens. That is the upshot of Aristotle's
statements about the Prime Mover (*Met.* 12. 6–10), though elsewhere he seems to have accepted the popular view that the gods
attend to human affairs (*EN* 1179a24–5). Nevertheless, the position
standardly attributed to him in the Imperial period was that providence extended only to the heavens, not to the sublunary region;
cf. DL 5. 32; SE *PH* 3. 218; see Sharples 1987. 1216–18. Plato
already knows of men who hold that 'there are gods, but they take
no thought for human affairs'; cf. *Laws* 885b, 888c, and see Guthrie
iii. 231 on their identities. But since Plato does not make precisely
the same distinction as here between the affairs of heaven and earth,
E is probably influenced mainly by the Aristotelian formulation of
the idea.

  'A fourth group says that it takes thought for things on earth and
for human affairs, but only in a general way, not for the interests
of individuals.' Grounds for holding this view included not only
the undeserved suffering or happiness of men, but also the idea
that it was actually beneath god's dignity to concern himself with
individuals. Such a view originated with the Stoics (see below),
but became common property; cf. [Arist.] *De Mundo* 398a–399a;
Nemesius, *NH* 43 (p. 127 Morani); Justin, *Trypho*, 1. 47, etc.; for
discussion see Sharples 1983: 25–6; Moraux 1984: 498–500. In
the third and fourth group we could conceivably include later
Platonists. Plato actually combats such opinions at *Laws* 899d–903a.
And later Platonism officially remained true to his position that
providence was all-embracing. But middle and neo-Platonists
differentiated levels of providence, holding that god looks after
the heavens directly, delegating mundane interests to subordinate
divinities or *daimons* (an idea possibly foreshadowed in *Laws* 903b;
cf. 713d; *Pol.* 271d). Cf. [Plut.] *De Fato* 568E, 569D–F, 572F–
574A; Apuleius, *De Platone* 1. 12; see Dörrie 1977; Baltes and
Dörrie 1993: 322.

Pohlenz 1964: i. 339 notes that E identifies with the fifth and final group: those who uphold god's omniscience, and trust to his control over everything that happens. In 1. 14 E expressly upholds the doctrine of divine omniscience that he ascribes to Socrates here. That he should favour this position is consistent with Stoic pan-providentialism, which contrasts with the restricted providence of the Peripatetics. Cf. Plut. *St. rep.* 1056C: '[Chrysippus] says that nothing at all, not even the slightest, stays or moves otherwise than in conformity with the reason of Zeus, which is identical with destiny.' Cf. also *St. rep.* 1050A, C–D; Cic. *ND* 2. 75: 'I assert that it is by the providence of the gods that the world and all its parts were first compounded and have been governed for all time.' As part of his effort to rationalize evil in the world, however, Chrysippus entertained the thought that god was careless of particulars and heedless of individuals. Cf. *St. rep.* 1051B–C: 'In the third book on substance [Chrysippus] mentions the fact that [bad] things happen to virtuous men and then says: "Is it because some things are neglected, just as in larger households some husks and a certain quantity of wheat get lost, though affairs as a whole are well managed?"' The idea is not uncommon in later Stoicism. Cf. Sen. *Ep.* 95. 50: 'The way to worship the gods . . . is to know that they are supreme commanders in the universe, controlling all things by their power and acting as guardians of mankind, even though they are sometimes unmindful of individuals'; Cic. *ND* 2. 167: 'The gods care for great matters, they disregard small ones.' Cf. also *ND* 3. 86, 90; *Div.* 1. 117–18; Sen. *Ep.* 110. 2; *Prov.* 3. 1; Philo, *Prov.* 2. 54–5. This never established itself as standard Stoic doctrine, however, and E implicitly rejects it, since, as Long and Sedley (1. 322) point out, it is 'scarcely compatible with their usual theology'.

Pépin (1976: 115–17) discusses this passage, and suggests that the fourth group must be Stoics, on the grounds that E distinguishes their view from that of the third group, who can only be Aristotelians. But Moraux (1984: 499 n. 21) refutes him, pointing out that both the third and fourth groups can accommodate Aristotelians. As indicated earlier, E is not concerned to assign these opinions, only to highlight their variety. The fourth group can include Stoics, but also Aristotelians and later Platonists. The fifth can be Stoics, and includes Plato as well as Socrates. For Socrates' faith in god's omniscience and care for individual men, cf. Xen. *Mem.* 1. 1. 19, 1. 4. 18, 4. 3. 12. Simplicius, *In Ench.* 237a–48c, argues for god's unqualified

providence on his own as well as E's account; at 239b–42a he con-
tests the view that this entails an unbecoming condescension on
god's part.

The quotation in **§3** is from the *Iliad*, 10. 279–80, where Odysseus
addresses Athena.

§§4–7 as a whole is superficially similar to those Stoic arguments
for the existence of gods from the existence of piety, or from the
consequence to piety if the existence of gods should be denied;
see Pease ad *ND* 1. 3, where this passage is cited. But Pease is
wrong, as this is a different argument, to the effect that the study of
physics, theology in particular, is a necessary prelude to ethics. It
derives from Plato's *Laws* 888b: 'The supreme decision is whether
or not to have the right ideas about the gods, and so live well.' The
early Stoics assumed some such priority. Cf. Plut. *St. rep.* 1035B–
C: 'Chrysippus habitually puts theology first and makes the preface
to every ethical enquiry, for it is obvious that, whether the subject
is ends or justice or good and evil or marriage and child-rearing or
law and government, he says nothing unless, as those who introduce public decrees prefix the phrase "Good Fortune", he has pre-
fixed Zeus, destiny, providence, and the statement that the universe,
being finite and one, is held together by a single power—none of
which can carry any conviction for one who is not conversant with
physical theory.'

E reprises the argument at 2. 14. 9–13; cf. also 1. 20. 15–16; *Ench.*
31. 1; and Cic. *Fin.* 3. 73: 'Natural science has with justification
also been honoured, on the grounds that a man who wants to live in
harmony with nature must start from the universe and its government. Surely no one can make a true assessment of good and evil
unless he has grasped the principles of both nature and divinity,
and understands whether or not the nature of man accords with
that of the universe. Moreover, without natural science no one can
appreciate the full meaning of proverbs propounded of old by wise
men, which bid us "yield to occasion", "follow god" "know thyself",
and "nothing to excess".'

The ideal that both Cicero and E (in **§5**) invoke, 'Follow god',
had a long history. Tradition assigns it first to Pythagoras; cf. Stob.
2. 49. 16; Iamblichus, *Vita Pyth.* 18. 86; Boeth. *Cons.* 1P4. It
appears a few times in Plato, i.e. *Phdr.* 248a, *Rep.* 613b, *Laws*
716a–b, and was elevated into a cardinal doctrine of later Platonism.
Cf. Alcin. *Epit.* 28. 3: 'Sometimes Plato says that the end (*telos*) is to

become like god, sometimes that it consists in following him.' The formula is not perspicuous, but could be construed in various ways. Often it functions as a virtual doublet of the injunction to 'become like god'. As he was the paragon of virtue, so god was the supreme model to imitate. In Stoicism the ethical end was conformity with nature. But because nature was identified with god, it was possible to assimilate the two formulas. This more and more tended to happen, initially probably under the influence of Posidonius; see Theiler 1930: 106–9; 1982: ii. 395; Reale 1989: 54–5. Cf. Sen. *Ben.* 4. 25. 1: 'Our goal is to live in accordance with the nature of things, and to follow the example of the gods'; Marc. 12. 31: 'Address yourself to the goal of following reason and god.' Cf. Sen. *Ep.* 90. 34, 95. 50; *VB* 15. 5; SE *PH* 9. 91; E 1. 20. 14–15; Marc. 3. 9, 7. 31, 10. 11, 12. 27; Plut. *De Sera num.* 550D–E.

In §5 E is obviously right to imply that the injunction to follow the gods is absurd if they are non-existent. But the suggestion that the formula is empty of meaning if the gods care for nothing is less self-evident. After all, Epicureans also imagined that they were 'following' the gods in imitating their detachment. §7 indicates that E has another idea in mind: for him, to 'follow the gods' means to obey them. Cf. Sen. *Ep.* 90. 34: '[Philosophy] has taught us, not merely to know the gods, but to follow them, and to accept whatever happens as the commands of god'; 107. 9: 'Whatever you cannot change it is best to endure, and without complaint to follow god, under whose authorship everything proceeds. For it is a bad soldier who complains when his general gives the command'; 16. 5: '[Philosophy] will teach us to follow god and endure what happens.' Thus the Stoic use of the formula 'Follow god' may have derived from the Platonic tradition, but was differently interpreted, in line with their distinctive doctrine of fate. Man should follow god like the smart dog follows the cart in the famous Stoic analogy; cf. LS 62A; Sen. *Ep.* 107. 11; E 4. 1. 131.

The Greek for 'communication' in §6 is *diadosis*. It is also used of intercourse between man and god at 1. 14. 9, and by Marcus in a passage (1. 17. 7) which, in the view of Rutherford (1989: 193), draws on this one. It reads: 'To have had clear and frequent impressions about what life according to nature is like, so that as far as the gods are concerned and the communications (*diadosesi*) from the other world, and assistance and conceptions, nothing hinders my now living in accordance with nature, though I yet fall short of this through my own fault, and through not observing the reminders and, as it were, the instructions, from the gods.' What kind of communication is this, and how does it operate? Marcus sometimes speaks of dreams and oracles as forms of intelligence from god (see Rutherford 1989: 195–200). But not here. E for his part never mentions dreams, and deprecates divination (see 1. 17. 18–29 with comment). For him, communication from the gods is simply the universal pattern of events. Marcus indicates that god's communications are not always intelligible, though he blames his own obtuseness. At 2. 6. 9–10 and 2. 10. 5–6, E likewise implies that it is not always possible for the individual to anticipate god's plan for him. It can be inferred retrospectively only from what happens— and then must be welcomed as divine dispensation.

The analogy of the universe to a city in §7 was standard in Stoicism. Cf. 3. 24. 107: '[Whenever anything happens, ask yourself,] "And who has sent the command? Our leader or general, the city, the law of the city? Give it then. For I must always obey the law in every particular."' Cf. Cic. *Fin.* 3. 64: 'The Stoics maintain that the universe is governed by divine will, and that it is a kind of city and state composed of men and gods, and that each one of us is a part of this world. Hence it naturally follows that we prefer the common good to our own.'

For the definition of freedom in §9, cf. 4. 1. 1; Arist. *Pol.* 1310a31; Cic. *PS* 34: 'What is freedom? The power of living as you wish. Who then lives as he wishes, but the man who follows what is right, who rejoices in proper function, who has considered and worked out his way of life in advance, and who does not obey the laws out of fear, but follows and respects them because he judges them to be most beneficial?' Cf. Cic. *Fin.* 3. 26: 'Since the ultimate goal is life in conformity and harmony with nature, it necessarily follows that all wise men are all their lives in a state of happiness, perfection, and good fortune, without any restriction or hindrance.' Freedom is predicated on life in accordance with nature. It demands apprehension of the process of nature; it requires study, like any art. In §§9–15 E develops this characteristically Stoic conception of virtue as an art of living; note in particular the analogy in §§13–14. For the overall idea see Annas 1993: 396–411.

[Like Schenkl, I accept Schweighäuser's deletion of *d'* after *ta* in §12. It can hardly be shameful for things to happen in accordance with one's every wish, just unlikely; and it seems that both the appearance and the wishing in §11 can be characterized as 'random', since wishing and appearance are in practice indistinguishable. E distinguishes them in §12 only for the sake of rhetorical fullness.]

Submission to the divine will, the message of §15, is a recurrent theme in Stoic ethics. Of course, it was not arbitrary; on the difference with Judaism and Christianity in this respect see Dihle 1982. Divine will is an expression of the same reason that inheres in man; it commands man's assent naturally; cf. Sen. *Ep.* 74. 20–1.

§16 essays two types of theodicy, as part of the overall argument that evil in the world does not necessarily prove that god is careless of individuals and mundane affairs, but can be explained on other grounds. The first is the principle of the unity, or inseparability, of opposites, good and evil in particular; for its use by other Stoics cf. DL 7. 91; Plut. *St. rep.* 1050F; *Comm. not.* 1066D; Simpl. *In Ench.* 82c–84a.

The second is the principle he invokes at 1. 1. 11: i.e. the hypothetical necessity (as Aristotle would have it) of matter and everything material, especially the body. Cf. SE *M* 9. 90 (quoting Cleanthes): 'Man cannot be the best animal . . . for he is in need of countless aids such as food and clothing, and all the other requirements of the body, which lords it over us, demanding its daily tribute and threatening us with disease and death unless it is satisfied.' The body and other externals are sources of vexation. But they are gifts of god nevertheless, intended to accommodate the conditions of life on earth. E says that god gave them 'to each of us' (*hēmōn hekastō*), suggesting that he personally took charge of distributing them. This supports his main thesis. The list of material things and externals at the end of §16 fixes the sequence of argument in the remainder of the discourse.

§17, with its reference to 'hypotheses', is based on an analogy between logic and life; cf. 1. 25. 11–13, 1. 29. 39, 2. 5. 11. For a discussion of hypotheses and hypothetical arguments in their proper context, cf. 1. 7. 15–16, 22–5. For the thought of §§17–21 cf. 3. 13. 1–7, 4. 4. 25–7: 'In like fashion you say, "I don't like leisure, it is desolation, I don't like a crowd, it is a tumult." But if matters bring it about that you must spend time alone or with few people, call it peace, and use the condition for its appropriate end.' That being alone makes one 'the equal of the gods' (§21) assumes the distinctively Stoic doctrine of the world conflagration. Cf. 3. 13. 4: 'If being alone is enough to be desolate, you will have to say that Zeus is desolate in the world conflagration'; see Long 1985: 23–4, citing also Sen. *Ep*. 9. 16.

That 'Socrates was not in prison, for he was there willingly' (**§23**) is a Stoic paradox with a long afterlife, through Lovelace's 'Stone walls do not a prison make | Nor iron bars a cage', and beyond. It is based on what Socrates says at Pl. *Phd*. 98e–99b.

In **§§24–26** we find two older ideas in novel combination: (1) the priority of the whole to the part; (2) belief in a personal fate assigned by the gods. As indicated, the two were traditionally supposed to be incompatible. But E wants to counter that assumption. Just because sacrifice for the good of the whole is required of someone does not imply that god neglects him. Sacrifice may be just what god demands of him personally. Elsewhere E argues that sickness, death, poverty, etc. are not evils in the true sense, thereby removing a traditional obstacle to belief in god's consideration for man. Cf. 3. 26. 28: '[God does not] neglect his own creatures, his servants and witnesses, whom alone he uses as models for the uninitiated, to prove both that he exists, and governs the universe well, and does not neglect the affairs of men, and that no evil can happen to a good man either alive or dead.' This thesis is based on the Stoic revision of values; cf. 1. 22. 15–16; 2. 5. 25, 2. 6. 10; *Ench*. 31. 1–2. He does not argue for it here, however, possibly because it does not presuppose god's interest in individuals, but reflects the general dispensation. For the whole–part distinction and its importance in Stoic theodicy see Long 1974: 179–84; Annas 1993: 175.

For the sentiment in **§24** compare 4. 1. 101 ff.; *Ench*. 11. With **§25** cf. *SVF* 2. 913, 914, 1092, and Cornutus, ch. 13, where the mythical Fates ('Moirai') are similarly equated with destiny. E chooses this trope because the Fates traditionally superintended the destiny of individuals. For one man's smallness in relation to the whole (**§26**) cf. 2. 5. 13, 26; 2. 16. 42. It is a characteristically Marcan perspective; cf. 2. 4, 12. 32, etc. It is characteristic of E, however, to offset this with a cheerful reflection on what makes man 'no less than the gods'. For the sentiment, cf. Arist. *EN* 1177b33–1178a2: 'We must, so far as we can, make ourselves immortal, and strive to live in accordance with the best thing in us. For even if it be small in bulk, the mind surpasses everything in power and value.' It was an ancient commonplace that the mind, though small or even without extent, could be judged by its far-reaching effects; cf. Pl. *Laws* 898d–e; Xen. *Mem*. 1. 4. 8; Sen. *Clem*. 1. 3. 5. For the decisive influence of 'judgements' (*dogmata*) on human behaviour see note on 1. 19. 8.

With §27 cf. 1. 3. 3–6, with comment. With §§28–9 cf. 1. 29. 39; *Ench.* 30; Sen. *De Brev. vitae* 15. 3. With §§30–1 cf. 1. 6. 30 with comment. §§32–5 restates the message of 1. 1. 7–9; see comment there.

[In §30 I have adopted Meibom's emendation of *prosagontōn* to *prosagomenōn*.]

CHAPTER 13

How Each Thing May be Done in a Manner Pleasing to the Gods

The title adverts to a Stoic ideal of virtue that permeates every department of life. It is invoked in the opening section. The title is a little inapposite, however, since most of this brief essay is taken up with the subject of the humane treatment of slaves. Stoicism has sometimes been supposed to mark an advance here. How true this is remains at issue. For discussion see Bonhöffer 1894: 97–101; Milani 1972: 179–92; Griffin 1976: 256–85; Bradley 1986; Erskine 1990: 43–63; Manning 1986; Garnsey 1994. Most of the literature concerns Seneca. On the present discourse, however, see Bonhöffer 1894: 98; Pohlenz 1964: i. 337–8; Milani 1972: 254; Sandbach 1975: 168–9.

With §1 compare the openings of 1. 14, 3. 6, and 3. 22 for other instances where a question from an unnamed source serves as a pretext for the entire discourse. Comparison with 3. 13. 23 indicates that eating 'justly and . . . equitably' means with due regard for others, that they too get enough to eat. To eat 'with restraint and self-control' is self-explanatory; E often inveighs against gluttony (4. 8. 13, 17, 20; 3. 15. 10–11; *Ench.* 33. 7; 41).

[The translation assumes the existence of another *kai* after *isōs*, and renders *isōs* 'equitably', making it co-ordinate with the other adverbs. This reading has the support of a second hand in S. For *isōs* co-ordinate with *dikaiōs* cf. Dionysius of Halicarnassus 10. 40.]

With §2 compare Griffin 1976: 261: 'The Stoic doctrine of the wickedness of all passions was naturally applied to that relationship which most of all encouraged anger and licentiousness [i.e. slavery]. In *De Ira*, Seneca draws some of his most vivid examples from this area of life.' In one's dealings with slaves it is the most dangerous of the passions, anger, that E is also concerned to control. Griffin (ibid. 262) adds that this advice reflects a limitation in the Stoic attitude toward slavery, in that it consults 'the moral well-being of the master, not the treatment of the slave, as is particularly clear when it is handled by Epictetus', and she cites 4. 1. 119 ff. We should not discount the possibility that E favoured an egoistic appeal simply because he judged it would be most effective. For the thought of this section cf. *Ench.* 12; 14. 1; 26.

For testimony concerning old Stoic attitudes toward slaves and slavery cf. *SVF* 3. 349–66 with Pohlenz 1964: i. 136, ii. 75. Philo at *SVF* 3. 352 states that 'No man is a slave by nature', a view credited to several ancient thinkers, but thought in this instance to derive from Chrysippus. For discussion see Griffin 1976: 459, accepting Chrysippus as the source. DL 7. 121–2 differentiates three kinds of slavery: moral, political (diminished sovereignty), and chattel (what we normally think of as slavery). It was the first of these, moral slavery, that mainly preoccupied the Stoics; cf. Cic. *PS* 33–41. Their tendency to treat slavery less as a social reality than as an ethical metaphor, along with their depreciation of externals, undercut whatever reforming spirit was latent in their attitude. That, at any rate, is the received view, well represented by Griffin, but recently challenged by Erskine (1990). He argues that Stoic theorizing about slavery presented more of a challenge to the institution than is usually thought. For an assessment of Erskine's view see Van der Waerdt 1991.

The image of men as seeds sown by god alluded to in §3 is a development of basic Stoic doctrine. Cf. Cic. *Laws* 1. 24: 'A time came for sowing the seed of the human race. And when this seed was scattered and sown over the earth, it was granted the divine gift of mind.' All men are united especially by their common share in reason, which they have from god. In Aristotle's eyes, slaves could listen to reason, but did not themselves possess it; see Taylor 1995: 254–7, with bibliography. The contrast with the Stoics is clear, since it was just by their (assumed) share in reason that slaves had a full share of citizenship in the commonwealth of god and man. In trying to account for this change in viewpoint, we cannot overlook the new political realities of the Hellenistic and Roman periods: for instance, the residence in Rome of slaves who were more cultured and intelligent than their Roman masters. This reminds us that E was once such a slave himself. De Ste Croix (1981: 142) calls him 'an ex-slave who had thoroughly acquired the outlook of a master'. I doubt this opinion can be squared with the present passage. Contrast Pohlenz 1964: i. 337: 'Epictetus is the first Stoic who, owing to his own experience, felt the truth of the kinship of all men with his whole being.'

In §4 E says that slaves are 'brothers by nature'. Aristotle, by contrast, maintained that non-Greeks were 'slaves by nature' (*Pol.* 1254a18–1255a2, esp. 1255a1–2). Here is evidence of a more liberal outlook on the Stoics' part, though Aristotle was notoriously reactionary in his attitude toward slaves, and more enlightened ones (similar to E's) preceded him; cf. *Pol.* 1253b20–2, and see Guthrie iii. 155–60. For the sentiment in this section cf. Sen. *Ep.* 47. 10: 'You want to remember that the man you call your slave sprang from the same stock as you, breathes the same air, and lives and dies on equal terms. You can just as easily see him free as he could see you enslaved.' *Ben.* 3. 28. 1: 'Can anyone doubt that a master may sometimes be benefited by a slave? . . . We all spring from the same source, have the same origin; no man is more noble than another except in so far as his nature is more upright.' Declarations of the brotherhood of man, extending even to slaves, could become a complacent platitude; cf. Trimalchio (a storehouse of clichés) at Petronius 71. 1.

For the terms of comparison in §5 see the note on 1. 19. 9, discussing the image of the body as a 'corpse'. The image is reinforced by reference to the earth, the element out of which bodies are composed, and to which they are returned. For the implicit dualism of this passage see note ad 1. 3. 3. The word for kinsmen, *sungeneis*, is cognate with *sungeneia* there. The contrast is also bound to recall the *nomos–physis* controversy applied to slavery (cf. Arist. *Pol.* 1253b20–2). The bill of sale represents the law of man; nature represents the law of god. The law of god here is the law governing the city of gods and men, to which, as indicated, slaves also belong.

CHAPTER 14

That the Deity Oversees All Men

This chapter is organized around two terms with interesting histories: *sympatheia* and *daimon*. Reinhardt (1926: 115–19) identified much of the discourse as Posidonian in inspiration. This was accepted by Theiler (1982), who excerpts §§1–10 as Posidonius F 355, §§11–14 as F 388. The collection of Edelstein and Kidd admits only fragments in which Posidonius is mentioned by name. Hence none of this discourse is included. But E does not often cite authority for his statements. I think the influence of Posidonius is in fact likely, although he revitalized doctrines the seeds of which were already present in the old Stoa.

The doctrine of universal sympathy originally depended on the idea of thorough blending. This was made to do a lot of work. Just as it held the universe together, so it helped hold Stoic philosophy together, which was important, since Stoics took pride in their system's coherence. Cf. Alex. *De Mixt.* 227. 5–10: '[The Stoic] theory of blending does not rely on anything else, but their views on the soul depend on it, and their notorious fate and universal providence gain credence from it, if indeed their theory of principles and god, as well as the unification and sympathy (*sumpatheia*) of everything, also rely on it. For the god that pervades matter is all these things to them.' Cf. 216. 14–16 (= LS 48C1): 'Chrysippus' theory of blending is as follows: he maintains that the whole of matter is unified, because of *pneuma* that permeates all of it, by which the whole is held together, is stable, and is in sympathy (*sumpathei*) with itself.' Being in sympathy with itself means that an affection in one part of the universe is felt throughout. The doctrine fitted the Stoic view of the universe as an organism, with god its soul, matter its body (Plut. *Comm. not.* 1077D–E; Cic. *Ac.* 2. 125). For other evidence of the doctrine of *sumpatheia* in the old Stoa cf. [Plut.] *De Fato* 574D and Cic. *De Fato* 7.

Panaetius denied the doctrines of universal unity and sympathy as part of his challenge to astrology and divination. He found it difficult to suppose that things as distant as the stars could affect the earth (Cic. *Div.* 2. 87–97 = fr. 75 van Straaten; see Alesse 1994:

239–54). Posidonius came to the doctrine's defence with an array of new arguments drawn especially from astronomy. He reaffirmed its validity at precisely those points where Panaetius had raised doubts. Reinhardt (1926) went so far as to maintain that *Sympathielehre* was Posidonius' exclusive intellectual property. Pohlenz (1964) challenged him, however, and the consensus today is that his thesis cannot stand in so absolute a form. Its old Stoic origins are generally recognized. See Reinhardt 1926: 54 n. 2; 1954: 654; Pohlenz 1964: i. 102, 217; ii. 58; Graeser 1972: 68–9; Sandbach 1975: 130; Talanga 1986: 87–90; Duhot 1989: 106–28, esp. 117–19.

What E does in this discourse is continue the tradition of finding new use for the suggestive doctrine of *sympatheia*. He applies it here to a topic he shows an interest in elsewhere (e.g. 1. 12): viz. the extent of god's knowledge. The discourse exploits a fertile source of argument: the Stoics' penchant for identity statements and their capacity to view the same phenomena under different aspects. So here E assumes the traditional Stoic identification of Zeus with the pervasive *pneuma* (cf. Alex. *De Mixt.* 224. 36; Aet. 1. 7. 33–8). From this he draws an inference about god viewed in personal terms: he sees all things due to his immanence. And the influence is reciprocal. Even though man does not enjoy god's omniscience, he has a share in divine reason. This is the *daimon*, the fragment of god distributed to each. The influence of Posidonius on this part of the discourse (§§11–14) has also been hypothesized. I would accept that, but it is evident more in the terminology and details than in the substance of the argument. E's thesis could be derived from old Stoic suppositions.

Posidonian influence on the discourse is accepted by Pohlenz (1964: i. 338). The first ten sections are anthologized in Stob. 1. 1. 34. The whole may be analysed thus:

§§1–6 An argument for god's omniscience based on the doctrine of universal sympathy.

§§7–9 An *a fortiori* argument for god's omniscience in comparison with man's mental capacities.

§10 An additional argument *a minori ad maius* based on Stoic pantheism.

§§11–17 A consequence of pantheism drawn: god is present in each of us, in the fragment called the *daimon*. This functions as the human conscience; and so assists in the process of moral surveillance that motivated the original question of the discourse, concerning the extent of god's knowledge.

With §1 compare 1. 13. 1, where a question from a student or member of the audience serves as the ostensible pretext for the whole discourse. Such questions are probably a contrivance on E's part to lend the discourse an air of spontaneity. In §11 an imaginary interlocutor raises an objection that leads E to introduce a new, if related, motif, concerning the extent of man's knowledge. Both these manoeuvres have their roots in the dialogue tradition, as Hirzel (1895: ii. 247–50) explains.

E embarks on his rather circuitous argument to prove god's omniscience. For the background to belief in divine omniscience, and challenges posed to it in earlier philosophy, see Barnes 1982b: 451–6. Classic statements in support include Xen. *Mem.* 1. 1. 19, 1. 4. 18; Pl. *Laws* 901d. For what purports to be a comprehensive list of views concerning the degree of god's attention to mankind, cf. 1. 12. 1–2.

In stating in §3 that plants perform their several functions in obedience to god, E highlights the divine power animating the world system. Cf. Cic. *ND* 2. 19, where the point is illustrated, as here, with reference to the behaviour of plants; [Arist.] *De Mundo* 400b30–401a10, with reference to plants as well as animals: 'Under god's motionless and harmonious rule the whole ordering of heaven and earth is administered, extending over all natural things through the seeds of life in each both to plants and to animals, according to genera and species . . . "Pear trees and pomegranate, and apple trees glorious-fruited", and animals both wild and tame, feeding in the air or on earth or in the water, all are born and come to their prime and decay in obedience to the dictates of god.' Cf. also Simpl. *In Ench.* 222b–c: 'Not only men, but also irrational animals and plants and rocks and, in sum, all beings, each according to their capacity, act in obedience to god'; E fr. 3: 'All things obey and serve the universe, both earth and sea, and the sun and other stars, and plants and the animals of earth.' See Theiler 1982: ii. 280 for more parallels.

There is a certain incoherence in §3, in that E states that god tells plants to bloom and ripen, etc., but then qualifies the thought by saying that these things happen 'as if by god's command'. (Hard translates 'as if by god's express command', which side-steps the problem.) Two perspectives on the deity are competing for attention: immanence, similar to, if not based on, the Aristotelian insight that nature has its efficient cause within it (see Solmsen 1960: 95; Lapidge 1973), and transcendence, which is implied by the image of

god standing outside nature, issuing orders. The former is the orthodox Stoic view, but the awkwardness of expression can be explained
as reflecting the influence of the other, more popular one.

With §4 compare Cic. *ND* 2. 19 (= Posid. F 356 Theiler): 'Consider the sympathy, unity, and affinity of things; will this not convey the truth of what I say? Would it be possible for the earth to be
at one time in bloom, and then all bare, or for the spontaneous
transformation of so many things around us to mark the approach
and retreat of the sun at the summer and winter solstices, or for the
tides to ebb and flow in the seas and channels with the waxing and
waning of the moon, or for the different courses of the stars to be
maintained by the revolution of the entire sky? These processes . . .
could not take place were they not sustained by a single divine, all-
pervading spirit.' The regular cycle of things on earth (seasons and
tides, etc.) follows the rhythms of the heavens. Straightforward
accounts of these phenomena are credited to the Stoics at DL 7.
151–2. When adduced in connection with *sympatheia*, however, they
raise the possibility of Posidonian influence. Posidonius particularly
liked to substantiate the doctrine by citing the effects of celestial
phenomena on terrestrial life, with the former bestowing their
vital influence *in distans*; cf. DL 7. 140 (F 6 EK); Cic. *Div.* 2. 33–5
(F 106 EK); Macrob. *Sat.* 1. 23. 2 (F 118 EK); SE *M* 9. 78–89
(F 354 Theiler); Cic. *ND* 2. 119 (F 365 Theiler, part); Cleomedes
4. 2 (F 276 Theiler). This was the most dramatic evidence for
sympathy, not only because the effects are obvious, but because the
elements are so far apart.

Other ancient authorities would broaden the extent of lunar influence; at Cic. *ND* 2. 119 the moon is called 'the source of conception
and birth and of growth and maturity'. Some poetic or pre-scientific
ideas were at work here. (See Pease ad *ND* 2. 50 for parallels.) E
does not dwell on the moon's influence, but reference to 'the things
on earth' in §4 suggests that he may be thinking of the tides. Edelstein and Kidd (ii. 523–5) accept that arguments for sympathy based
on the relation of tides and lunar phases derive from Posidonius.
He was not the first to discern the connection (cf. Aet. 3. 17. 3–5),
but owing to his travels he was able to put it on a firmer empirical
basis. Reference to 'our own bodies' in §5 suggests that E may also
be thinking of menstruation.

With §§5–6 compare Cic. *Div.* 1. 110 (= Posid. F 375 Theiler,
part): 'Since everything is filled to repletion with immortal intellect

and divine mind, human souls must be moved by their sympathy with divine souls.' E's argument depends on the dualism between body and soul, here given Stoic colouring. Plants and our bodies are connected to god on the principle of unity enunciated above; but our soul is a fragment (*apospasma*) of the world soul, which is identical with god (DL 7. 142–3). For the expression in **§6**—'does not god perceive their every movement as a movement of that which is his own'—cf. Lucan 9. 580, and the Greek verse quoted in Acts 17: 28: 'In [God] we live and move and have our being.'

The word *apospasma* recurs at 2. 8. 11: 'You are a fragment (*apospasma*) of god, you have within you a part of him.' Cf. 1. 17. 27: 'If god had so constructed that part of his own being that he has taken from (*apospasas*) himself and given to us, that it could be subject to hindrance . . . he would not be god.' The word has been taken to be distinctively Posidonian on the strength of DL 7. 142–3, where Posidonius is cited by name. It is registered as F 304 Theiler, F 99a EK. The human soul is also called an *apospasma* of god, or the world soul, at Marc. 5. 27; Philo, *Mut. nom.* 223; and DL 8. 28 (the latter purports to be Pythagorean doctrine, but is heavily Stoicized; cf. Cic. *ND* 1. 27 with Pease ad loc.)

[**§5** *ta phuta* is the reading of Stobaeus, which Schenkl and Oldfather rightly prefer to the MS reading *phulla*.]

With **§7** compare the Stoic definitions of wisdom at SE *M* 9. 125 and Sen. *Ep.* 104. 22, as 'knowledge of things human and divine'. If man can know about god, god can certainly know about man. That is the essence of the *a fortiori* argument E presents in **§§7–9**. It derives from older Stoic arguments for divine intelligence by comparison with man's (cf. 1. 6. 10 with comment). In **§§7–8** E dwells on the complex workings of reason, which start with sense impressions, approving some, rejecting others, holding dubious ones in abeyance or refusing to pronounce on them, remembering and synthesizing the approved ones into experience and the arts. The theme was traditional; for similar descriptions of the mind's ability to sort and process information, cf. 1. 6. 10, 1. 16. 18. The length at which it is elaborated here is surprising, but E returns to the subject of man's share in reason in **§11**, and this may anticipate it.

The Greek for 'communication' in **§9** is *diadosis*. It is also used of intercourse between man and god at 1. 12. 6 and Marc. 1. 17. 7; see Rutherford 1989: 192–3; Graeser 1972: 46. God's ability to perceive everything is tantamount to making contact with it. Knowledge here comes strictly by acquaintance, by actual physical presence (*sumpareinai* in §9) before the objects of cognition. Inasmuch as god is suffused throughout nature, his ability to perceive things is to that degree complete. This may seem rather a crude argument, but for the Stoics knowledge ultimately derived from the senses. Physical proximity was therefore its pre-condition. That god is intelligent and capable of processing this information is simply taken for granted.

On the association of god and sun in §10, cf. 1. 19. 11 with note. 'Shadow' refers to the hemisphere of the earth that is turned away from the sun and in darkness at any one time. It appears here as the sun's one limitation, by comparison with god's ability to reach into every quarter of the universe. For the argument *a minori ad maius*, compare Minucius Felix 32. 7–9: 'How is god far away, when all things on earth and in heaven, and even outside the starry sphere, are full of gods? He is not only near us, wherever we are, but inside us. Just consider the sun: it is fixed in heaven, but diffused throughout all lands. Equally present everywhere, it pervades everything and suffuses everything, its brilliance nowhere diminished. How much more is god, the creator and witness of all things, from whom nothing is hidden, present in the shadows, and present in our thoughts like so many shadows. We not only live under him, but as I just said, we live with him.' A virtually identical argument is made by Simplicius at *In Ench.* 242b–c. For the details of light and shadow, see Theiler 1982: ii. 265 with parallels. That the earth's shadow is a 'small space' derives from the *topos* of the earth's insignificance on the cosmic scale; see Farquharson ad Marc. 4. 3. 3.

The objection in §11 by a suppositious interlocutor is best taken as a response to what is said about the mind in §§7–8 (where the wealth of detail may anticipate the present section). In the context of the entire discourse, the purpose of the objection is to motivate a new theme, that of the *daimon*. E is done with the argument provoked by the opening question. In what remains, he develops a topic loosely connected to it. *Daimon* is the part of the Stoic god that inheres in each of us personally. The subject is introduced here especially to draw an ethical consequence of god's immanence. Thus it prepares for the protreptic section that ends the discourse.

Daimon is a word that resists translation. No English word has its range. Attempts to inventory the different meanings have been made by Bonhöffer (1890: 81–6), Rutherford (1989: 215 n. 102), and Kidd 1995. For the sake of convenience, three can be distinguished: (1) beings intermediate between man and the gods, especially (2) guardian spirits; (3) the faculty of reason, the portion of god implanted in man, his true self. This last was the distinctively Stoic sense. It essentially internalizes elements of the first two senses.

That this move originated with Posidonius is maintained by Theiler (1982: ii. 316–20). Galen (*PHP* 5. 6. 4–5) reports Posidonius as saying that 'the cause of the passions, that is, of discord and unhappiness, is that men do not follow in everything the *daimon* in themselves which is akin and by nature related to the divinity that rules the whole universe; but sometimes they turn aside in the company of that part of them which is inferior and beast-like, and let it carry them along.' Reason, the *daimon* in man, is here contrasted with his lower impulses. It is evident that Posidonius adapted this concept to his complex psychology. Like his psychology in general, he derived it from Plato. Cf. *Tim*. 90a: 'God gave the sovereign part of the human soul [i.e. reason] to be the *daimon* of each'; cf. *Tim*. 90c. The introduction into Stoicism of this concept, which corresponds to the third meaning above, is probably due to Posidonius' mediation.

E does not adopt Posidonius' psychology. But his use of the term *daimon* otherwise largely agrees. As the *daimon* was an inferior divinity, so E concedes that our reason, the *daimon* in us, is inferior to god's. But it is different in degree, not in kind. For clarification, cf. Cic. *Div*. 1. 127: 'Since all things happen by fate . . . , if there were some human being who could see with his mind the connection of all causes, he would certainly never be deceived. For whoever grasps the causes of future things must necessarily grasp all that will be. But since no one but god can do this, man must be left to gain his foreknowledge from various signs that announce what is to come.' From this it transpires that man in principle has access to the knowledge god has, only by a more laborious process of inference. It is interesting to note that this comes from a Posidonian section of the *De divinatione* (= F 107 EK). It might suggest that Posidonius determined the whole course of E's argument. For man's diminished knowledge in comparison with god's, cf. 2. 6. 9; Sen. *Ep*. 92. 27, 120. 14; see Kerferd 1978; LS 1. 259.

Marcus is the most eloquent exponent; he often formulates the ethical end as an obligation to do nothing contrary to the *daimon*, but to keep it pure; cf. 2. 13, and see Pohlenz 1964: i. 349. Cf. Sen.

Ep. 41. 1: 'God is near you, with you, within you. This is what I mean: a holy spirit dwells inside us, one who watches over us and observes our good and bad deeds.' In such passages, *daimon* functions much like our notion of conscience. That the connection with conscience is relevant to this passage is suggested by E's advice to swear to it as to a tutelary spirit. As with earlier philosophers, E's interest in god's omniscience evidently relates to the problem of divine justice. If god is to reward virtue and punish evil, he has first to observe them. E says that god has implanted the *daimon* in man to be his guide toward virtue. (For virtue as the perfection of reason cf. Cic. *Laws* 1. 25.) This implies that god has delegated to the individual responsibility for looking after his own moral welfare.

In **§15** E indicates that soldiers in the Imperial period were obliged to swear a loyalty oath to the *daimon* (Latin *genius*) of the emperor and his family. For an analogous application of the idea to an oath of the state religion, cf. Cic. *Off.* 3. 44: 'When a judge has to give a verdict under oath, he should remember that he is calling as his witness a god, which is to say, as I see it, his own mind; for that is the most divine thing that god has given man.'

With **§§16–17** compare the formula for happiness at DL 7. 88: 'This constitutes the virtue of the happy (*eudaimōn*) man and the smooth flow of life, when all actions promote the harmony of the *daimon* dwelling in the individual with the will of the manager of the universe.' (On the background to this play on words see Dillon ad Alcin. *Epit.* 28. 3.) The goal of man is agreement with nature, including the nature of the universe (DL 7. 87–8; Stob. 2. 75. 11–2. 76. 8). This constitutes virtue, and produces happiness. E assures us that this does not demand sacrifice, but is consistent with egoism. Cf. 1. 19. 11–15, with comment, for the spirit of self-interest he defends at the close.

CHAPTER 15
What Philosophy Professes

As noted in the commentary on the opening sections of 1. 11, E concentrates on duties that are determined by social roles such as brother, father, etc. This preoccupation reflects the influence of

Panaetius' functionalist ethics; see LS 1. 368, 428. It constitutes
E's second field of study. Cf. 3. 2. 4: 'The second field deals with
proper function. For I should not be impassive like a statue, but
should maintain my relations, both natural and acquired, as a pious
man, a son, brother, father, and citizen.' For the duties incumbent
upon a brother particularly, cf. 2. 10. 8: 'Next know that you are a
brother. This role demands deference, complaisance, kind words,
and an unwillingness to lay claim to any of the things with regard
to your brother that are outside the realm of moral choice, but
to surrender them gladly, so that in the things that lie within the
realm of moral choice you may have the better of it.' Cf. also *Ench.*
30: ' "My brother is doing me wrong." Well, maintain your relationship with him. Do not consider what he is doing, but only what
you must do to keep your moral choice in agreement with nature.'

The present discourse elaborates on a point hinted at in these
passages, that performing our duties to friends and relatives does
not ensure that they will respond in kind. Nor does it matter,
because we can keep our character in accord with nature regardless.
Actions are measured not by their success or failure (which is determined by factors outside our control), but by the underlying intention.
Analysis:

§§1–5 Philosophy is focused on one's own actions and character, not
on that of others.

§§6–8 Therefore we are not relieved of our moral responsibilities if
others decline our help.

In **§2** E supports the assumption that actions are judged by intention by invoking a standard Stoic definition of philosophy as 'the
art of life'. For parallels cf. 4. 1. 63, 118; Sen. *Ep.* 95. 7; SE *M* 11.
170, 181, 184. The analogy of philosophy, or its subject-matter, to
the arts, was fertile ground for controversy; cf. Cic. *Fin.* 3. 24, and
see Striker 1986 for discussion of the issues. Stoics maintained that
wisdom, or virtue, was a 'stochastic' art: i.e. that it could be judged
by the quality of the intention involved, not by the outcome, which
was unpredictable owing to extraneous factors. E then assumes that
the 'life' in question is one's own. This reflects the agent-centred,
virtue-based character of ancient ethics generally. To define philosophy's subject-matter, E invokes what he elsewhere calls its general principles (*ta katholika*); cf. 4. 12. 7–8: 'No one is master of
another's *prohairesis*, and in this alone lies good and evil. No one,

therefore, can secure the good for me, or involve me in evil, but I alone have authority over myself in these matters.' (On *prohairesis* see comment ad 1. 1. 23.) In §3 the *prohairesis* of others is classed with externals, the things E regularly calls *aprohaireta*, which are 'not in our control'. E treats these on a level with things subject to fate, like health and reputation. Thus his analysis of social duties assumes the fundamental Stoic distinction between target and end. Cf. Cic. *Fin.* 3. 22: 'For if a man's object were to aim a spear or arrow straight at something, his doing everything in his power to aim it straight would correspond to our doctrine of the final good. On that kind of analogy, this man must do everything to aim straight. And this doing everything to attain his object would be his end, so to speak, analogous to what we are calling the final good in life, whereas his striking the target would be something "to-be-selected", as it were, not "to-be-desired".'.

This is related to the definition of philosophy, or its subject-matter, as a stochastic art. In this case, the brother's target would be to maintain a proper relationship. But since that partly depends on his brother's co-operation, it is not his to maintain unilaterally. His end is simply to do for his part what he can to secure that rela-tionship, by performing his fraternal duties. The rest is subject not to fate, but to something equally outside his control, his brother's *prohairesis* (or free will). The point is made clearer at 3. 24. 46–7, where E advises someone to perform his duty by his estranged brother and visit him: 'Am I telling you, "Go like a man who is certain to get what he wants," and not simply, "Go in order to do what becomes you"? Why then go at all? So as to have gone, so as to have performed the function of . . . a brother.' On the Stoic dis-tinction between target and end see further Inwood 1986. For the general lesson, cf. Marc. 8. 56: 'To my *prohairesis* the *prohairesis* of my neighbour is as much a matter of indifference as his little por-tion of breath or flesh. For however much we may have been born for one another, nevertheless each is master of his own ruling prin-ciple.' 'Ruling principle' here and in §4 of this discourse is *to hēgemonikon*, the distinctively Stoic designation of the chief part of the human soul; cf. Aet. 4. 21. 1–4, and see Long 1982*c*.

In §4 we are to imagine Philosophy speaking, declaring its aims, after we have just learned what those aims are not. In §5 it is the frustrated brother speaking, and E responding. The mention of anger complicates, but does not alter, the fundamental point, that moral health is a person's own responsibility. Stoics were concerned to expunge emotions like anger, as well as to fulfil social duties. E explains that, in either case, one's concern is primarily with the self, not with others.

[In **§2** the translation assumes the change adopted by Schenkl from *anexetai* to *anadexetai*.]

§§6–8 serve to complicate the picture somewhat. E does not want to let us off too lightly: there is more to virtue than the rote performance of prescribed duties. So in the passage from 3. 24 quoted above, after enjoining the addressee to visit his brother, he adds, 'your good is not to be found in merely going, nor in standing at gates, but in one's judgements within' (§§54–5). For the time and difficulty involved in acquiring correct judgements, cf. 1. 20. 13–19 and 1. 11. 40 with note. Correct judgements transform 'proper functions' (*kathēkonta*) into 'right actions' (*katorthōmata*): cf. LS 59E–H. Even if E does not invoke that distinction directly, he is, I think, alluding to the effort involved in acquiring a character from which right actions will flow. Acquiring a perfect character should be our goal, but demands patience and a lifetime of effort. The rarity of the sage, which Stoics acknowledged, reflects that difficulty. Yet, as E says, 'Even if you are not yet a Socrates, still you ought to live as one who wishes to be Socrates' (*Ench.* 51. 3). E employs the metaphor to like effect at 4. 8. 35–6; cf. Marc. 9. 10.

CHAPTER 16

On Providence

This discourse complements 16 (also entitled 'On Providence'), but here E modulates to a minor key. The diatribe's attention to neglected and apparently insignificant things, its wry humour, even its brevity, contribute to its charm. It is anthologized and briefly commented on by Wilamowitz (1902: i. 326–7, ii. 202–3) and Russell (1991: 210–13). Summary:

§§1–5 The beasts' greater self-sufficiency relative to man is no proof of god's neglect of him, but the contrary.

§§6–14 Natural phenomena cited that attest to divine providence regarding man, including apparently useless effects. The latter appear on a level with similar traits in the beasts. But they are more effective, demonstrating anew man's superiority.

§§15–21 Man's superiority consists above all in his capacity to appreciate and bear witness to providence.

§1 'Do not wonder': the verb 'wonder' (*thaumazō*) was used in Greek as a polite way of signalling controversy or dissent. Like 1. 6, this discourse tacitly opposes the Epicureans with their proofs purporting to discredit Stoic belief in providence and show that nature is a cruel stepmother, since she lavished on the beasts advantages for survival that she omitted to give mankind. Cf. Lucr. 5. 222–34, and see Russell 1991: 212 for background to the debate.

E's argument in §§1–5 is noteworthy in that it seems to concede to the Stoics' rivals their claim about the beasts' greater fitness for survival. But E turns this to account, by integrating it with the Stoic version of the *scala naturae*. Although it is true that beasts do not require clothes and shoes, etc., their self-sufficiency is actually provided for man's convenience. It saves him the trouble of having to tend to them as much as to himself; the anthropocentric thesis is thereby vindicated. With the assumption in §2 that animals are put on earth for man's benefit and entrusted to his care, cf. 1. 6. 18 and Cic. *Fin.* 3. 67, *SVF* 2. 1152–67. The image of shoeing and clothing animals is meant to be ridiculous. (The practice of shoeing horses did not begin until the Middle Ages.)

Nun de ('But as it is' in §6) usually introduces the reply to an unreal condition (as in §20 below), but in E more often introduces a note of reproach, and a transition from how things ought to be to how they unfortunately are: cf. 1. 1. 14, 1. 3. 3, 1. 4. 8, 1. 26. 16, etc. In this passage E counts on rousing our sense of justice to give credit where credit is due, especially for everyday things we take for granted. By 'great things' in §8 he means cosmic phenomena, such as the interchange of the elements fire, air, earth, and water. This was standard in Stoic discussions of providence; cf. Cic. *ND* 2. 84, 3. 30–1; Lucr. 1. 782–9 (*contra*); Sen. *NQ* 3. 10. 1; Philo, *Prov.* 2. 45. But here E elects to speak of humbler things, like the transformation of grass into milk, milk into cheese. Such examples have the advantage of touching mankind more nearly. This is not, then, just an argument from design, but one from god's solicitude for mankind specifically—the fourth and last in Cicero's classification of Stoic theological arguments (*ND* 2. 3).

§§9–14: as part of their systematic teleology Stoics essayed explanations of nature's apparently trivial or gratuitous effects. They were able to do this by recognizing not just utility, but also beauty and variety as teleological principles. In this they outdid Aristotle, for though they may have agreed that the different colours of the eye served no useful purpose (Arist. *GA* 778a30–b1, b16–19), they would not necessarily have agreed that it served no purpose at all. For an appeal to secondary or incidental effects in nature (*ta parerga* in **§9**) that have their own, especially aesthetic, *raison d'être*, cf. Plut. *St. rep.* 1044B–D: '[Chrysippus] wrote in his books *On Nature* that beauty is the purpose for which many of the animals have been produced by nature, since she loves the beautiful and delights in diversity. . . . The tail of the peacock is an especially impressive example of this, for here nature makes it plain that the creature exists for the sake of the tail, not the opposite, and the male, which had this origin, brought the female along with it.' Cf. Philo, *Prov.* 2. 47; Marc. 3. 2. On the significance of the apparently superfluous beard, cf. Cic. *Fin.* 3. 18 and Galen at *SVF* 2. 1164: 'For even the hairs on the chin not only cover the face, but also serve for adornment.' Chrysippus at Athenaeus 13. 565 comes out against shaving for this reason. At 3. 1. 44–5 E suggests that a man no more ought to shave than a lion be shorn of his mane. On the subject, see Zanker 1995: 108–13.

For the coda in **§§15–21** E modulates to a virtual hymn of praise. Compare the closing lines (33–5) of Cleanthes' hymn to Zeus: 'hymning your works continually, as befits one who is mortal, since neither for mortals nor for the gods is there anything greater than always to praise duly the common law' (*SVF* 1. 537 = LS 541). 'Great is god' is a hymnic formula: cf. h. Hom. *In Apoll.* 198; Pind. *Ol.* 7. 34.

Praise for the wonderful mechanism of the hand (**§17**), especially as the means given man to attain his present level of culture, was an ancient *topos*; cf. Xen. *Mem.* 1. 4. 11; Arist. *PA* 687b3; Cic. *Off.* 2. 12; Lucr. 4. 830–1 (*contra*). The Greek for 'gullet' is *kataposis*; cf. Muson. 97. 5 and E *Gnom.* 22. Oldfather translates 'power to swallow', but the parallel with Cic. *ND* 2. 135 indicates that E is thinking of an organ, not a faculty, as Wilamowitz (1902: ii. 202) recognized. Biological organs were a regular feature of arguments from design; see note ad 1. 6. 1–7.

The ability to grow unconsciously and to breathe while asleep (**§17**) are, in Galen's terms, *aprohaireta*, biological functions under the control of the heart. Voluntary motions, *kata prohairesin*, are regulated by the brain (*PHP* 2. 8. 23–5). The point is worth making, since the former interest E only in so far as they allow us to focus on the latter, the things he calls *ta prohairetika* (cf. 1. 17. 23, 3. 3. 15, 3. 8. 3, etc.). E would evidently endorse the view of Descartes (*Entretiens avec Burman*, ed. Adam, 70), that irrational animals and our bodies are machines which function unconsciously, requiring minimal attention from our conscious selves. E pauses here over things we normally do not give a thought to, and his point is that that is how god wanted it: we are meant to concentrate on more important things. E implies that these signs of unconscious life are overlooked signs of providence, and in fact I have not found them in other ancient sources.

On 'the power to understand', *dunamis parakolouthetikē* in **§18**, see on 1. 6. 14. As at 1. 6. 19, E represents it as the gift that enables us to appreciate the others. '[A] lame old man': this self-reference in **§20** has a note of Socratic irony to it; cf. Dio Chrys. 7. 1, 12. 1 ff. For the role E deems appropriate to his age cf. Hesiod fr. 321 M–W: 'Deeds are for youth, counsel for middle years, prayers for old age.'

§21 'I . . . will not desert the post'; military analogies abound in E, Seneca, and Marcus; see Brunt 1975: 32–5; Rutherford 1989: 240–1. The associated image of our station (*taxis*) in life as a post we should not desert was inspired by Socrates; cf. 1. 9. 24 with note. Plotinus elaborates the idea at 3. 2. 17. 64–91 and 3. 3. 2. 3–15.

[The reading *aidonta*, 'sings', in **§19** is Schweighäuser's certain emendation for *diadonta* in S.]

CHAPTER 17

Concerning the Necessity of Logic

The title applies only to §§4–12. A better title for the whole would be 'On Self-Sufficiency'. The discourse proceeds, first, by arguing that the faculty of reason is self-sufficient, then, with that established, by arguing for the self-sufficiency of the rational animal, man. Analysis:

§§1–3 Reason is self-correcting.

§§4–12 Logic is the discipline that proves reason's ability to regu-
late itself; E extols it on that basis.

§§13–19 E deplores the practice of consulting interpreters and not
applying what one learns. Since reason is self-correcting and capable of enlightenment independently, interpreters are largely superfluous anyway.

§§20–9 That interpreters should be used rightly is demonstrated in
connection with divination. This provides an opportunity to reflect on
fate and free will. The upshot is that mankind is self-determining
in the way reason is.

§§1–3 is designed to show that human reason is self-correcting.
The argument, though complex, is clear enough, and the text mainly
sound, for all the difficulty Schweighäuser (ii. 194–7) found with it.
'Obviously, it must be by itself, or by something else' (**§2**): E wants
to prove the first alternative. To do so, he sets out to disprove the
second, by way of a dilemma: the 'something else' is either reason
or something superior. He quickly dismisses the second possibility;
it was an axiom of Stoic philosophy that nothing was superior to
reason (Cic. *ND* 1. 37; 2. 16, 133, etc). He then attacks the first with
two objections. The first is a regress argument. If reason B is to
correct reason A, what will correct reason B, and so forth? A possible reply is that reason B corrects itself, as well as reason A. E
anticipates this by objecting that if reason B is self-correcting, it
must be by virtue of something in reason that it is so; and reason
A, *qua* reason, should have the same capacity. This is a somewhat
more refined version of the Stoic argument at SE *M* 7. 441–2 (on
which see comment ad 1. 1. 1–6).

But E's logic is flawed. If he is prepared to admit that there are
varieties of reason, the distinctive mark of one in particular might
be just that it is capable of self-correction. Why does he need the
argument? The theme of the whole essay is self-reliance. In this
section he wants to argue that reason—everyone's reason—is self-
determining. Below, the argument for the superfluity of oracles and
interpreters assumes that the reasoning faculties of these supposed
authorities are by definition no better than anyone else's, which is
the point he tries to prove here. Thus man has no grounds to look
outside himself for guidance.

On the ability of reason to reflect on and organize itself, cf. Cic.
Ac. 2. 91: 'What will the dialectician judge? What a true conjunction is, what a true disjunction, what is said ambiguously, what
follows from each thing, what conflicts with it. If [reason] judges
these and similar things, it is its own judge.'

[Schenkl, Oldfather, and Souilhé propose to change *huph' autou*
in §2 to *huph' hautou*. But oblique forms of *autos* regularly function
as reflexives in the Imperial period, so no change is needed.]

The title of the piece, 'Concerning the Necessity of Logic', properly relates to §§4–12 only. We have to bear in mind that logic in
the Stoic sense comprised, *inter alia*, the elements of discourse, what
they called rhetoric (DL 7. 41; Cic. *Ac.* 2. 92; see LS 1. 188–9).
E works a variation on a motif that appears again in 2. 24. 13–15
and 2. 25, urging that the process of communication, on whatever
topic, assumes competence in logic in the expanded sense. For the
background to this argument see O'Meara 1994.

The imaginary interlocutor in §4 fulfils one of his customary
roles in motivating a transition in the argument. The gist of his
objection is that moral matters take precedence over logical ones.
This is a view that E himself appears to vouch for at times; cf. 3. 2.
3. We may imagine the interlocutor, in effect, to be accusing E of
inconsistency. But in §5 E repeats the interlocutor's own words
back to him to show that it is actually his own opinion that involves
him in self-contradiction.

In §6 E alludes to the three divisions of philosophy, logic, physics, and ethics, and to their order of study within the Stoa. There
was disagreement about this: cf. DL 7. 40–1; SE *PH* 2. 13; *M* 7.
20–3; see Ierodiakonou 1993: 68–71. Zeno and Chrysippus, however, put logic first, and this can be regarded as the standard Stoic
view; cf. DL 7. 40; Plut. *St. rep.* 1035A; SE *M* 7. 22. E endorses
that arrangement here. He implies in §§7–9 that, before anything
can be known, a criterion of knowledge must be established; and in
the Stoa matters of epistemology also fell within the province of
logic (DL 7. 41–2).

In other passages, however, E relegates logic to last place. It
corresponds to his third and final *topos*; and the *topoi* are ranked
in the order they are to be mastered (3. 2. 5, 17–18; see comment ad
1. 4. 5–11). In another passage that uses the same imagery as the
present one, but in other respects appears to flatly contradict it, E

again implies that logic comes last: 'You practice to avoid being shaken by sophisms; shaken from what? First show me what you are protecting, what you are measuring or weighing; *then* show me the scale or the bushel basket. Or how long will you continue to measure ashes?' (3. 26. 16–17). Bonhöffer (1890: 20; 1894: 123) has suggested that the contradiction can be resolved on the supposition that E envisaged two levels of logic, elementary and advanced. Considering how much logic represented for the Stoics, training in its rudiments could hardly be avoided. It was the medium through which all thought, all philosophy, was conducted. Training in more advanced topics could be postponed until later.

This is plausible. E's three *topoi* do not completely correspond to the three divisions of philosophy; see note ad 1. 4. 5–11. The fact that he approves the standard ordering of the latter, putting logic first, does not necessarily contradict what he says about the organization of the former, because he is partly talking about different things. There is some inconsistency, to be sure: the third *topos* does represent the study of logic. But when regarded in the context of the *topoi*, logic is normally not conceived in the broad sense in which E regards it here. There it is conceived more narrowly as dialectic. Cf. 3. 2. 6: 'Philosophers today neglect the first and second *topoi* and concentrate on the third: changing arguments, ones that conclude in a question, hypotheticals, lying arguments.' The rhetorical and epistemological sides of logic are usually overlooked in this connection. These two different conceptions of logic, expansive and restricted, are evident already in the old Stoa; see Hülser 1987–8: pp. lxxxii–lxxxiii. The reason they are more prominent in E is that they are assimilated to other categories of thought, especially theory and practice. Dialectic is *theōria* (cf. 1. 26. 1–3), while rhetoric and epistemology bear more directly on *praxis*; see note ad 1. 4. 5–9. Some of E's inconsistent statements pertaining to logic can be explained on this basis.

For the analogy of logic to weights and measures in §§6–7 cf. 1. 28. 28 and 2. 11. 13–24; also SE *PH* 2. 15; *M* 7. 31–3; Stob. 2. 2. 12. In §9 the interlocutor, retaining the image of logic as an instrument of measure, says that it 'bears no fruit'. The gist of his objection is that logic has no relevance to ethics, 'bears no fruit', that is, in virtuous action. E defers consideration of this for another time; he refutes it, in fact, in 1. 7, where he argues that dialectical virtue is a species of ethical virtue. The point made here likewise assumes that the three divisions of philosophy are interrelated (DL 7. 40). But it relies on the further Stoic assumption that logic has a certain priority. Cf. DL 7. 83: 'All things, they say, are discerned through logical study, everything that falls within the province of physics, as well as of ethics.'

Concerning the 'examination of terms' mentioned in §12, and its (contested) status as a division of logic, cf. SE *PH* 2. 205–6: 'The dogmatists take great pride in their technique of definition, which they list in the logical part of what they call philosophy. . . . They always present definitions as indispensable either for apprehension or teaching.' On the controversy regarding whether definition was part of logic see Hülser 1987–8: pp. lxxxiv–lxxxvi. Cf. DL 7. 41–2: 'Some divide logic into the two sciences of rhetoric and dialectic, while some add that which deals with definitions. . . . The part to do with definitions is accepted as a means of recognizing the truth, since things are apprehended through concepts (*ennoiai*)'; Aug. *CD* 8. 7 (= LS 32F): '[The Stoics say that from the senses] the mind forms conceptions . . . of those things that they articulate by definition. The entire method of learning and teaching, they say, starts and spreads from this.' See Atherton 1993: 62–4. E confirms that the examination of terms is equivalent to the articulation of concepts; cf. 2. 14. 14–15, 2. 17. 10–13; see Bonhöffer 1890: 199. §§10–11 are registered as Hülser fr. 95 and by von Arnim as *SVF* 1. 48, 1. 483, and 2. 51, as evidence of interest in definition on the part of Zeno, Cleanthes, and Chrysippus, respectively. Atherton (1993: 109) gives references to show that the importance of defining terms at the start of an argument was a commonplace of later Greek philosophy. Of course it had roots further back. In §12 E characteristically makes Socrates sponsor of the view he seeks to promote. Socrates' interest in definition is attested by Xenophon at *Mem.* 1. 1. 16 and 4. 6. 1, and often by Plato and Aristotle: cf. Pl. *Chrm.* 159a; Arist. *Met.* 1078b27, etc. For Antisthenes cf. DL 6. 17. E's testimony is registered as V A 160 Giannantoni. It is discussed in the context of Antisthenes' philosophy by Giannantoni (1990: iv. 248–9, 365–85) and Brancacci (1990: 85–129).

[In §4 'passions, and opinions' is a supplement to the text proposed by Wolf. It has been adopted for three reasons: (1) it is too much to suppose that *therapeuō* is being used in an absolute sense; 2. 21. 15, *pace* Schweighäuser, is not a true parallel, since the verb there is in the passive voice, and so has an object implied. (2) The

phrase *kai ta homoia* ('and the like') is too elliptical to serve as an
addendum to the interlocutor's remark, especially as the original
text probably lacked quotation marks. (3) 'Them' (*ekeinōn*) in the
next sentence needs an antecedent. The supplement adopted is
suggested by comparison with *SVF* 3. 479–80, 490, etc. The translation also assumes Upton's change of the first word in **§4** from
einai to *nai* ('yes'); cf. 1. 6. 30, 1. 28. 8, 1. 29. 11, and **§9** of this
discourse.]

§§13–19 transmit one of E's most common complaints: people
are content if they can understand Chrysippus and other authorities on to how to behave. As for putting what they read into practice, this they completely overlook (cf. 1. 4. 5–17, 1. 26. 8–9, Gellius
1. 2, 17. 19. 1–4). As in **§§1–3**, another regress looms: if we need an
interpreter for the will of nature, we are liable to need an interpreter
of that interpreter, and so on: the process becomes endless. E's
impulse is to stop it before it starts. The need of a commentator to
elucidate Chrysippus reflects that author's notorious obscurity; see
note ad 1. 4. 5–11. Some people evidently felt it was enough to puzzle
his meaning out; but understanding him is just the beginning.

The means–end distinction is a common motif in E. Among the
things he calls means are the body (2. 23. 32–5), our station in life
(1. 29. 41), even life itself (2. 23. 36–7). Yet I think Schweighäuser
(ii. 191) is wrong to suppose that E directs his fire here against the
pursuit of logic as an end. The development of the interpreter motif
is used here not to attack logic, but to support the theme of self-
sufficiency. As reason is self-sufficient, so man, the rational animal,
should be self-sufficient. He does not need help from extraneous
sources whose reason, as argued in **§§1–3**, is in principle no better
than his own. On the thought of **§§18–19**, cf. 3. 1. 37.

The doctrine that 'all men err unwillingly', treated as a truism in
§14, is argued for at length in 1. 18 and 1. 28. It is a corollary of
Stoic rationalism; originally, of course, it was a Socratic paradox
(Pl. *Prot.* 395d; Xen. *Mem.* 3. 9. 5). On the phrase 'the will of
nature' (§13), cf. 3. 20. 13; *Ench.* 26; Marc. 5. 1; see Inwood 1985:
26–7, 106–11. It is synonymous with the will of Zeus, and with
'right reason'. Here again logic demonstrates its usefulness, since
understanding the workings of reason is tantamount to understanding the will of nature. This is needed in order to anticipate the
course of events and adjust one's will, or expectations, accordingly.
In **§§18–19** the description of portents perceived through augury as

a species of 'sign' was traditional in Stoicism; cf. Cic. *Div.* 1. 82–3, 117–18, 127.

[The punctuation of **§16** differs from earlier translations, in that I assume that the phrase 'as if it were written in Latin' is not part of the interlocutor's remarks, but E's sarcastic comment on the practice of seeking a gloss on Chrysippus. He implies that one type of interpretation is much like any other, and all are subordinate disciplines.]

In **§§20–9** E's complex attitude toward divination is evident. The old Stoics had defended it because it supported belief in divine providence (cf. Cic. *Div.* 1. 82–3), and fate (cf. Cic. *ND* 1. 55; *SVF* 2. 939–44). E does not challenge its validity, as Panaetius had done (Cic. *Div.* 1. 6; *Ac.* 2. 107; see Alesse 1994: 230–9). But he questions its utility. Cf. *Ench.* 32. 1: 'When you have recourse to divination, remember that you do not know what the outcome will be, and you have come to learn it from the seer; but if you really are a philosopher, you know beforehand what kind of thing it will be. For if it is among the things outside our control, it can by no means be either good or bad.' Bonhöffer (1894: 45) points out that divination is concerned solely with externals, things indifferent; whereas it is E's constant refrain that such things are outside our control. And since things really good or bad are at all times within our power, the wise man does not worry about the future (cf. 4. 10. 4–13; *Ench.* 18, 32). The usefulness of divination was much debated in later Greek philosophy; cf. Cic. *Div.* 1. 5–7; *De Fato* 26–33; DL 10. 135. E's doubt is shared by other later Stoics; cf. Sen. *Ep.* 88. 14; *NQ* 6. 29. 3. The Stoic saint Cato in Lucan's *Pharsalia* (9. 566–72) declines to consult the oracle of Zeus Ammon, on the grounds that it cannot tell him anything of value he doesn't already know. That philosophy helps render divination otiose is a point also made by Cicero at *Div.* 2. 10–11. By equating his seer with a philosopher in **§29**, E implies as much. This ideal seer fulfils his duty by transmitting the message for mankind ascribed to Zeus at 1. 1. 10–13. He evangelizes about inner freedom in a familiar manner; cf. 1. 1. 21–5, 1. 18. 17, 2 .15. 1, 3. 22. 105, 3. 26. 24, 4. 1. 68–75, 99–100, 4. 7. 8, etc. This Stoic—or better, Epictetan—seer is paradoxical because he would end up putting himself out of business.

In **§§20–1** E parodies the action of a seer inspecting the lobes of the liver, and other organs. There is a pun on two meanings of *topos* ('place' and 'subject-matter'). E's doctrine of the three *topoi* is fully laid out in 3. 2; see comment ad 1. 4. 5–11. In the present section these motions of the mind are equated with what he calls, for short, *prohairesis*. This complex word could accommodate all these senses, because its associations were both intellectual and emotional; Aristotle had defined it as 'rational desire' (*EN* 1139b5). The translations offered in 21, 23, and 26—'choice' and 'power of choice'— get at another aspect of the word, but are no more than stopgaps. *Prohairesis* in **§27** is the part 'which [god] has given to us as a fragment of himself (*apospasas*)'. The expression contains an echo of Posidonius; cf. 1. 14. 6 with comment.

The epigrammatic claim in **§26** that 'choice compelled choice' reads oddly in English, but benefits in Greek from the semantic range of *prohairesis*, covering both active and passive senses. It could be rendered, for instance, 'choice determined policy', *vel sim*. E's meaning here, though, can only be paraphrased in English. The idea is that man is autonomous and self-determining, and like all self-movers, free. The import of **§24** is that no person or thing can force us to a course of action without our assenting to it. Everything we do is ultimately a consequence of our own decision. Aristotle's analysis at *EN* 1110a4–b17 of acts performed under duress is more subtle, but can be usefully compared. Both assume that such acts are essentially voluntary (cf. esp. *EN* 1110a11–14).

On **§§21–8** see further Hahm 1991: 39–42. He draws attention to similarities between E here and Origen at *SVF* 2. 989 (= *On Prayer* 6. 1–2), and concludes that both were drawing on a common Stoic source. Perhaps he is right, but in view of Origen's familiarity with E (acknowledged by Hahm, ibid. 45 n. 32), I think it just as likely that Origen is drawing on E directly.

CHAPTER 18

That We Should Not Be Angry with Wrongdoers

This discourse treats of some of E's most typical themes. It is a good example of how they are interrelated. Analysis:
§§1–10 Evildoers should not be hated: they simply make the wrong judgements about good and evil. Anyone inclined to hate them is therefore himself misguided.

§§11–14 Such a person is also misguided in the same way as the object of his indignation, in that he evidently shares his values. He should scrutinize his own judgements before criticizing another's.

§§15–20 The false values that both share involve attachment to externals. The secret to invincibility lies in putting trust in the virtues of character.

§§21–3 He who has realized this will look upon theft and such accidents of fortune—as well as material temptations—as so many opportunities to display strength of character and firmness of judgement.

With §§1–4 compare 1. 28. 1–5, and see comment there. This passage is identical in drawing a parallel between assent and impulse, in asserting that both are psychologically determined, and in going on to make this grounds for indulgence of the morally misguided.

Oldfather says that 'it is not known just what persons are referred to' by 'the philosophers' in §1, whose doctrine E outlines in §§1–2. But by 'philosophers' E normally means Stoics (cf. 1. 4. 1, 2. 1. 22, 2. 10. 5, 24, etc.). And the doctrine is arguably Stoic, though couched in terms unusual for a Stoic. E posits a single psychological principle to account for both opinion and action: 'feeling' (*to pathein*). Stoicism defended a unified view of the soul, ascribing such (apparently) diverse functions as sensation, impression, impulse, and assent to a single faculty, the *logos* or *hēgemonikon*; see comment ad 1. 1. 1–6. This may be a popular paraphrase of that idea. 'Feeling', in Greek as in English, can denote cognitive as well as affective states. Our passage suggests that the two are actually aspects of the same thing. As one modern philosopher, G. Frege, put it, 'a conviction or a belief is the ground of a feeling' (Black and Geach 1952: 52). E uses *to pathein* with like implication at 1. 28. 3; cf. 1. 2. 3, 1. 18. 1, 1. 20. 12. But however well adapted *to pathein* was to Stoicism's integrated psychology, there is no evidence that it was earlier employed in quite this way (possibly because it is cognate with the Greek for 'passions', *pathē*, which Stoics wanted to eliminate). I do not think that E's unorthodox terminology is too troubling; he is evidently formulating the Stoic position in a new, compelling way. It is worth noting, however, that Sceptics used *pathos*, *to pathein*, and their cognates in this very same sense, to denote the basis of one's beliefs. Cf. SE *PH* 1. 22: 'We say that the standard of the Sceptical persuasion is what is apparent (*to phainomenon*), implicitly meaning by this the appearances; for they depend on passive

and unwilled feeling (*pathos*).' In the passage parallel to ours, 1. 28.
1–3, E also adduces *to phainomenon* in conjunction with 'feeling'.
And the point of both passages is that there is an involuntary element to human behaviour, in so far as it is conditioned by appearance, or feeling. This is upheld in Sceptic sources; cf. SE *M* 8. 316:
'Some things, as we have frequently said, are believed to be evident, others non-evident; and evident are those which are grasped
involuntarily through appearance and feeling.' In view of these
similarities, I think it probable that E's choice of vocabulary was
influenced by the Sceptics. For other evidence of their influence,
see introductory comment to 1. 22. For the tendency of later ancient philosophers to borrow selectively from their rivals, see Annas
1993: 281.

With **§§3–10** compare 1. 28. 8–10, and see comment ad loc. As
Long and Sedley (1. 385) remark, 'passages such as [these] (which
abound in Marcus Aurelius and Epictetus) indicate that committed
Stoics tempered the harshness of their absolute moral categories
by a charitable attitude towards those whose values are mistaken'.
Marcus and E were certainly committed Stoics. But there is evidence that they abated somewhat a less compromising attitude among
earlier Stoics. Cf. DL 7. 123: '[Wise men] are not pitying and make
no allowance for anyone; they never relax the penalties fixed by the
laws, since indulgence and pity and even equitable consideration
are marks of a weak mind that prefers kindness to punishment';
see Rist 1978*b*. In **§9** E says that 'if you must be affected in a way
contrary to nature by the evil of another, pity, do not hate, him.'
Because pity is a passion, it is 'contrary to nature' (cf. 3. 22. 13, 3.
24. 43, 4. 1. 4). E is so far consistent with traditional Stoicism. But
he sanctions pity as an alternative to the more harmful emotion of
anger; and that is a change.

[The translation of **§8** assumes the emended text of Schenkl.]

§§11–14 depends on the fundamental Stoic point that external
goods are not essential to happiness. In so far as we become attached to them, in fact, they inevitably subvert our happiness when
we lose them, either through natural causes, or through the actions
of wicked men. And since we are masters of our judgements, any
unhappiness that we incur through loss of external goods will be
our own fault. In characterizing the opinion of others as 'the very
thing that you imagine' (**§13**), E shifts the focus back on to the

reader, suggesting that he should examine his own opinions before criticizing those of others.

The argument of §§15–16 depends on an additional point, summed up by the somewhat cryptic remark in §16 that 'a man loses what he has'. This can be read two ways. It may be taken to suggest that we should jettison worldly goods, since they only involve us in difficulty. This is a Cynic sentiment; the person in §15 who stole E's lamp (cf. 1. 29. 21) may be regarded as teaching him the hard lesson that the child taught Diogenes (DL 6. 37): viz. that we can manage without many of the conveniences we imagine to be indispensable. The other way to interpret his words is that we should count ourselves lucky to have such things in the first place. Being robbed only shows us that we are more fortunate than people who feel compelled to steal. I think this is the more likely explanation, since it reinforces the controlling theme of the discourse, that we should pity wrongdoers instead of despising them.

This incident is alluded to again at 1. 29. 21. According to Lucian, *Adv. ind.* 14, E's lamp was later sold for 3,000 drachmas to someone who wanted a souvenir of the famous philosopher.

[The principal MS, S, is damaged in the area of §§9–11. This was decisive in establishing its primacy, since all other MSS indicate a lacuna at this point, or ignore the passage altogether; see Schenkl, p. lv; Souilhé, i. pp. lxxii–lxxiii. A facsimile of the damaged page is included in Schenkl's edition. Enough of S is legible at this point to permit the general sense to be inferred, but the text in §10 cannot be certainly restored. Our translation of this section is based on the following reading (conjectural supplements in parentheses): *mē e(isenen)kēis tas phōnas tautas has hoi polloi tōn ph(ilopsougoun)tōn 'toutous oun tous kataratous kai miarous mōrous'. estō. su pōs pot' apesophōthēs aphnō (houtōs hin' allois) khalepos ei.*]

For the importance to Stoicism of the traditional wisdom to 'Know yourself' (§17) cf. 1. 6. 25 with comment. Beginning with this section, E makes the (apparent) injury done us by others pretext for a point he often makes, that we cannot be harmed by outside forces. It assumes familiarity with the subtle Stoic teaching about externals, the goods of the body included. E does not deny that they have value, but it is only selective value. Hence, 'I do not say that it is not permitted to groan; only do not groan in the centre of your being' (§19). For comparable advice cf. *Ench.* 16; Sen. *Ep.*

54. 6–7; Plot. 3. 2. 15. 47. We would prefer to keep such things, but can still be happy without them, and even derive benefit from their loss; see comment ad 1. 1. 22 and 1. 6. 35–6. **§18** is meant to imply that the loss of so small a thing as a pot can be turned to account by inuring us to the more serious losses that all flesh is heir to. Cf. 4. 1. 111 and *Ench.* 12. 2: 'Begin, then, with little things. A bit of oil is spilled, a bit of wine gets stolen; say to yourself, "This is the price of calmness, of serenity."' With **§19** cf. also 1. 13. 2 regarding slaves, with comment.

In **§20** E implies that we ought not trust to our leg, our neck (**§17**), our head, our ears (**§19**), or any part of our anatomy, but to our soul and mind: this is the true self, which cannot be affected by things outside us. To identify with the body is to put oneself on a level with the beasts. For the thought cf. Sen. *Ep.* 15. 2, with Summers (1910) ad loc.

[On the omission of *dei* in **§20** see textual note ad 1. 25. 18.]

§§21–3 restates the point that difficulties such as wrongdoers cause can be useful for weaning us from dependence on externals, the only things wrongdoers influence. So, if we start with small things (**§18**), we develop resistance to the more upsetting influences of derision and death—as well as the distracting effects of women and fame (**§22**). The wise man is proof against all these. Cf. Sen. *Cons. sap.* 2. 3: 'The wise man is safe, and no injury or insult can touch him'; DL 7. 117: 'The wise man is free from vanity, for he is indifferent to good or evil report ... Again, they say that wise men are ascetic, for they have no dealings with pleasure.' In **§23** E rehearses the ultimate tests of the wise man: drunkenness, sleep, and temporary insanity. In all such circumstances his judgement remains sound. Cf. Cic. *Ac.* 2. 51: 'There is only one way to repulse delusive impressions, whether they are bodied forth in ... sleep, or under the influence of wine, or insanity: we shall say that all such impressions lack clearness, which we are bound to cling to tooth and nail.' Cf. SE *M* 7. 245–7; DL 7. 118, 127; on 'melancholy-madness' cf. esp. E 3. 2. 5 and see Pease ad Cic. *Div.* 1. 81. For the commonplace comparison of the philosopher to an athlete, cf. 1. 24. 1–2; *Ench.* 51. 2; and see Cherniss 1957 ad Plut. *De Facie* 943D. It helps with E's advice in this final section to look upon hardship as a test of one's mettle—a sly way to get one to view it opportunistically.

CHAPTER 19

How One Should Behave toward Tyrants

E opens the discourse by dwelling on familiar themes, but at §§11–15 advances an argument that is rather provocative and has drawn its share of comment in the past. It defends egoism as an ethical principle. The tyrants of the title serve two functions in this context. As the traditional embodiment of flawed egoism, they offer an opportunity to explore what true egoism consists in. (This can be traced back to Plato's tyrant at *Rep.* 587e, whose life is at 729 removes from true pleasure.) Second, they appear to pose a threat to our happiness, our own egoism. Now, Stoics maintained that no outside force can inhibit our access to virtue, and therefore our happiness. Tyrants, on this supposition, are exposed as an empty threat. (Cf. 1. 29. 1–15, 4. 1. 132–4, 4. 5. 34, etc.) But there was a tension within Stoic ethics concerning external goods, as we have seen (cf. 1. 6. 32–6, with comment). E reflects that tension in weighing the degree of importance that should be conceded tyrants. The discourse may be outlined as follows:

§§1–10 Tyrants are deluded in supposing that they merit exceptional attention.

§§11–15 This is because everything that has a claim on our attention must appeal above all to our self-interest.

§§16–29 But first we must be clear ourselves about where self-interest lies. If not, we will vainly search for it in external honours, and tyrants, who have power to dispense or withhold such honours, will be encouraged in their perverse egoism.

'[Q]uite inevitable' in **§1** is *pasa anankē*. The phrase is repeated in §16 below. Belief in determinism made the Stoics, when they turned to ethics, more than usually sensitive to factors that influenced human behaviour decisively one way or the other: see Long 1989: 90. The thought resembles what is said about Medea in 1. 28, whose crimes stem from her ignorance of good and evil; cf. 1. 28. 8–9 with comment.

The argument in §§2–4 presupposes E's standard list of psychic functions: desire, impulse, and assent; see note ad 1. 4. 5–11. They are adverted to again in §25, and referred to collectively in §23 as *ta prohairetika*. Excellence in respect of these faculties constitutes the real superiority as far as E is concerned. That a tyrant is paradoxically powerless is the inverse of Stoic claims that the wise man alone is king; cf. Dio Chrys. 3. 25 sq.; *SVF* 3. 597, 599, 600, 603. The test of his influence that E applies, his ability to confer (real) favours, informs some of Seneca's arguments about rulers in *On Benefits*. Cf. *Ben.* 5. 6. 1: 'Alexander the Great used to boast that no one had outdone him in benefits. . . . Socrates could have boasted the same thing, and Diogenes the Cynic likewise, by whom, in fact, Alexander was outdone. Was he not outdone on that day when, puffed up beyond the limits of human pride, he saw someone to whom he could give nothing, from whom he could take nothing away?' Cf. ibid. 7. 3. 1–7.

[The *Hoti* in §1 is elliptical, designed to introduce E's thoughts: compare fr. 8, lines 2 and 4, and 3. 21. 1; the titles of the essays afford other parallels (e.g. 1. 8, 1. 17, 1. 18, 1. 28, etc.). Schweighäuser preferred to delete *hoti*, and Upton changed it to *hotan*, which gives excellent sense, but since the reading of S can be defended, I think it should be kept.]

§§3–4 is pure Socratic induction: the expert in every skill is the 'one who knows'. For the comparison with other skills (*technai* in §4) in connection with political leadership, especially the associated activities of driving a chariot and piloting a ship, cf. Xen. *Mem.* 4. 4. 5; Pl. *Rep.* 341c–342e. The parallel was used, especially by Plato and Socrates, to discredit pretenders to power who lacked the requisite expertise. E puts it to similar use. The tyrant errs in putting his own happiness before that of the state, or in failing to realize that he attains his own good by furthering the common good. His ignorance is more a matter for pity than pride. For the analogy cf. 4. 1. 63, 117–18; Sen. *Ep.* 85. 30–7, 109. 14.

In §§4–6 E develops a different argument, which depends, in large part, on the semantic range of the verb *therapeuō*. It is translated 'care' or 'attend to' above, but, depending on context, can mean 'respect', 'flatter', even 'worship'. (For similar play on the word see 2. 22. 31.) The fact that there is a single term for such different things helps account for the tyrant's confusion. The meanings lie along a continuum. He can mistake care of one sort, i.e. tending to an annoyance (himself), for care of a much warmer kind, amounting almost to worship. **§5** 'Who cares for you as a man?' 'As a man' here means, as the possessor of certain virtues; cf. 2. 10. 23 and Sen. *De Ira* 1. 5 for a list. For the thought, especially the contrast with animals, cf. 3. 14. 14.

'[A]ll men care for themselves, but care for you as they would for their donkey.' The first half of this statement in **§5** is argued at greater length in **§§11–15**. As for the second, it might seem that the tyrant cannot claim even the degree of attention a donkey receives, inasmuch as donkeys confer a benefit (quite a big one, according to Cic. *ND* 2. 159), whereas the tyrant is just evil. Does E concede to the tyrant any care at all, or is this reserved for people and things that are beneficial? Comparison with **§§9–10** suggests that the tyrant is valued on a level with things that affect the body, whether for good or for ill, and so is entitled to a measure of the same respect that the body deserves. E is in line with other Stoics regarding the class of things 'in accordance with nature', including the goods of the body; cf. 1. 2. 15–16 with comment. This is supported by the picture of Zeus in **§12** as tending above all to our bodily needs.

Romans set up altars and temples to abstractions: cf. Cic. *ND* 2. 61. On the altar of Fever in Rome (**§6**), cf. Cic. *ND* 3. 63, and see Latte 1960: 52. The cult was apotropaic; cf. Valerius Maximus 2. 5. 6: 'The other gods they worship for their benefits, but propitiate Fever with temples to minimize its harm.' Stoics rejected such usages, on the grounds that gods could only be the cause of good; cf. Philo, *Prov.* 2. 53; Sen. *Ep.* 95. 49. Sandbach (1930: 50) cites Cic. *ND* 2. 14 to demonstrate that Cleanthes regarded the gods as potentially harmful, but the phenomena listed there are not so much harmful as awe-inspiring, and Sandbach concedes in any case that the argument is without parallel. See further Cherniss 1976: 708 note b.

§6 'Who wants to be like you?' The ancients believed that imitation was the sincerest form of flattery, even, or especially, where the gods were concerned; cf. Sen. *Ep.* 95. 50: 'Do you wish to appease the gods? Be good. Whoever imitates them has worshipped them sufficiently.' No such impulse toward the tyrant is possible, so that, whatever he imagines, the respect due him is of a meaner sort. On the respect and following Socrates commanded, cf. 3. 7. 34. 'What is by nature free' in **§7** is *prohairesis*, the source of a man's opinions. External force has influence over the body, but our thoughts are free. (E did not know about brainwashing.) Cf. Marc. 8. 48: 'Our mind is a citadel, for a man has no fortress more impregnable. If he resorts to it, he will remain free for ever.' For a contemporary testimonial to the truth of this idea, see Stockdale 1995.

For the imperturbability of the wise man in the tyrant's presence (**§§8–10**), compare 1. 1. 21–5, 1. 29. 21–5; Cic. *Off.* 2. 23–6. The word translated 'opinions' in **§8** is *dogmata*. The sentiment is similar to 1. 1. 23–5 and 1. 29. 5–8. It reflects Stoic rationalism, which E subscribes to completely: cf. **§16** below and notes ad 1. 28. On the sovereignty of *dogma* cf. 2. 16. 22, 40; 3. 3. 18–19, 3. 9. 2–11, 3. 16. 8, 3. 19. 3, 4. 5. 28–9; *Ench.* 5; see Barnes 1990*b*: 2630.

For Zeus as father, and we his sons (**§9**), cf. 1. 3. 1 with comment. The note of the scholiast to S (p. 26b) is interesting: 'He calls the souls of men god's own children, and their body a corpse.' (On the scholia in S see Schenkl pp. lxxix–lxxxii.) Cf. Plut. *Plat. quaest.* 1001B, in the course of explaining in what sense Plato at *Tim.* 28c calls Zeus 'father': 'There are two constituent parts of the universe, body and soul. The former god did not beget, but he formed and fitted matter together once it had submitted to him.' The scholiast, then, gives us a Platonic interpretation, but E's language seems to invite it. When he says, 'Zeus has set me free,' E evidently distinguishes 'me' from the body, which is subject to the tyrant's will. For *prohairesis* ('moral character') as the true self, cf. 1. 1. 21–5 and comment. See MacMullen 1966: 64 on this passage and others like it; on the Platonic strain in Stoicism see Nussbaum 1994: 326.

For the comparison of the body to a corpse in **§9** compare 1. 9. 19, 33; 1. 13. 5, 3. 10. 15; fr. 26; Simpl. *In Ench.* 6b. The sentiment is Platonic, but the image is not. Within the Platonic, tradition the body was usually characterized as a prison, a tomb, or as fetters on the soul. 'Corpse', however, is properly speaking not an image at all, but a *reductio* in the manner of the Stoic paradoxes. It is rare in classical texts, but caught on with Christian authors; for references see Farquharson ad Marc. 4. 41 (= E fr. 26) and ad 12. 33.

§11 'This is not selfishness (literally "self-loving": *to philauton*).' 'Selfish' was an invidious term, then as now: that is why E disavows it. But what E promotes in **§§11–15** is in fact a kind of selfishness, only not as most men practise it, or as the word is popularly construed. (Oldfather and More translate, 'not mere selfishness'.) E expounds the principle of psychological egoism, the view that an agent acts only so as to promote his own real or perceived interest.

In E's case this is reinforced by his psychological determinism, which dictates that agents must choose the good wherever they find it (cf. 1. 18. 1–2, 1. 28. 1–7, 3. 3. 2–4). In the remainder of this section he undertakes to reconcile this truth with altruism, and find the necessary connection existing between individual and general interests. The passage is commented upon by Rist 1978*a*: 265; Inwood 1983: 197; Striker 1983: 153; Bosworth 1988: 33; Striker 1991: 37–8; Annas 1993: 275 n. 88.

Since in **§15** E ties the argument to the distinctively Stoic theory of appropriation (*oikeiōsis*), it is best to start there. In brief, the theory of *oikeiōsis* holds that a creature's fundamental tendency is to come to an awareness and appreciation of its own physical and mental faculties, and to try and protect, exercise, and develop these as far as possible. For other references to *oikeiōsis* in E cf. 2. 22. 15, 3. 24. 11; *Ench.* 30. In characterizing it as 'one and the same principle (*archē*) for all beings', E invokes it in a genuinely Stoic way; other Stoics called it the 'first impulse (DL 7. 85), and with *archē* compare *principium* at Cic. *Fin.* 3. 16. Stoics viewed the process under two aspects: personal appropriation to the self and social appropriation toward others. The extant sources treat mainly of the former; cf. LS 57A–C; Cic. *Fin.* 3. 16–25; Gellius 12. 5. 7–9. Accounts of the latter usually start with parents' love for their offspring. This is cited as proof that concern for others is also innate; cf. Plut. *St. rep.* 1038B; Cic. *Fin.* 3. 62; *Off.* 1. 12. Appropriation toward others was held to be the basis of justice and society.

What relation these two kinds of *oikeiōsis* have to each other is variously explained in both ancient and modern sources; see Striker 1983; Inwood 1983: 193–201; Annas 1993: 262–76; Schofield 1995. Schofield argues that no definitive account emerged from the old Stoa, so that later Stoics were forced (or free) to devise varying explanations of their own. This is what I think E does here. Annas, for her part, maintains that all Stoics held to 'a two-source' view. In her words, 'self-concern and other-concern are two distinct sources of human behaviour, neither developing from the other. *Oikeiōsis* is a disjunctive notion: it covers the rational development of both self- and other-concern. What these have in common is simply that they are both cases of rational development of the agent's initially narrow, instinctive attitude to a wider and rationally based concern' (Annas 1993: 275). This is a controversial interpretation, and I think belied by what E says here. He states flatly that there is 'one and the same principle for all beings', and that it is 'appropriation to themselves'. He obviously does not negate altruism, but denies in so many words that it constitutes, or results from, a distinct form of *oikeiōsis*. How then, does he get from egoism to altruism?

There are several things to notice about the argument. E may appear to deduce behavioural norms from the examples of Zeus and the sun, on the principle that what is good enough for them should be good enough for us. But in fact he is not trying to use Zeus and the sun as role models. He is invoking the cosmic perspective that had an established place in Stoic arguments for other-concern. Cf. Cic. *Fin.* 3. 64: 'The Stoics hold that the world is governed by divine will; it is as it were a city and state shared by men and gods. [In Stoicism both Zeus and the sun were gods.] Each one is part of this world. From this it is a natural consequence that we prefer the common advantage to our own.' To maximize self-interest, our actions should be referred to the situation we find ourselves in. E suggests that our interest is served not by sacrificing individual good to the common good (there is no suggestion of sacrifice here), but by cultivating gods and men and getting benefits in return.

The second thing to notice is that E refers to man as 'the rational animal' (**§13**). There is a point to the periphrasis. As an animal, man shares certain needs with other animals, 'the primary things in accordance with nature'. These are the needs Zeus tends to when he is 'Rain-giver' and 'Fruit-giver' (**§12**). In calling man an animal, E implies that he does not outgrow these needs when he attains the age of reason. In this respect his account of appropriation differs from earlier Stoic accounts, by reacting to criticisms of them on this score; cf. Cic. *Fin.* 4. 26–42. And why 'rational'? In the statement (**§14**) that 'it is no longer anti-social to do everything for one's own sake', E implies that it is to our advantage to be altruistic. Other ancient accounts of appropriation also tie reason to altruism and the social virtues: cf. Cic. *Laws* 1. 23, 33; *Off.* 1. 12; Dio Chrys. 36. 31–2, 38. But they do not make the connection altogether clear. In E's version, reflexive self-regard is converted to altruism by becoming rational in the sense that calculation, not just instinct, is involved. Zeus, the embodiment of reason (DL 7. 135–6), demonstrates enlightened self-interest in satisfying man's needs. The tyrant, who is deficient in reason, practises a mistaken form of selfishness in his own community. Zeus is compensated with the esteem he craves, the tyrant only thinks that he is.

The force of E's presentation of the doctrine of appropriation derives from its integration with the picture of the universe as a community. He concedes that there are things of value that others can give and take away, the 'primary things in accordance with nature'; and implies that the human state and the state composed of gods and men exist in order to facilitate access to them. If that conflicts with his insistence elsewhere (e.g. 4. 12. 7–8) that virtue is the only good and depends solely on ourselves, this was a conflict in Stoicism generally. It had elicited the charge that Stoics promoted two ends and, as a corollary, two forms of appropriation. As Striker (1983: 164) puts it, 'Since both egoism and altruism were prescribed as natural, conflicts were bound to arise that could not easily be solved by another appeal to nature.' E tries to avoid them by upholding egoism as the one comprehensive principle in nature, and rationalizing altruism on that basis. Wolf compares Epicurus' defence of justice and society by appeal to egoism. Schweighäuser (ii. 234) tried to avoid that inference by interpreting the phrase 'his proper goods' in §13 in strict Stoic terms, to refer to virtue alone. His reading is ingenious, but I'm afraid that E is using 'goods' in the material sense, and that Wolf's comparison has merit.

According to Annas (1993: 275 n. 88), on the other hand, 'What the passage says, is that self-concern properly understood is compatible with other-concern, not that other-concern is just an expanded form of self-concern.' I think the latter interpretation is, in fact, the correct one, only I would put it a little differently: other-concern grows out of self-concern. The process of maturation involves seeing that concern for others helps meet our self-centred needs. And since appropriation is a developmental idea, care for others will more and more enter into our plans and actions. But it continues to be self-interest that lies behind them. It may be that E makes this argument partly for rhetorical reasons. After all, the conclusion he reaches is bland enough: viz. that concern for others is a good thing. But such a platitude is more compelling when it is argued for with such boldness and apparent contempt for sentimental ideals. Be that as it may, this is, in fact, E's argument, and I think it can be supported by others where he says much the same thing. Cf. 2. 22. 15–19: 'For in general, make no mistake, every creature is appropriated (*ōikeiōtai*) to nothing so much as its own interest. So whatever appears to be an obstacle to this, whether it be brother, father, child, lover or beloved, the creature hates, rejects, and execrates

it. . . . For wherever is located the "I" and the "mine", to that must
the creature incline.' Cf. further 3. 3. 5–10, 4. 5. 30–2. His exclusive
focus on motives of advantage constitutes what we might call his
Realphilosophie.

'Even the sun does everything for its own sake' (**§11**). For how
much the sun does by way of benefit, compare 3. 22. 4–5, a passage
that tends to confirm that in our passage also the universe is viewed
in the aspect of a state: 'So it goes also in this great state. For here
too there is a master of the household who assigns everything its
place: "You are the sun, and by your revolutions you have the
power to give rise to the year and the seasons, and give increase and
nourishment to the fruits of the earth, and raise and calm the winds,
and give warmth to the bodies of men. Go, set out on your circuit,
and impart motion to all things, from the greatest to the least."'
Stoics believed that the sun, like the other stars, was alive. Cf. Cic.
ND 2. 41: 'Since the sun resembles those fires which are contained
in the bodies of living creatures, the sun must also be alive; and so
too the other heavenly bodies.' It possessed functions like nutri-
tion; cf. Cic. *ND* 3. 37: 'The sun, moon and other heavenly bodies
draw sustenance in some cases from bodies of fresh water, in other
cases from the sea. This is the reason Cleanthes gives why "The sun
turns back, and no further proceeds | Than the summer solstice",
and the winter one too: it is that he may not wander too far away
from his food.' Cf. DL 7. 145; Philo *Prov.* 2. 64, 84; E 3. 23. 27.
This explains why E says that it 'does everything for its own sake'.
It bestows its vital energy incidentally, while in search of its proper
nourishment. See further Mansfeld 1979: 150–1.

§12 'When Zeus wishes to be "Rain-giver" and "Fruit-giver" and
"Father of gods and men".' Cf. 1. 22. 16. Such epithets are frequently applied to Zeus in Stoic sources; cf. the inclusive description 'many-named' in the first line of Cleanthes' *Hymn to Zeus* (LS
54I1). This could refer to the Stoic tendency to treat the various
gods of Greek and Roman polytheism as manifestations of the one
true god (DL 7. 147; *SVF* 2. 1070). But at *St. rep.* 1049A–B,
Plutarch says that Chrysippus always lavished 'fair and humane'
epithets on Zeus specifically. According to Cic. *ND* 2. 64, Zeus'
name in Latin, Jove, comes from *juvare*, 'to help'. The prolifera-
tion of cult titles was traditionally meant to underscore the scope of
a deity's power. But Chrysippus and his successors were concerned
above all to highlight god's beneficence. For the epithet 'Father of

gods and men', see note ad 1. 3. 1; for 'Fruit-giver' cf. Plut. *Comm. not.* 1075F; for 'Rain-giver' cf. Cornutus, ch. 9.

That Zeus attains his private ends by contributing to the public good follows from the contractual nature of Graeco-Roman religion, *do ut des*. Zeus wants to be addressed with these titles because he wants to be cultivated in turn. Stoics found a place for a less calculating god, one who did not consult his own interests, but performed benefits from the goodness of his heart: 'Why does god perform benefits? It is his nature' (Sen. *Ep.* 95. 48). Moreover, it seemed to detract from god's dignity to suggest that he stood in any need of man's attention; cf. Plut. *St. rep.* 1052E; Sen. *Cons. sap.* 8. 2; Simpl. *In Ench.* 219a. This was an old, particularly philosophical idea; cf. Xen. *Mem.* 1. 4. 10, Pl. *Tim.* 34b; Lucr. 1. 48; see Pease ad Cic. *ND* 1. 45. E's picture resembles more the gods of poetry and popular religion. But it suits his purpose here to play up the element of gain, to make the point that, even on such a calculating basis, generosity and altruism are not excluded.

As often toward the end of a discourse, in **§§16–29** E has recourse to humour and anecdote; cf. 1. 1. 27 ff., 1. 2. 25 ff., 1. 7. 32–3, 1. 9. 27–34, etc. On Epaphroditus see comment at 1. 1. 20 and cf. 4. 1. 148–50, where Felicio appears again; he too was a freedman of Nero. For similar reversals of fortune, leading to similar transpositions of master and slave, cf. Sen. *Ep.* 47. 9.

The presentation of the honours accorded the successful petitioner for office in **§§24–5** is in asyndeton, with many vivid details. For the significance of lamps being lit cf. 2. 20. 9; it evokes a quasi-religious atmosphere (see Koester 1982: i. 170). With **§25** compare 1. 4. 32, 3. 24. 117–18, 4. 6. 31–2. Reference to good desires and impulses assumes E's standard list of the psychic functions within our power, what are referred to in **§23** as *ta prohairetika*; cf. 1. 4. 11, 1. 12. 27, 2. 1. 5, 10; *Ench.* 31. 4.

The essay concludes (**§§26–9**) with a brief dialogue between E and an unnamed figure who aspired to be one of the priests of Augustus in Nicopolis. E has moved from the philosophical *topos* of the tyrant, retailed anecdotes drawn from Nero's court in Rome, and finally adduces a local and contemporary parallel to his theme. On the functionaries of the Imperial cult, especially in the provinces, see Nock 1972: i. 348–56. As a priest of Augustus in one of the provincial towns, he would often be invoked as a witness in the execution of contracts and official papers; so Oldfather 1925:

i. 136–7, no doubt rightly. On this passage see Millar 1965: 147; Bosworth 1988: 118; Bowersock 1973: 182–3, with comment on 210. According to Reinhold (1988: 207), 'Greek intellectuals of the 2nd c AD were complacent about the imperial cult.' Cf. also Mattingly 1966: 96: 'Philosophy had its martyrs, but they were usually political, not religious.' There is little evidence, in other words, of protest by philosophers about emperor worship. But if there is no explicit criticism here, the tone of the whole passage is so negative that we can hardly suppose that E approved. In the context of a discourse devoted to criticizing excessive flattery, especially toward tyrants, the cult of the emperor (real-life tyrants in the case of Nero and Domitian) was bound to impress the reader as just another example.

CHAPTER 20

About Reason, How It Investigates Itself

This discourse opens with a theme that recurs elsewhere, concerning the self-examining power of reason. The style of argument, however, is unique. The chief interest, perhaps, attaches to the refutation of Epicurus at the end. Summary:

§§1–6 Reason is by nature self-correcting; it is therefore our duty to correct it.

§§7–12 We expend a disproportionate amount of effort to achieve certainty in things of less importance than reason.

§§13–19 Perfecting reason requires a lot of work—not to learn the principal doctrines of the philosophers, but to articulate their terms and fit them into a coherent scheme. This process also illustrates reason's ability to operate upon itself, as even Epicurus would have to admit.

In §§1–6 E employs an argument from arts (or crafts), to make the point that wisdom (*phronēsis*) is unique in its ability to scrutinize itself. Philosophical arguments involving the arts figured prominently in later Greek philosophy. One was mobilized in connection with the Stoic distinction between target and end (on which see comment ad 1. 15. 1–3). Opponents denied that the distinction was tenable, and devised a craft argument to give their criticism colour. So Carneades (at Cic. *Fin.* 5. 16) maintained that 'no science or art begins with itself; its subject-matter must always lie outside it. There is no need to advance the point with examples; for it is obvious that no art is occupied with itself; an art is one thing, its subject-matter another. Therefore, since medicine is the art of health, and navigation the art of sailing, and wisdom is the art of living, it follows that wisdom must also have something on which it is based and from which it derives.' For the purpose behind Carneades' argument, see Striker 1986: 202. A variant is found in Pyrrhonist sources, again in anti-Stoic contexts. Cf. SE *M* 11. 186: 'If wisdom is itself a good thing and deemed to be a science of good things, it will be a science of itself [the Stoic position]. This is absurd. For the things of which there is an art are conceived prior to the art.' For analysis of the passage see Bett 1997: 202–5. In positing a reflexive art, Stoics were drawing on their Socratic heritage; cf. Pl. *Chrm.* 165c–169c; *Euthd.* 291d–293a. E's argument here is similar to 1. 1. 1–6 and 1. 17. 1–3 above. The craft analogy properly applies to wisdom (*phronēsis*). To strengthen the conclusion he wants to draw from it, E makes the case in **§5** that reason (*logos*) is self-correcting. Cf. Galen, *PHP* 5. 3. 1: 'Reason is a collection of certain conceptions and preconceptions.' Stoics conceived of reason as both a critical faculty and a repository of memory and experience. E elsewhere speaks of the 'articulation' of preconceptions as the essential task of education (cf. 2. 11. 18, 2. 17. 7, 13). The process thereby demonstrates reason's ability to operate on itself. Cf. Marc. 11. 1. 1: 'The properties of the rational soul are as follows: it sees itself, articulates itself, makes it into the sort of thing it wants to be, itself reaps the fruit it bears.'

[**§2** *anomogenēs* is Meibom's easy correction of the reading *an omogenēs* in S.]

§6 assumes the standard Stoic definition of wisdom (*phronēsis*) as 'knowledge of things good, bad, and indifferent', or 'good, bad, or neither'; cf. DL 7. 92; SE *M* 9. 162, 11. 170. Because *phronēsis* is a particular kind of knowledge, it could be regarded as a kind of craft. In Stoicism all the virtues were forms of knowledge (DL 7. 93). The term 'good' was restricted to the virtues (DL 7. 102–3). Thus wisdom, a good, comes to be self-reflecting. Cf. Cic. *Fin.* 3. 24, in the context of comparing wisdom to other kinds of art: 'Wisdom is wholly directed toward itself, which is not the case with other arts.'

Having argued that there is an art or faculty, reason, that takes itself as its subject-matter, in **§7** E appends an *ergon* ('duty') argument. This effects a transition from the abstract opening argument, to a protreptic section. E maintains that the possession of this particular art or faculty entails the obligation to exercise it in precisely this way. For other *ergon* arguments in E, cf. 1. 6. 16 and 1. 16. 21 with comment. In **§§8–11** E supplements the *ergon* argument with an *a fortiori* argument intended to persuade us of the unfairness of treating casually our judgements about good and bad. For similar analogies involving the art of testing coinage, cf. 1. 7. 6–7, 2. 3. 2–4, 3. 3. 3–4, 4. 5. 15–18. The analogy, variously applied, was traditional; cf. Plut. *Comm. not.* 1063E with Cherniss ad loc. For a close parallel cf. Aristippus at DL 2. 78. **§12** contains another *a fortiori* argument to the same effect, for good measure. For the terms of comparison (also traditional) cf. 1. 11. 9–11 and 1. 18. 6.

Starting in **§13** E owns up to one respect in which the analogy to testing coinage (at least) is imprecise: viz. in the amount of application each art requires. (E uses the interlocutor in his usual way here, i.e. to introduce an objection that motivates a new argument.) The remark in **§14** that the 'the principal doctrine of the philosophers is itself very short' reflects a Cynic, anti-intellectual outlook. Cf. Antisthenes at DL 6. 11: 'Virtue resides in deeds, and does not stand in need of much argument or learning'; Demetrius the Cynic at Sen. *Ben.* 7. 1. 3: 'It is far more profitable for you to lay hold of a few precepts of wisdom, but those at the ready and in constant use, than to learn a great many, but not to have them handy.' Aristo the Stoic endorsed some such view; cf. comment ad 1. 25. 3–4; see Ioppolo 1980: 130–3. Later Stoics sometimes defend it, including E himself; cf., besides 1. 25. 3–4, 2. 9. 15: 'For who of us cannot give a philosophical discourse about goods and evils? Namely, that of things some are good, some evil, and some indifferent. Goods are virtues and things that partake of virtues; evils are the opposite; indifferents are wealth, health, and reputation.' Cf. also Muson. 1. 7–9, 60. 18–61. 2. But while allowing that ethics can be summarized in a few, key doctrines, E here makes the point that they need to be supported with a good deal of abstract argument. Even apparently simple doctrines involve terms and issues that need further explication, explication that depends on reason. Thus its primacy is established—and the traditional Stoic penchant for lengthy argument (Chrysippus was reputed to be the most prolific of ancient philosophers) defended against the superficial Cynic attitude to learning.

The doctrine that E ascribes to Zeno in §§14–15 is registered as *SVF* 1. 182. Von Arnim's typography indicates that he had little confidence in it as a direct citation, and I think he is right, *pace* Oldfather, Souilhé, and (apparently) Schenkl, to regard it as a paraphrase of Zeno's thought. It resembles too much E's own formulations of Stoic doctrine. On 'follow the gods', cf. 1. 12. 5 with comment.

'So what is god, and what is an impression?' (§16). On the importance later Greek philosophy attached to the definition of terms, cf. 1. 17. 10–12 with comment. '[W]hat is individual nature, and what is the nature of the whole?' This distinction, worked out in Stoic physics, was central to Stoic ethics; see Long 1974: 179–84.

In §§17–19 E employs against Epicurus a self-refutation argument of a kind often encountered in later Greek philosophy; see Burnyeat 1976. Epicurus himself used such arguments; cf. *KD* 23; LS 20C3–7; Lucr. 4. 469–70. That 'the good ought to lie in the flesh (*sarx*)' (§17) is a conclusion that may be derived from Epicurean statements about the pleasures of *sarx* (*KD* 18, 20; *Vatican Sayings* 33, 51; Plut. *Non posse suaviter* 1089D; *In Col.* 1125B), together with Epicurus' assertions that 'The root and origin of all good is pleasure of the stomach', and 'I cannot imagine the good if I set aside the pleasures of taste and sex and listening to music' (Athenaeus 546F; cf. Cic. *TD* 3. 41). But Epicurus also recognized a class of mental pleasures (DL 10. 132; Lucr. 2. 7–8), called wisdom the greatest good (DL 10. 132), and defined philosophy as 'an activity that secures the happy life through reason and discussions' (SE *PH* 11. 169). So E infers on the basis of Epicurus' own suppositions that reason, not flesh, is the instrument of happiness.

Clearly Epicurus acknowledged reason as the arbiter of how to conduct oneself. But he saw no contradiction in supposing that reason could also identify pleasure as the end. How successful is E in refuting him? His argument seems to rely on an ambiguous use of *prohēgoumenos* (translated 'dominant') in §§17 and 18. Admitting that reason determines our decisions does not mean that it is dominant in all respects; in particular, it does not entail that it should be our dominant concern. E's point, though, is practical rather than logical: we have to decide what to devote most time to, reason or the flesh. And, as he argues in **§§16–19**, satisfying reason takes a lot of time. Questions about the essence of god and nature, in particular and in general, are involved and protracted. Inevitably we will end up preoccupied with these questions rather than tending to the satisfaction of the flesh. E's argument has certain affinities with Plato's at *Rep.* 582d–e: 'That which is the instrument of judgement is the instrument, not of the lover of gain or the lover of honour, but of the lover of wisdom. . . . And since the tests are experience and wisdom and discussion, it follows . . . that the things approved by the lover of wisdom and discussion are most valid and true.' Because the 'lover of gain' is the person devoted to pleasure, Plato's point could be used against Epicurus' principled hedonism. This is essentially how E uses it, though he is concerned less with the authority of the person than with the soundness of the criterion he appeals to. E attacks Epicurus in the same manner at 2. 23. 20–2 and 3. 7. The frequency and vigour of his attacks on Epicurus are noted by Diogenes Laertius at 10. 6.

The description in **§17** of the flesh as 'the shell' has a Platonic flavour; cf. *Phd.* 87e. Strictly speaking, Epicurus located the good in the belly, not the flesh (cf. Plut. *Non posse suaviter* 1087D). But since the 'flesh' (*sarx*) was standard metonymy for sensuous experience, and flesh is on the surface, E is able to describe it as 'the shell' (*keluphos*). This (by analogy with a snail) leads to an argument about the unlikelihood of it being the seat of the good, the point being that 'the shell' exists for the sake of the thing it covers and protects, not the other way around.

On Epicurus' industriousness, adduced in **§19** in rather condescending fashion to prove that he was not the hedonist he professed to be, cf. DL 10. 26: 'Epicurus was a most productive author, and exceeded all others before him in the number of his writings.' See Usener 1887: 87–8 for other testimony to Epicurus' output. The close is meant to suggest that all rational enquiry, even into the motives behind Epicurus' industry, proves the superiority of reason in investigating such a problem. It also seems intended as another self-refutation, this time of Epicurean egoism. The point is developed at greater length in 1. 23.

CHAPTER 21

To Those who Want to be Admired

This discourse develops in brief the point that virtue is its own reward: look for no other. The lesson is intended for the young, who crave outside approval. For the thought cf. Plut. *Prof. in virt.* 80E–81B: 'The lover of virtue and wisdom, in the intercourse with virtue that comes through his actions, should keep his pride to himself and keep silent, feeling no need of eulogists and an audience. . . . Among young men who study philosophy, those who are most frivolous show assurance and a certain pose and gait, as well as a haughty and disdainful countenance toward everyone. But as they begin to be educated and to reap the fruits of learning, they lay aside their swagger and superficiality.' E develops the point at length in 3. 23; cf. also 3. 15. 13 for the kind of attitude towards others he discourages here.

'[S]tation' in **§1** is Greek *stasis*. Cf. *Ench.* 48: 'The station (*stasis*) and character of a layman is never to expect help or harm from himself, but from outside. The station and character of a philosopher is to expect help or harm only from himself. Signs of one making progress are that . . . he has suspended desire, and transferred aversion only to the things within our power that are contrary to nature. He uses qualified impulse toward everything. If he seems to be ignorant or a fool, he doesn't care.' E particularly warns against expertise in logic as grounds for ostentation; cf. 1. 26. 9, 2. 19. 8–10.

§2 (and *Ench.* 48, quoted above) alludes to E's three *topoi*; cf. 1. 4. 1–2 with comment. 'Purpose' (*prothesis*) and 'design' (*epibolē*) were species of impulse (*hormē*) in Stoic psychology; see Inwood 1985: 231–3.

The Stoic in training is in the habit of calling laymen mad (**§4**), because in Stoic ethics anyone who was not wise was automatically mad; cf. Alex. *De Fato* 199. 17; Stob. 2. 68. 18. For the thought compare Sen. *Ep.* 52. 11: 'Why are you delighted to be praised by men whom you yourself cannot praise?'

CHAPTER 22

Concerning Preconceptions

This chapter relates to an important topic in Hellenistic epistemology. For modern discussions pertaining to the Stoics see Bonhöffer 1890: 187–232; Sandbach 1930; Pohlenz 1964: i. 56–9 and ii. 33–5; Todd 1973; Striker 1974: 90–102; Schofield 1980; Obbink 1992. LS 40S excerpts §§1–3 and 9–10 of the present discourse. The topic is explored again at 2. 11 and 2. 17. For further Stoic testimonia see Hülser frs. 300–21.

The subject was involved and provoked controversy. In E's case we find anomalous features that call for special comment, features that can plausibly be read as responding to the criticism this doctrine had aroused. As usual, his terminology and much of his treatment are within the Stoic tradition. Details, however, are unique. As Long and Sedley (1. 253) write: 'Epictetus tries to retain community of preconceptions by referring disagreement to their application to particulars. For this quite promising move to work, the scope and content of preconceptions would need to be far more restricted than the Stoics were willing to admit. On this aspect of the debate over criteria of truth, the sceptics can be judged to have carried the day.' Sceptics had challenged the existence of a consensus of opinion, pointing out that philosophers cannot agree on anything, and producing other counter-arguments besides (cf. SE *M* 8. 331–2; *PH* 1. 89, 211; Cic. *ND* 1. 62).

It is reasonable to suppose that it was precisely searching criticism from Sceptics, among others, that motivated E to a measure of retrenchment in this regard. In 2. 11, also devoted to the subject of preconceptions, he writes: 'Here is the beginning of philosophy: a recognition of the conflict in the opinions of men, and a search for the origin of that conflict, and a condemnation of mere opinion, together with scepticism toward it' (§13). Inasmuch as he makes dissonance, rather than shared belief, the starting-point of his philosophy, E's attitude seems Sceptic in inspiration (cf. DL 4. 28, 9. 78; SE *PH* 1. 32, 165; Cic. *Ac.* 2. 118–19, 129–34; see Barnes 1990*d*: 1–35). Not that he is content to remain there. As Long and Sedley point out, E defines preconceptions more narrowly than earlier Stoics had done, but his ultimate purpose is to save community of belief by making it a smaller target.

E does two things that are new. First, as Stoic appeals to preconceptions had been overly ambitious, E elects not to gloss the fact of disagreement, but to deflect it, away from conceptions, on to particulars. 'Where . . . does conflict arise? (§1) In applying preconceptions to particular cases' (§2). This 'quite promising move' not only saves consensus (albeit on a more modest scale), it serves to redefine education: 'What, then, does it mean to get an education? It means learning to apply natural preconceptions to particular cases in accordance with nature' (§9). E elsewhere calls this process the 'articulation' (*diarthrōsis*) of preconceptions; cf. 2. 11. 18, 2. 17. 7. Now, 'articulation' had figured in early Stoicism, in connection with things like ethical conceptions (or preconceptions) such as 'the good'; cf. DL 7. 199; Plut. *Comm. not.* 1059C. E's use is in line with this. But he extends 'articulation' to the level of particulars, where he says disagreement occurs: 'Who among us does not use the words "good" and "bad"? . . . For who among us does not have a preconception of each? But is it articulated and complete? . . . Doesn't one man apply his preconception of the good to wealth, another to pleasure, another to health? In brief, if all of us who use these words possess no mere empty knowledge of each, and do not need to practice the articulation of our preconceptions, why do we disagree, why fight, why blame one another?' (2. 17. 10–13). E then identifies the process of articulation as the act of associating preconceptions with particular instances.

Second, as education becomes a matter of applying universal terms to particulars, attention shifts from how preconceptions are acquired (the focus of earlier discussions, e.g. LS 39C–E) to how they are applied. Preconceptions themselves are taken for granted. That was true for earlier Stoics in so far as they treated preconceptions as part of normal human development. But E goes further. He sometimes describes them as innate: 'We come into the world without an innate conception of a right-angled triangle, or of a quarter-tone or a half-tone; but we learn about these through systematic instruction, and for this reason those who have no knowledge of them do not imagine that they do. But who has ever come into the world without an innate concept of what is good and evil, honourable and base, appropriate and inappropriate, what happiness and misery are, what is fitting and incumbent upon us, and what we ought to do and not do? Thus we all make use of these terms and try to apply our preconceptions to particular cases' (2. 11. 1–4).

Sandbach (1930: 49) has suggested that E reflects the syncretism of his day in adopting a Platonic belief in innate ideas. (Cf. Boeth. *Cons.* 5. M4; Philo, *Prob.* 78; and Aug. *CD* 8. 7, for rejection of these by the majority of Stoics.) The suggestion that preconceptions exist apart from and prior to particulars does hint at a partial retreat from traditional Stoic empiricism. But E never goes so far as to refer to Forms or recollection (*anamnēsis*), the way others did in grafting Platonic doctrine on to the terms *prolēpsis* and (*koinai*) *ennoiai*: see Cherniss ad Plut. *Plat. quaest.* 1000E; Whitaker 1987: 114–17. And the question of whether preconceptions appear at birth, in the fourteenth year, or, as some sources report, the seventh (Aet. 4. 11. 4), is not especially important. We have to interpret E's words in light of the traditional Stoic belief in innate seeds of virtue. To associate these with preconceptions is understandable, since Stoics identified character with mind or its contents. Cf. 3. 6. 8: 'There are some things which men who are not entirely perverted perceive in accordance with the common impulses (*aphormai*).' As Bonhöffer (1890: 224) remarks, 'Under the common impulses here we should in essence understand the common conceptions.' Cf. Alex. *Probl. eth.* 129. 10–12: 'Those who have not been completely perverted, but retain the common and natural notions, do not lack understanding of better things.' Cf. also Cic. *Fin.* 2. 20–1, a Stoic account of moral development that makes possession of the concept 'good' a key component.

The discourse may be analysed thus:

§§1–8 All men share preconceptions like 'the just', and agree on their definition. Where they disagree is in applying such preconceptions to particulars, and in deciding what things, for instance, are just. Examples given from ethnology and myth.

§§9–16 E proceeds to apply the ethical preconception 'good', arguing for the paradoxical, but standard Stoic, view that virtue alone qualifies.

§§17–21 A coda anticipating the prejudice on the part of the unphilosophical against such paradoxical views.

As E does in **§§1–3**, earlier Stoics had appealed to the preconception of good and bad in their ethics; cf. SE *M* 11. 22: 'The Stoics, sticking fast to the common conceptions, define the good as follows: "Good is benefit or not other than benefit".' Our passage is similar in upholding moral preconceptions as a point of departure: if not as self-evident truths, then as propositions that need only be clearly articulated to command assent. What does E mean in §1, that 'Preconception does not conflict with preconception'? The point recalls what Epicurus says about sensations, that one cannot refute another; cf. DL 10. 31–2, 146. Both are making an important claim for their value as criteria of truth. In E's case there is an ambiguity, however. Does he mean (1) that X's preconception of *a* does not conflict with X's preconception of *b*, or (2) that X's preconception of *a* does not conflict with Y's preconception of *b*?

The context supports the latter interpretation. Talk of common conceptions, or, as here, preconceptions, alerts us to an argument from widely held belief (cf. Plut. *Comm. not.* 1058E–F, 1060A). Consensus arguments were common in Greek philosophy; but they were made a corner-stone of the Stoic system, and a criterion of truth (LS 48C5). Preconceptions here include not only ethical abstractions like good and bad, but the common understanding of these terms, their definition. Thus, 'who of us does not assume that the good is beneficial and choiceworthy, and in all cases to be strived after and pursued? Who of us does not assume that justice is fair and appropriate?' (§1). E is referring to the sorts of identity statements that functioned as axioms in Stoic ethics. Cf. DL 7. 98: 'All good is expedient, necessary, useful, serviceable, beautiful, advantageous, choiceworthy and just.' Stoics took it that such propositions were uncontroversial. But from these ethical postulates they were able to derive paradoxes such as the doctrine that only virtue is good. In §12 E indicates that this is where disagreement arises.

The distinction in §2 between universals and particulars is expressed in similar terms at *SVF* 2. 224. For the phrase *epi merous* used of particulars, cf. Arist. *EN* 1107a29–31; *Met.* 359b31; Alcin. *Epit.* 6. 1. '[A]ssume' (in §1) is *tithenai*, another technical term. E is laying down here what is non-controversial in the manner of Aristotle with his *endoxa* ('reputable opinions'), and because he has taken the measure of Sceptic criticism, he avoids the difficulties in which earlier Stoics became involved; he relieves preconceptions of some of their doctrinal load. For the sense of this passage cf. 4. 1. 43–5.

That humans, and humans only, have preconceptions of 'the good', 'the just', etc. was an old and far-reaching idea. Cf. Arist.

Pol. 1253a15–17: 'It is a characteristic of man that he alone has a sense of good and evil, of just and unjust, and the like.' Stoics, like Aristotle, made this cognitive capacity the foundation of society and the virtues: cf. Cic. *Fin.* 3. 20–1, 5. 59; Dio Chrys. 7. 138.

The distinction between someone who is brave and one who is crazy, which forms the basis of the putative debate in §3, alludes to the fact that rashness or insanity can pass for courage. Socrates explores the idea at Pl. *Prot.* 350b–c, 351a; *Laches* 197b.

In §4 we find examples drawn from ethnology. These are common in Sceptic sources, and another reason to suppose that E's treatment of this topic was formulated in response to Sceptic attacks on the Stoic use of common notions. Cf. SE *PH* 3. 223: 'A Jew or an Egyptian priest would sooner die than eat swine's flesh; by a Libyan it is regarded as most impious to eat mutton, by some of the Syrians to eat a dove, and by others to eat sacrificial victims.' In the revival of Pyrrhonism, the juxtaposition of *ethē* or *nomoi* to discredit one another constituted Aenesidemus' Tenth Mode; cf. SE *PH* 1. 37, 145; see Annas and Barnes 1985: 151–71. This served as an attack on *sunētheia* (SE *PH* 1. 146), an occasional synonym of *prolēpsis* in the sense of shared belief: cf. Plut. *Comm. not.* 1084B. E concedes the point, but seeks to salvage the doctrine by confining the damage to particulars. With this section cf. 1. 11. 12, 2. 11. 15.

A taboo on pork prevailed in the Roman province of Syria (Lucian, *Dea Syr.* 54) and Egypt (Hdt. 2. 47; Plut. *Is. et Os.* 353F). At *St. rep.* 1051E Plutarch cites the views of 'Jews and Syrians' as evidence that there was no common belief 'about gods'. This criticism had especial force, since advocates of common belief traditionally appealed to shared belief about the gods (cf. Cic. *ND* 2. 5, 13; see LS 1. 253, Schofield 1980). But Plutarch's counter-examples demonstrate the danger of getting specific as to details, and E is shrewd to cite them for difference rather than unanimity.

In §§5–8 E demonstrates his point with reference to the dispute between Achilles and Agamemnon that opens the *Iliad*. On this section see 1. 28. 13 with comment. The admissions elicited from Achilles and Agamemnon appear trivial. That is the point. E shows how large-scale conflict can be traced or reduced to simple, innocent breakdowns in reason about particulars—and particulars are always trivial in comparison with general principles, about which most everyone agrees. They nevertheless have far-reaching consequences,

demonstrating in stark terms the need of a standard; see comment
ad 1. 28. 28.

With the definition of education in **§9**, cf. 1. 2. 6, 4. 5. 7; *Ench.* 5.
In **§§9–16** E proceeds to the task of applying particulars to the
general preconception of the good. He argues that the class of good
things is coextensive with the class of things in our power. Stoics
in general restricted the scope of the word 'good' to virtue; for texts
and comment on this fundamental point see LS 60. They with-
held the designation 'good' from advantages such as health, on the
grounds that they were not in all circumstances beneficial. In particular, they denied the term to bodily states and externals; cf. SE
PH 3. 181. E's list here assumes the traditional Greek tripartite
division of goods; for a fuller version of the argument cf. Cic. *TD*
5. 40–6. E puts a twist on the tradition by introducing the notion of
what is in our power (*eph' hēmin*), a category of thought borrowed
from discussions of free will (see on 1. 1). The upshot is that all
the resources needed to attain happiness, viz. 'the good', are in our
control.

In **§§13–16** E demonstrates how the sort of selfishness he sanctions, involving restriction of the good to the things in our power,
preserves piety and social cohesion, whereas any other value system
tends to subvert them. This is a candid argument from consequences; cf. 2. 22. 17, and see Bonhöffer 1894: 5. It may be paraphrased
thus: things that are good should be productive of happiness, and
consistent with our thoughts about god; but locating the good outside virtue leads to wars and irreligion; therefore 'good' must be
restricted to 'things within our power'. E is typically blunt: 'If it is
in my interest to have land, it is my interest to steal it from my
neighbour.' This is a sample of his *Realphilosophie*, whose force
depends on its frank eudaimonism. It reflects the utilitarian mind-
set among Stoics generally, who defined 'the good' in terms of
'benefit'. On the cult of Fever, see comment on 1. 19. 6. Penalties
for the crime of stealing clothes from a public bath are mandated in
the *Digest of Roman Law* 47. 17. On this whole section, including
the cult titles of Zeus, cf. 1. 19. 11–15 and comment.

§§17–21 The attention to detail in the concluding vignette is
noteworthy. The old man's many gold rings are a badge of world-
liness, but lend an air of fatuity. See M. Smith ad Petronius 32,
noting that 'in the Empire the wearing of rings reached ridiculous

extremes'. The whole scene seems to dramatize the attitude which
Callicles represents in the *Gorgias* (484c–486d), deprecating flight
from the world for the sake of philosophy. At 1. 26. 5 E proposes a
defence to offer parents who are upset because their children, his
students, consort with philosophers; cf. Muson. 86. 18–87. 18.

'The man who truly philosophizes and is in travail of thought'
(**§17**) employs a Platonic metaphor (cf. *Tht.* 148e, 210b; Plut. *Plat.
quaest.* 999C–1000E; see Vlastos 1994: 5 n. 19). Ignorance of what
is good and bad is tantamount to madness; for the metaphor, or
analogy, in **§18**, cf. Marc. 11. 38 (= E fr. 28). The sense of the
riposte in **§20** is that if, as the old man insists, the young man
knows what he is doing better than philosophers, then he must
know what he is doing in resorting to them, and therefore should
not be reproached for doing it; cf. 1. 26. 5–7.

CHAPTER 23

Against Epicurus

The general thrust is clear enough, but this chapter is obscure
in details owing to a corrupt text and more than usually elliptical
expression. E tries to convict Epicurus of being inconsistent on the
score of man's sociability. §§1–3, §5, the first part of §6, and §7, are
collectively registered as Epicurus fr. 525 Usener. For E's hostility
to Epicurus, besides 1. 20. 17–19 and the present discourse, cf. 3.
24. 38 and DL 10. 6: 'Epictetus calls him a spokesman for immoral-
ity and abuses him mightily.'

Analysis:

§§1–6 Epicurus belies his doctrine that man is not by nature social
when he warns his followers against social activities that will involve
them in grief.

§§7–8 Not even the beasts engage in the kind of anti-social behaviour that Epicurean doctrines promote.

§§9–10 Common sense and experience are enough to prove that
parental love is natural.

That 'we are by nature social (*koinōnikoi*)' (**§1**) is a characteristically
Stoic claim; see Bonhöffer 1894: 118 n. 70 for many citations. It is

not a view Epicurus shared; he did not regard society as 'natural', but artificial, the product of the social contract. Section 2. 20. 6–7 (= fr. 523 Usener) makes it clear that this is the position E ascribed to him: 'For what does [Epicurus] say? "Be not deceived, not led astray, nor mistaken, men: there is no natural society (*koinōnia*) among rational animals, believe me. Those who say otherwise trick and deceive you." ' The evidence that E cites to prove that Epicurus nevertheless agreed, *malgré lui*, that man was by nature social, comes in **§§3–6** below, by way of his tacit admission that the concern for others inherent in familial and political relationships can cause pain. And they would not cause pain if, in fact, we were by nature asocial creatures, indifferent to the welfare of others.

As 1. 20. 17 shows, *keluphos* in **§1** (here translated 'husk') is E's contemptuous designation for the body. It is like his other term, 'corpse' (on which cf. 1. 19. 9, with comment), in implying that the body is lifeless, while the soul is the true self. 'Placed our good in the husk' is E's way of saying that Epicurus was a sensual hedonist. The claim that 'having once placed our good in the husk, he is no longer able to say anything else' is important, because it provides the basis for E's inference that Epicurus warned against incurring family and political obligations because they bring pain or distress. In designating pleasure as 'the good', Epicurus had to justify all action by this criterion. E endorses the basic principle in **§2** (and elaborates it at 3. 3. 5–10 and 4. 5. 30–3.) Epicurus could have discouraged politics and child rearing simply on the grounds that they are unnatural for man, just as Stoics encouraged them on the contrary assumption. But this would not give E what he needs for his argument. He wants to convict Epicurus out of his own mouth, as it were, making his case against him stronger. So E argues in **§§3–6** that Epicurus deters us from these entanglements to spare us the pain, but he does not then draw the proper consequence: viz. that concern for others is natural. He fails to draw this consequence because of his identification of the good with the interests of one's own body ('husk'), which, unlike the soul, cannot be improved by other-concern.

[In **§3** I prefer the received reading *huponoētikoi* ('suspicious') to Wolf's emendation, *eti koinōnikoi* ('still social'), adopted by Old-father. What we are suspicious of is spelled out in the rest of §3 and §4: what motivated Epicurus, a wise man in his own conceit, to discourage other wise men from raising children when he raised one (Mouse) himself. I also think we can do without the changes proposed by Souilhé in the text and punctuation of this section. In **§4**, however, I would alter *empiptei* ('does he come to grief') to *empipteis* ('do you come to grief'). An abrupt change from the second to the third person in referring to Epicurus takes place somewhere in §§4–5, and I think the sense improved if we assume it happens here. My translation also assumes a change at the end of §4 from *autou* to *autōi* ('to him').]

That 'Mouse' in **§4** is a proper name was first recognized by Bentley; see Oldfather 1921: 45–6. Mouse is mentioned at DL 10. 10 and 21, where we learn that he was manumitted under the terms of Epicurus' will.

Before going further, we must face a doxographical problem. Is E right that Epicurus opposed the raising of children? At DL 10. 119 the received text reads: 'And indeed the wise man will both marry and raise children, as Epicurus says in the *Problems* and in his work *On Nature*. But sometimes, according to the circumstances of life, he will marry.' Obviously the text is corrupt, leading most editors to emend the first sentence in such a way as to actually discourage marriage and child rearing for the wise man; see Chilton 1960 and Brennan 1996 for discussion. This passage has been used to support the change; cf. also 3. 7. 19 (also part of fr. 525 Usener), where E ascribes to Epicurus a similar opinion as here: 'In god's name, can you imagine an Epicurean state? "I won't marry." "Nor I. For one should not marry, nor raise children."' The Christian authors Clement, Lactantius, and Theodoret (fr. 526 Usener) also report that Epicurus was against child rearing. According to Seneca (fr. 45 Haas), 'Epicurus says that it is rare that the wise man will consent to marry because marriage involves many inconveniences.' And one of those inconveniences would no doubt be children.

So far, then, E seems to represent Epicurean doctrine fairly. It might be objected that Epicurus condemned marriage and children only for the wise man. But the wise man undoubtedly served as a model for others; cf. how he is apparently equated with 'the man of sense' in §6 below. In any case, E is scrupulous, indeed eager, to preserve this qualification in reporting Epicurus' view in §3, since it enables him to ask why, then, Epicurus himself raised Mouse as his child, if he thought that wise men (like himself, presumably) should not raise them. This is supposed to be another way Epicurus contradicts himself.

A more serious objection is that Epicurus seems to have admitted instances when the wise man would marry, 'according to the circumstances of life'. These circumstances are not spelled out in our sources, but the important point is that, if he did marry, he would probably raise children. Brennan also draws attention to passages in Epicurus' will (DL 10. 16–21) that enjoin members of his school to look after various children until they come of age—again, as Epicurus apparently looked after Mouse. Moreover, Epicurus had an explanation for child rearing that fitted in with his theory of society as a whole, i.e. his contractual theory. He argued that people who raise children act from selfish motives, because children can help them in their work, or support them in their old age. Cf. Plut. *De Amore prolis* 495A (= fr. 527 Usener): 'In our theatres men applaud the verse of the poet who said, "Who loves his fellow man for pay?" And yet, according to Epicurus, it is for recompense that a father loves his son, a mother her child, children their parents.' This could provide an Epicurean with a reason to bring up a child.

Does E, then, distort Epicurus' position on child rearing? I hardly think so. If he does, then so do the Christian authors cited earlier. But their agreement suggests that Epicurus did proclaim a universal ban on child rearing in his treatises, as Brennan (1996: 350) likewise concludes. If he hedged or qualified the doctrine elsewhere, these putative prohibitions left him open to misunderstanding. But whatever exceptions he admitted, Epicurus still did not believe that parental love was natural. That is the important point, as it is the doctrine E challenges in §3: 'How then are we suspicious, if we have no natural affection for children?' That Epicurus did not regard love for offspring as natural is well established. It is the testimony of Demetrius of Laconia, PHerc 1012 cols. 66–8; see Puglia 182–3, 297–302. Cf. Plut. *In Col.* 1123A (= fr. 528 Usener): 'Do you [Epicureans] not dismiss the instinctive love of parents for their offspring, a fact accepted by all?' According to Lactantius (*Divin. instit.* 3. 17. 5 (= fr. 529 Usener)), the lack of natural affection was mutual: 'Epicurus infamously claims that there is no bond of nature toward parents.' So the fact that most people, including even the sage in some circumstances, would engage in a practice that Epicurus otherwise deprecates is not so important as the fact that, like all social attachments, it is normally undertaken for reasons of policy, not from natural instinct. That is the view which E fairly credits Epicurus with and tries to prove that Epicurus himself unwittingly discredits. Lucretius at 5. 1013–23 purports to describe the process whereby mankind's finer feelings developed from experience of family life, but I think it is too brief and poetic an account to be considered a significant addition to Epicurean views on parent–child relations.

In §6 the argument shifts ground. This section assumes the Epicurean ban on politics. Cf. DL 10. 119: 'The wise man will not take part in politics, as is stated in the first book *On Life*'; cf. *Vatican Sayings*, 58. Although this view is more reliably attested for Epicurus than the ban on child rearing, Long (1986) argues that the situation is complex here too. Still, it is the attitude he was generally identified with. E then implies that he discourages participation in politics for the same reason that he warns against raising a family: because naturally we will be induced to make sacrifices for others, which is painful. Stoics, for their part, definitely supported child rearing and involvement in politics. Cf. DL 7. 121: 'The Stoics say that the wise man will take part in politics, if nothing hinders him . . . He will also marry, as Zeno says in his *Republic*, and beget children.' Marriage and politics were associated in the Stoic mind, since the family was supposed to be the corner-stone of society; cf. Cic. *Off.* 1. 54; Muson. 73. 8–74. 1.

The further remark in §6 about flies is obscure. Like Oldfather, I take it to mean that it is possible to live among one's fellow creatures without any sense of community, but that is the exception, not the rule. Flies do not bestow any care on their young, and show no sign of co-operating among themselves, although they are not solitary animals but are often seen together. So it is just possible to imagine being part of a community while still remaining aloof from one's kind—but, for a human being, neither natural nor likely. Wolf thought we were to imagine that the sentence is spoken by Epicurus, who compares being involved in politics with being surrounded by bothersome flies. This seems ruled out by the start of §7, 'But as if [Epicurus] did not know these things . . .', where what follows clearly contradicts what went immediately before. There is even less to be said for Schweighäuser's suggestion that abstention from politics in the Epicurean manner leaves one free to do nothing but catch flies all day!

[Oldfather and Souilhé are surely right to adopt Upton's proposed change from the aorist *politeusasthai* to the future *politeusesthai* in §6, a reading supported by comparison with DL 10. 119.]

A final question to raise in judging the justice of E's remarks is whether Epicurus dissuaded his followers from politics and parenthood for the reason given: i.e. for the sake of the 'husk'. We saw that identifying the good with the 'husk' means identifying it with bodily pleasure. Epicurus said (DL 10. 128) that happiness consisted in *ataraxia*, freedom from disturbance. And he clearly advised against fathering a family and taking part in politics on that basis. He also said that *ataraxia* was synonomous with pleasure: 'When we say that pleasure is the end, we do not mean the pleasures of the dissipated . . . , but freedom from pain in the body and from disturbance in the soul' (DL 10. 131). So E is in general right that Epicurus' social doctrines are dictated by his hedonism. But is he right to reduce matters to the 'husk': i.e. the pleasures of the body? After all, E himself says that Epicurus feared that a father 'may be involved in sorrow' (§3), and the word for sorrow, *lupē*, was standard for mental anguish, not physical pain. Moreover, as we saw, Epicurus placed freedom from disturbance in the soul alongside freedom from physical pain as the constitutents of pleasure; see also the comment ad 1. 20. 17–19 for his attention to mental pleasures. But it was a standard criticism of Epicurus that he makes mental pains and pleasures ultimately dependent on bodily ones (frs. 429–39 Usener). E undoubtedly assumes this criticism in locating the Epicurean good in the 'husk'.

'But a sheep does not desert its own offspring, nor a wolf; and does a man desert his?' With §7 cf. Plut. *De Amore prolis* 495A for a similar style of attack on Epicurus. In §8 E must mean that we would actually be more foolish than sheep, and more savage than wolves, if we abandoned our children. But since sheep were standard symbols of foolishness, as wolves were of savagery, he cites them here. There is no evidence that Epicurus sanctioned the abandonment of children. 'Let us not raise children' in §7 involves a subtle distortion in so far as it purports to represent him accurately. The verb, *anhaireō*, can mean to 'raise' an infant in the sense of picking it up and formally acknowledging it as one's own, rather than deserting it. E is drawing the most provoking implication he can from Epicurus' twin doctrines that love between parent and offspring was not natural, and that child rearing was improvident. What Epicurus seems to have discouraged for the wise man was simply procreation (although he extolled the pleasures of sex), on the assumption that the parent would then have to care for the child. But E takes his advice not to raise children in close conjunction with his denial of paternal love, to infer that he actually approved of abandoning children. In the absence of any explicit testimony to this effect, this goes too far.

[I accept Schenkl's emendation of *ho* to *hōs* at the start of §7.]

§9 makes explicit the point implied in §4 above, that parents' affection for their children is innate. §10 restates the point with a sardonic jest.

CHAPTER 24

How We should Struggle with Circumstances

This discourse shows E's interest in the Cynics. It has much in common with 3. 22, 'On Cynicism'. Together they attest to a revival of interest in Cynicism in the early Empire. This development is also evident in the work of Seneca, who admired the contemporary Cynic philosopher Demetrius. For an overview of the neo-Cynic movement, see Reale 1989: 145–63.

Stylistically, the diatribe is remarkable for its wealth of metaphors applied to the life of man. It may be analysed thus:

§§1–5 Difficult circumstances should be looked upon as tests of one's character.

§§6–10 They cannot defeat us. Diogenes had tested the limits of hardship, and lived to tell about it—not only lived, but thrived, stronger for the experience.

§§11–13 Like Diogenes, we can survive with few possessions, and should even be prepared to sacrifice our body if necessary. This readiness brings a new freedom.

§§14–18 The more one has, the more one has to lose. The rich and powerful are tragic figures by definition.

§§19–20 If a circumstance really does prove unbearable, there is always the option of escape through suicide.

With §1 compare Proclus, *In Tim.* 18c Schneider (*SVF* 3. 206): 'The Stoics often say, "Give a circumstance and you get the man."' This presupposition underlies many of Seneca's arguments in *Cons.*

CHAPTER 24   201

sap. and *Prov.*: see comment ad 1. 6. 36. For life as an Olympic contest (§§1–2) see Cherniss ad Plut. *De Facie* 943D, who assigns the metaphor to Plato originally. For its use by Roman Stoics see Billerbeck 1978 ad 3. 22. 56.

[The translation in §1 assumes Wolf's emendation of *beblēken* to *sumbeblēken* ('matched'). This is also adopted by Schenkl and Oldfather.]

In §§3–5 E switches to the metaphor of life as a term of military service, also traditional; see Rutherford 1989: 240–1. The spy metaphor enhances the image, since spies performed the most dangerous military duty; cf. 3. 22. 24–5. Seneca writes: 'Why does god visit bad health, and loss of those dear to them, and other troubles on the best people? Because in the army the most dangerous tasks are assigned to the bravest soldiers. . . . No one who goes out on a dangerous mission says, "The commander has mistreated me," but "He has thought well of me"' (*Prov.* 4. 7–8). E dispatches the spy to Rome because Rome offered the most temptations (such as are referred to at 1. 10), and the most trials, including exile (§4) and ill repute (§6)—over and above the generic circumstances of poverty and death.

[In §3 I have, with Souilhé, accepted Upton's change of *ge* to *se*.]

The 'cowardly spy' in §3 is wrong on several counts. In the Stoic dispensation, death, exile, and the rest are not evils, because they are not moral wrongs. Cf. 2. 19. 13: 'Of things some are good, some are bad, some indifferent. The virtues and everything that shares in them are good, while vices and everything that shares in vice are evil, and what falls in between these, namely wealth, health, life, death, pleasures, and pain, are indifferent.' Cf. Sen. *Ep.* 82. 14: 'Day restores light, night steals it away. Thus it is with the things we call indifferent and "middle", like riches, strength, beauty, titles, kingship, and their opposites: death, exile, ill health, pain, and all such things, the fear of which upsets us more or less. It is virtue or vice that bestows on them the name of good or evil.'

§§6–9: On E as a source for our knowledge of Diogenes the Cynic, see Goulet-Cazé 1986: 12, citing the principal passages, including this one. That the Cynics made light of death, and ill repute (§6), is also attested at DL 6. 11, 68 and Cic. *TD* 1. 104. As regards pain and pleasure (*ponos* and *hēdonē* in §7), they held an attitude directly opposed to that of most people. Cf. DL 6. 2–3: 'Antisthenes demonstrated that *ponos* is a good thing by instancing

Heracles and Cyrus. . . . He would repeatedly say, "I would rather go mad than feel pleasure."' This was not inconsistent with Stoicism, although Stoics, unlike Cynics, certainly did not regard pleasure as evil, or pain as good; cf. 1. 2. 16, and see comment ad 1. 6. 32–6. They merely held that pleasure was produced by, and pain should be endured for the sake of, the one true good, virtue; cf. DL 7. 85–6; Cic. *Fin.* 2. 69; Sen. *Ep.* 121. 7–8; Philo, *De Sacrif.* 115 (= *SVF* 3. 505).

'[S]imply clothed' in **§7** is Greek *gumnos*, which does not have to mean 'naked' (*pace* most translators). Cynic asceticism included poverty, simple dress, and rude sleeping arrangements. Cf. DL 6. 104: 'They hold that we should live frugally, eating for nourishment only, and wearing a single garment. They despise wealth, fame, and high birth. Some, like Diogenes, are vegetarians and drink cold water only, and are content with chance shelters or tubs [for sleeping].' Most Stoics frowned on this sort of ironic ostentation. Cf. 3. 12. 1: 'Training should not be in things that are unnatural or fantastic, for in that case we philosophers will be no better than magic-men'; Sen. *Ep.* 5. 2–3: 'Rough attire, shaggy hair and beard, open scorn of silver dishes, a couch on the bare earth, and other such perverted forms of self-display, should be avoided. . . . Inwardly we ought to be different in all respects, but outwardly we should conform to society. Let your toga be neither too fine, nor too frayed.' E may appear to differ, but he is not actually advocating Diogenes' harsh regimen. He only suggests that we be prepared to endure the like if circumstances dictate, and not regard it as evil—advice all quite consistent with traditional Stoicism. Diogenes is a 'spy' because he has scouted out the extremes of hardship, and is in a position to report that nothing there is beyond endurance. But we are under no obligation to imitate him. On the comparison of Cynics to spies or scouts, see discussion by Giannantoni 1990: iv. 507–12; and parallels at V B 27 Giannantoni.

[In **§7** I read *gumnon einai*, a later correction in S of *gumnasion einai*, also advocated by Souilhé.]

'[F]reedom' (*eleutheria* in **§8**) was a watchword of the Cynic school; cf. 3. 24. 67, 4. 1. 152; DL 6. 71. It denoted freedom from convention and external encumbrances, as well as freedom of speech. Concerning Diogenes' 'gleaming, well-knit little body', cf. DL 6. 81: 'Athenedorus says he always had a gleaming body owing to his use of unguents'; Dio Chrys. 6. 8: 'Diogenes was not neglectful of his body as certain foolish people thought. When they saw him often shivering and living in the open air and going thirsty, they imagined that he was careless of his health and life, whereas this rigorous regime gave him better health than those who were always stuffing themselves, better than those who stayed indoors and never experienced hot or cold.' Cf. further E 3. 22. 88, 4. 8. 31; Julian 194D–195A. It is probably unnecessary to point out that these notices, written centuries after Diogenes' death, have no documentary value. They are part of a revisionist effort to rescue Cynicism's reputation by bringing it more into line with traditional Hellenic values. Stoics, for their part, certainly approved of physical culture; cf. DL 7. 123: 'The wise man will submit to training to enhance his body's endurance.' Muson. 25. 6–8 recommends that we inure ourselves to 'cold and heat, thirst and hunger, a meagre diet and a hard bed, abstention from pleasure and endurance of toil'; see Goulet-Cazé 1986: 185–8. The 'oil flask and wallet' in **§11** sound like Cynic gear (cf. DL 6. 13; Billerbeck 1978 ad 3. 22. 88), but it is probably just a matter of travelling light.

With **§§11–14** cf. 1. 1. 21–5 with comment. In **§12–13** the person giving the orders is indeed supposed to be the emperor, but *pace* Starr (1949: 24), I don't think we need to assume that the emperor is Domitian (whom E names only once, at 2. 7. 8). By this time the emperor had been identified with the tyrant of philosophical tradition. And although the trend may have been encouraged by the example of Domitian, E intended his lessons to be timeless. For this style of passage, where the victim exasperates the tyrant with his equanimity, cf. 1. 1. 22–5, and see MacMullen 1966: 72–3. For the comparison with the inn in **§14** cf. the comparison of life to a stopover at an inn at 3. 23. 36–7; *Ench.* 11; Plut. *De Exilio* 607D.

Starting in **§15** there is a new metaphor, also traditional, comparing life to a drama. It flourished among the Stoics; see Ioppolo 1980: 197–202; Rosenmeyer 1989: 47: 'Stoicism prompts theatrical tropes.' And since drama for the Greeks mainly meant tragedy, E can make the point that the protagonists, royalty for the most part, were regularly ruined by the last act; hence their (fleeting) prosperity should not be envied. This, at least, may have had contemporary relevance in view of the tragic ends of Caligula, Nero, and Domitian. The chorus consisted of citizens of middle estate who survive to comment on the great man's fall. 'Deck the halls' in **§16** is from a choral ode of an unknown play; it is registered as *Fragmenta*

Tragica Adespota 87 Nauck. The next quotation is *Oedipus Rex*, line 1390; Marcus also cites it at 11. 6. 1.

Calling a king 'Slave' (**§17**) was justified by Stoic standards; cf. DL 7. 121–2. With **§19** compare the act of redescription at 1. 12. 21, with note. Of course, there is an element of wry humour involved. In **§§19** and **20** E employs two of his most distinctive metaphors, comparing life to a game, and the option of suicide, when the game no longer attracts, to an open door. For the former, cf. 1. 25. 7–8, 2. 16. 37, 4. 7. 30; for the latter, cf. 1. 9. 20, 1. 25. 18, 2. 1. 19, 3. 8. 6, 3. 13. 14, 3. 22. 34. So Seneca similarly says that 'the road to freedom lies open'; cf. *Ep.* 26. 10; *Prov.* 6. 9; *De Ira* 3. 15. 4. Pliny (*NH* 2. 27) calls suicide 'the supreme boon that god has bestowed on mortals among the many penalties of life'. For Stoic teaching on suicide, see note ad 1. 2. 2. For a fuller exposition of the ideas in this section cf. 1. 25. 7–20.

CHAPTER 25

On the Same Theme

The title points to thematic continuity with the preceding discourse. This is not worth analysing in any detail, however, since the issues in common are featured in many other discourses. Perhaps the most notable similarity involves their use of the comparison of life to a play or (what comes to much the same thing) a game. Analysis: §§1–6 The self-evident nature of the basic ethical truths renders precepts unnecessary.

§§7–13 Regarding life as a play, or game, helps clarify the basic distinction between what is in our power, and what is not. The roles, or rules of the game, are dictated by forces outside our control, and are therefore not in our power. But it is within our power to play the game (or part) well. Thus it is with logic: hypotheses are dictated by others, but it is up to us to assess their implications correctly.

§§14–18 If we regard 'circumstances' as the arbitrary conditions of a game, they become easier to tolerate with good humour. This attitude encourages a certain complaisance. But ultimately it is our decision how long to remain in the game.

§§19–25 We need not 'remain in the game' under all circumstances.
If circumstances are too much to bear, suicide is an option. And the
promise of release, or escape, that death brings, emboldens us to
'break up the game' when conditions become intolerable.

§§26–31 The supposed difficulties of life are in any case mostly of
our own creation, or devised in unwitting collaboration with our
enemies.

§§32–3 A coda anticipating the objection that all this philosophy is
so much playing with words.

'[T]hese things' in §1, as the text implies, are E's usual doctrines,
i.e. that *ta prohairetika* (translated 'moral character' above) is the
only thing in our control, and the only thing worth caring about.
E elsewhere refers to these doctrines as 'general principles' (*ta
katholika*). Cf. 4. 12. 7–8: 'What are the things to which I ought to
attend? First of all, the general principles, and you should have
them at the ready, and without them neither go to bed nor rise, nor
eat, nor drink, nor associate with men: that no one is master of
another's moral character (*prohairesis*), and that here alone is good
and bad. Therefore no one has power either to secure me good, or
involve me in bad, but I myself am master of myself in respect of
these things.'

§§3–4 engages a controversy within Stoicism, concerning how
specific ethical instruction needed to be. The principal texts are
Sen. *Ep.* 94 and 95; see Kidd 1971, 1978; Ioppolo 1980: 130–3;
and, for a useful overview, LS 1. 427–9. Sen. *Ep.* 33 is similar to
the present passage in alluding to the controversy indirectly. The
principal proponent of the view that specific moral directions (what
Seneca calls *praecepta*) are superfluous was Aristo. His low opinion
of them related to his pared-down version of Stoic values. In his
view they were unnecessary, because it is easy to remember that
virtue is the only good, vice the only evil. In this discourse E invokes
the same dichotomy, and similarly concludes that precepts are otiose.

In §4 E implies that the principles he regularly espouses are
innate in each of us, so that moral instruction from others is unnecessary. Cf. 4. 3. 11–12: 'Guard your own good in everything; and for
the rest in so far as it has been given to you, as long as you can
make rational use of it, content with this alone. Otherwise you will
be unhappy and unfortunate, you will be hindered and obstructed.
These are laws sent from there [*ekeithen*, i.e. from Zeus], these are
his commandments.' To support his contention that knowledge of

what is ours and not ours is morally intuitive, he assimilates it to
the universal commandment not to steal; cf. 1. 24. 11. Context
indicates that 'from there' (*ekeithen*) in §4 also means from Zeus.
This passage might be further taken to suggest that the soul is
pre-existent, and comes into the world with a fund of knowledge
prior to its embodiment. But this would be more consistent with
Platonism than with orthodox Stoicism, and there is no need to
read it this way. Reference to 'trustworthiness', 'decency', etc. in
this section suggests that E equates the 'laws' and 'commandments'
of Zeus with the moral instincts that Stoics made the basis of the
virtues. That we have these 'from Zeus' derives from the Stoic
belief in our kinship with the gods. Cf. Cic. *Laws* 1. 25: 'Man
recognizes god because he recognizes and remembers, as it were,
his origin. Virtue exists in man and god alike, but in no other
creature.' With the last sentence in §4, cf. 1. 2. 14.

[The translation of §4 assumes an expanded text. S transmits
only 'Trustworthiness (*to piston*) is your own.' But 'trustworthiness' does not have enough relevance to the context to stand alone.
Oldfather and Souilhé (after Upton) add 'a sense of shame' (*to
aidēmon*). But even this is not enough, as Schenkl saw. Our translation assumes, *exempli gratia*, a longer list of proto-virtues, of a kind
E often serves up; see note ad 1. 28. 23.]

On 'preconceptions' (*prolēpseis*) in §6, cf. 1. 22. As indicated in
the introductory comment on 1. 22, E was unorthodox in sometimes treating preconceptions as the intellectual aspect of the innate
seeds of virtue. The former tell us what is good, the latter tell us to
pursue it. That is one reason why E invokes them in this connection. But in line with other Stoics, he could also regard preconceptions as the outcome of our moral training, which is another reason
he refers to them here. 'The proofs of the philosophers', as well as
'what you have often heard', and 'what you have read', and 'practised', all contribute to form preconceptions; see Bonhöffer 1890:
198. And preconceptions, E implies, are sufficient in themselves to
determine how to behave, without need of outside advice.

In §§7–20 E explores the implications of various metaphors for
life. Games and the theatre (§§8–10) were traditional; cf. 1. 24. 19–
20 with comment. The advantage of regarding life in these terms is
that circumstances come to be regarded with a certain detachment:
they are adventitious, and cannot touch the inner man. (Cf. Plot. 3.
2. 15 for a development of the idea.) All the same, E implies that we
should normally tolerate circumstances for the sake of the game (or

drama). Thus, we will perform the part assigned us at the Saturnalia, even if it is a humble one. But we will remember that we are playing a part, and will not suppose that we are actually 'in a bad way' (§9). It is always possible to opt out of the game if it proves unpleasant, even if that means renouncing life itself. The upshot is that we will have no grounds for complaint, whatever the circumstances, because we can either play along or excuse ourselves.

The comparison of life to a hypothetical argument found in §§11–13 seems to be original with E; cf. 1. 12. 17 with comment; also 1. 26. 1–2, 1. 29. 39–41, 2. 5. 11. Hypothetical arguments are similar to a game or a drama in that they depend on certain premisses. Thus, 'Let it be night' (§11). This must be accepted for the sake of argument. One could even propose a hypothesis of the form, 'Let it be that you suppose it to be night' (§12), from which the inference, 'You then suppose that it is dark', would follow. But the inference 'Suppose that it *is* night' is unsound as an inference from the hypotheses supplied. The point of E's argument depends in part on the fact that hypothetical arguments were judged not just by their internal coherence, but by their truth-conditions. To suppose that it really is night from the hypothesis 'Let it be night' is erroneous. Cf. SE *PH* 2. 149: 'An argument may conclude to something false even its assumptions are true, when it is said at night by lamplight. For the conditional "If it is day, it is light" is true, and so is the additional assumption "But it is light"; but the consequence, "Therefore it is day", is false.' The relevance of this for life is that we can play the part defined by circumstances, without imagining that it determines who we are. For in Stoicism character is determined not by circumstances but by our conduct in them. Cf. 2. 5. 1: 'Materials are indifferent, but the use made of them is not indifferent'; *Ench.* 17: 'Remember that you are an actor in a play, the properties of which are decided by the playwright. . . . If he wishes you to play the part of a beggar, remember to act even this role adroitly; likewise if your role be that of a cripple, a ruler, or a private citizen.' To apply the metaphor of the hypothetical arguments, one should normally accept the 'hypothesis' that one is a beggar, or a king. But it is wrong to accept it to the extent of identifying with it completely. Character is defined by *prohairesis*, not externals. We can be virtuous and happy, or vicious and unhappy, in any role.

§13 is a variation on the analogy of life to a hypothetical argument. E proposes a sorites argument, formulated as a series of hypothetical statements. (On the sorites see Barnes 1982*a*.) This one formally resembles the one at Cic. *Fin.* 4. 50. It attempts to equate bad fortune with badness *simpliciter*, by way of four predicates that are assumed to be equivalent. The Stoic would reject the inference, owing to his belief that only vice is bad. The argument tries to entrap him through its subtle and apparently innocent substitution of terms. Especially notable is the last step, from 'wretched' (*kakodaimoneis*) to 'in a bad way' (*en kakois*), based on the repetition of *kakon* ('bad'). It is here that the Stoic demurs, because he does not mistake unfavourable circumstances for real evil. Stoics allowed that the two were liable to be confused, however: cf. Cic. *Laws* 1. 31–2.

'[F]itting' in **§14** is Greek *prepon*, a term with Panaetian overtones; cf. Cic. *Off.* 1. 93–100. With **§17**, cf. 1. 2. 11. The image of 'smoke in the house' in **§18** denotes circumstances that are unendurable—in Stoic terms, an absence, or shortage, of the primary things in accordance with nature. Suicide was justified under these conditions; cf. Cic. *Fin.* 3. 60–1. The image is repeated at 4. 10. 27, and imitated by Marcus at 5. 29. On the phrase 'the door is open', alluding to the option of suicide, cf. 1. 24. 20, with note.

[A second hand in S, and the *deteriores*, supply *dei* in **§18**, but for the ellipse cf. 1. 18. 20 and 4. 10. 18.]

§19 contains one of E's tense stand-offs between the tyrant and the philosopher; cf. 1. 24. 12–13 with note. The latter remains unmoved despite the escalation of threats. The tyrant giving orders is tacitly equated with the factitious king of the Saturnalia in §§8–9 above. Both wield power, but how much depends in part on our compliance. This is explained, in the case of the tyrant, at **§§23–5**. Gyara (or Gyaros) is a barren island in the Aegean. In the early Empire it served as a place of exile. The residence 'open to all' in **§20** is, of course, the abode of the dead.

[I would delete **§21**; it adds nothing to the argument, and is imperfectly integrated with the context. The metaphor of the body as a garment is also used by Socrates at DL 2. 35 and by Seneca at *Ep.* 92. 13; cf. *Cons. Marc.* 25. 1. But 'the last garment' would make more sense in a context such as §30, or 1. 24. 12–13, where layers of clothing are successively removed to reveal the body at last. Upton suspected that the phrase 'that is, the poor body' (*toutesti to sōmation*) was an intrusive gloss that had displaced the main verb—the sentence lacks one as it is. He proposed *anatithemai*, and translates,

'And I put off the innermost garment; further than this, no one has any power over me.' This helps to establish a connection between §20 and §21 (and is adopted in Hard's translation). But I still find 'the last garment' too incongruous a phrase to suppose that it was intended for here.]

Demetrius (in **§22**) was the Cynic philosopher known and admired by Seneca; cf. *Ep*. 62. 3, and see Billerbeck 1979. His boldness in addressing Nero demonstrates the Cynic's freedom of speech. For the trope 'You threaten me with death, but nature threatens you', cf. DL 2. 13, 35; Xen. *Apol*. 27; see Goulet-Cazé 1986: 52. For the senatorial seats in the theatre as symbols of privilege (**§26**), cf. Horace, *Epist*. 1. 1. 67. For the thought in **§28** cf. 1. 1. 28 and 1. 19. 7–8, with comment. For the thought in **§29** cf. DL 2. 70. With **§30** cf. 1. 1. 23 with comment. That Socrates 'always had the same countenance' (**§31**) is the testimony of several ancient sources; cf. Cic. *Off*. 1. 90; *TD* 3. 31; Sen. *De Ira* 2. 7; *Ep*. 104. 28; Simpl. *In Ench*. 261b. It attests, of course, to his equanimity.

§§32–3 can be read as anticipating resistance to the foregoing lessons. The interlocutor's remark in **§32**, 'Philosophers speak in paradoxes,' seems provoked especially by the statement in **§31**, concerning the need to be 'free and unimpeded'. 'Philosophers' are Stoics, as usual in E; see comment ad 1. 18. 1. They famously argued that only the wise man was free (cf. Cic. *PS* 33–41). And they did not deny that such doctrines were paradoxical. Cf. 4. 1. 173: 'Cleanthes used to say, "Perhaps the philosophers speak contrary to opinion (*paradoxa*), but not contrary to reason (*paraloga*)"'; Cic. *PS* proem. 4: 'Even the Stoics call them paradoxes'. But, as E points out, paradoxes are found in other areas of study like medicine (with which philosophy was often compared; cf. 3. 23. 30; see LS 1. 385). Just because a doctrine is surprising doesn't make it untrue.

CHAPTER 26

What is the Law of Life?

The title is very ill-chosen, as reference to 'the law of life' occurs only in §1, and the theme is barely developed. The discourse is really another contribution to the role of logic in the philosophical

curriculum; as such, it should be compared with 1. 7, 1. 8, and
1. 17. In upholding the necessity of logical training it resembles
1. 7 and 1. 17. But, as in 1. 8, there are admonitions against excessive interest in the subject. The discourse is also interesting as giving
insight into how logic was actually taught in E's school. Analysis:
§§1–4 Theory exists for the sake of practice, logic for the sake of
ethics. But although it is ancillary, logic is indispensable.
§§5–7 The study of philosophy in general is indispensable.
§§8–12 But philosophy must be studied for the right reasons.
§§13–18 The study of philosophy, logic especially, affords an opportunity to test one's rational faculties in a secure environment.

For the narrative frame in **§1**, a relic of the dialogue tradition, see
introduction to 1. 11, and compare the openings of 1. 13 and 1. 14.
The 'person' in §1 is presumably one of his students; cf. §13. But
we need not assume with Schweighäuser (ii. 291) that someone else
reads the hypothetical arguments, because E was personally opposed
to logic. To judge from this passage, it was an established part of
his school's curriculum. That is enough to prove its importance as
far as he was concerned. The value he placed on it is defined in
what follows. On hypothetical arguments, cf. 1. 7. 22–9 with comment. For the parallel he draws between such arguments and life,
cf. 1. 25. 11–13 with comment. Here, at least, it is more than just
analogy. E's point is that scholastic training in logic sharpens the
mind's powers of inference, powers that are essential for life in 'the
real world', since the world, on the Stoic view, operates on rational
principles. Cf. Plut. *St. rep.* 1050A: 'Nothing, however small, can
come about otherwise than in conformity with universal nature and
reason.' The exercise of logic prepares for the activity whereby we
determine what behaviour is consistent with universal nature, and
with human nature; thus the allusion in §1 to the standard Stoic
formula for the end. Cf. DL 7. 87: 'The end may be defined as
living in conformity with nature, which is to say, in accord with
one's own nature and with the nature of the whole.' **§2** is intended
to show that this moral maxim can be couched in logical terms, the
point being that living rightly means living rationally. As E says at
2. 23. 40, 'One must advance toward the ethical goal through reason
and its instruction.' On the basic idea, see Long 1970a.

[Meibom and Koraes restored a form of *tis* ('someone') in **§1**, but
for the ellipse of the indefinite pronoun cf. 1. 18. 16, 1. 19. 24, 1. 25.
18.]

It is important to be clear about the contrast E is drawing in **§§3–4**. The 'more difficult things' are evidently equated with 'the matters of life'. The contrast, then, is between these things, and 'theory'. This does not advert to the controversy within Stoicism as to the order in which the three parts of philosophy—logic, physics, and ethics—should be studied; on this cf. 1. 17. 6. It is the contrast between theory and practice that E often rehearses, e.g. 1. 4. 6–17, 1. 29. 54–63, 2. 21. 15–22, 3. 10. 10, 3. 26. 13, 4. 4. 8–18, etc.; see Cherniss ad Plut. *St. rep.* 1033B for the importance of the theme in Stoicism generally. The contrast assumes that theory exists for the sake of practice; or, as E puts it elsewhere, 'The reading of books is a preparation for the act of living' (4. 4. 11). So there is not only contrast, but continuity: theory or book learning is a necessary first step. Inasmuch as it is clear from §1 that 'theory' includes formal logic, this passage contradicts others where E makes logic the last subject to be studied; cf. 3. 2. 5 and 3. 26. 14–20. For an explanation of the inconsistency, see comment ad 1. 17. 6–9.

In this section E adduces another reason why, although practice is the goal, theory cannot be skipped: it is necessary to start with easier, and progress to more difficult, things. The practical application of logical principles is more difficult, because 'in the matters of life many things divert the attention'. This refers to factors that, according to the Stoics, distort our natural good sense. Cf. Cic. *Laws* 1. 47: 'Our views are not perverted by parent, nurse, teacher, poet, or the stage, nor led astray by the opinions of the mob. But against our minds all sorts of plots are constantly being hatched, either by those whom I have just mentioned, who take possession of them while they are still tender and unformed, and influence and bend them as they wish, or else by that enemy that lies deep within every sense, that counterfeit of good, which, however, is the mother of all evils—pleasure.' These are 'the things that disturb the judgement' in §10; and are again referred to, in more technical terms, at 1. 27. 3.

Parents disapprove of philosophy for their children because they think it is impractical; cf. 1. 11. 39–40; 1. 22. 18–21; 2. 21. 15. In **§§5–7** E intends to combat that prejudice. He frames an argument similar to those at 2. 24. 13–15 and 2. 25, where he claims that the question of whether training in logic is necessary cannot itself be satisfactorily answered without some training in logic. So here he argues that the question of whether it is right to study philosophy itself falls within the province of philosophy, which Stoics defined as the art of life (cf. Plut. *Quaest. conviv.* 613B; Sen. fr. 17; see Lakmann 1995: 26). 'Philosophy' in this section refers not just to logic, but to the theoretical study of ethics. Cf. Philo, *Leg. alleg.* 1. 57 (= *SVF* 3. 202): 'Virtue is both theoretical and practical. For it also comprises theory, since philosophy, the road to virtue, does as well, by way of its three parts, logic, ethics, and physics.' E reinforces his point by assuming in §6 that the error of studying philosophy, if error it is, results from ignorance of good and bad—the very thing philosophy was supposed to amend. Cf. Sen. *Ep.* 89. 4: 'Philosophy is the love of wisdom, and the endeavour to attain it'; DL 7. 92: 'Wisdom is the knowledge of what is good and bad.' Stoics did, in fact, assume that it could be taught; cf. 2. 19. 31; DL 7. 91. The assumption in §6 is Socratic and Stoic; cf. 1. 18. In §7, E further reinforces his point by a Socratic analogy with the arts; and of course Stoics preferred reason, represented by philosophy, to irrational anger.

The point of §§8–9 is that the defence of philosophy (especially logic) offered in §§5–7 assumes it will be applied toward the conduct of life, not toward the vain display of erudition. E was aware that logic was liable to be abused. He sometimes deprecates it for that reason; see comment ad 1. 8. 6–10. For the danger posed by early exposure to logic, cf. Plut. *Prof. in virt.* 78E–F; for the overall idea, cf. ibid. 80A: 'Those who are ever studying, and looking for what they can take from philosophy to show off in the forum, or at a gathering of young men, or at a royal symposium, should no more be thought to practise philosophy than druggists are thought to practise medicine.'

'Here' and 'there' in §10 refer to the realms of theory and practice, respectively. The point continues to be that practice is more important. 'Matters' is *hulai* (sing. *hulē*). E is comparing the 'matter' of logic with the 'matter' of life. For the former, cf. 2. 21. 17: 'You should consider what you came to school for. You want to babble about philosophical theorems. Well, aren't you becoming more glib? Don't these paltry theorems supply you with the *hulē* for ostentation?' For the latter, cf. 1. 15. 2: 'For as wood is the *hulē* with which the carpenter deals, and bronze the sculptor, so the *hulē* of the art of life is the life of each person.' For logical exercises demeaned as 'games' or 'trifles' (*paignia* in §10), cf. Sen. *Ep.* 48. 8–9, 71. 6, 102. 20, 111. 4. For 'treasure' (*ploutos*) applied to the products of intellect, cf. Pl. *Euthphr.* 12a.

[The translation adopts Schweighäuser's clever emendation in **§10** of *ekei onta* to *ekseionta*, comparing 4. 9. 10. Schweighäuser (ii. 294) called attention to the lack of coherence in **§§10–12**. My solution would be to delete **§§11–12**. Like the anecdotes at 3. 8. 7 and 3. 15. 14, this one seems to have become detached from its original context. It was perhaps interpolated here by someone who took 'riches' in §10 literally, and interpreted 'here' and 'there' in a local sense. In view of these connections, deletion may seem drastic. But the passage has absolutely no bearing on the principal theme, the relation between theory and practice.]

§13 once again evokes the school setting in which this discourse is supposed to take place. E presided over the instruction. But he evidently had an assistant, perhaps a senior student, who took charge of assigning the readings in logic. The anecdote illustrates the difference between the exercise of reason in theory and practice. The logic of the student appointed to read the lesson is weak. E cuts him short for that reason. But the assistant committed a lapse of logic in calling on him in the first place. He is quickly reproved, because, as indicated in §17 below, E wanted his school to provide a supportive setting where one could face up to one's deficiencies without fear of derision. A different point is made at **§14**: the judgement of someone capable of error in such things as evaluating logical propositions— what E calls the 'small matters'—cannot be trusted in more serious matters. The thought is similar to that of 1. 21. 4.

On the conjunctive argument (*sumpeplegmenos*) cf. DL 7. 72: 'A conjunctive proposition is held together by certain conjunctions. An example is, "It is both day and light."' Stoics held that for a conjunctive proposition to be true, all of its component propositions had to be true. 'In every conjunctive, if one proposition is false, even if the others are true, the whole proposition is false' (Gellius 16. 9). See Frede 1974: 96–7; Mueller 1978: 8–9; Hülser frs. 966–71. For E's inveterate habit of viewing life in logical terms, cf. *Ench*. 36: 'As "It is day" and "It is night" have great validity with respect to the disjunctive proposition, but are invalid with respect to the conjunctive, so too to take the larger share at dinner is good for your body, but bad for the maintenance of the proper social feeling.'

[The translation of **§13** adopts Schenkl's restoration *taraxas* ('interrupted') of the partly illegible reading in S.]

With **§§15–18** compare 2. 11. 1: 'The beginning of philosophy for those who enter in by the front door is consciousness of one's

own weakness and infirmity with regard to the important things';
cf. also 2. 17. 1; DL 7. 23; Pl. *Soph.* 230a–e. This is where logical
exercises prove their utility, for they help to make one aware of
one's reasoning skills. Cf. Plut. *Prof. in virt.* 81F: 'The many who
sailed to Athens to go to school were at first wise in their own conceit, then they became desirous of wisdom, then orators, and laymen
as time went on. The more they lay hold of reason, the more they
put aside presumption and conceit.' In school we can tolerate correction, whereas in real life we tend to resist it. **§16**, I take it, is
directed not at students who seek to graduate from theory to practice too hastily, as in §§3–4, but at those who seek to become experts
in theory without mastering the fundamentals. They may be the
same as those in §§8–9 who are zealous for logic only because it
provides opportunities to show off. **§18** is a paraphrase of Pl. *Apol.*
38a. E implies that the formal study of logic, approached in the right
spirit, is the best way to begin the process of self-examination.

CHAPTER 27

In How Many Ways Impressions Arise, and What Aids We Should Provide Against Them

This is about E's principal theme, monitoring impressions (cf. 1. 1.
12 with comment). What makes it unique is that it addresses the
challenge posed to it by Scepticism. This had contemporary relevance owing to the Pyrrhonist revival. Analysis:
§§1–6 There are means to meet every difficulty facing the control of
our impressions.
§§7–14 Arguments offered that counter the impression that death is
evil, or that the gods take no thought for us.
§§15–21 Scepticism can also be met with an array of abstract arguments. But for most people it is enough simply to trust the evidence
of the senses.

With **§1** compare the stylistically similar opening of 1. 12. Bonhöffer
(1890: 145) observes that E's point is simple: viz. that 'our impressions and opinions in part correspond with reality, in part do not'.

Forms of the verb 'to be' can be read both veridically and exist-
entially here. Thus, things that 'are not, and yet appear to be' can
include illusions such as the oar that appears bent in the water (cf.
SE *M* 7. 244), things that appear good but are not (as in §3), and
things that do not exist, such as appear in dreams and hallucina-
tions (cf. SE *M* 7. 245; DL 7. 50). There is a more detailed Stoic
classification of impressions (*phantasiai*) at SE *M* 7. 241–58, which,
as in this discourse, refers to Stoic and Sceptic disagreement on the
matter. In §2 E characterizes the arguments of the latter as 'sophisms'. For the need of resources to meet them cf. Cic. *Ac.* 2. 45: 'So
that we may abide by conspicuous things more firmly and constantly, there is need of an art or discipline lest we be dislodged by
sophisms and trickeries from things that are obviously true.' This
section indicates that E, unlike Seneca (cf. *NQ* 7. 32. 2), was aware
of the Pyrrhonist revival.

   '[T]he plausibility of things' referred to in §3 was standardly
cited by Stoics as one source of moral perversion; cf. 1. 26. 3 with
comment, 2. 22. 6, and *SVF* 3. 228–36. It helps explains why impressions are wrongly interpreted. The danger posed by the plausibility of things goes hand in hand with the danger of bad habits
discussed in §§3–6, since the latter include misdiagnosing impressions and holding false opinions. Cf. 3. 12. 6–7: 'Since habit is a
powerful influence, and we are accustomed to employ desire and
aversion only on things which are not within the power of our will,
we ought to oppose to this habit a contrary one, and where there is
great slipperiness in the impressions, there to oppose discipline. I
am rather inclined to pleasure; I will incline to the contrary above
measure for the sake of discipline. I am averse to pain; I will strain
and exercise my impressions in order to stifle my aversion to every
such thing.' The idea of opposing one habit with its opposite was
originally Aristotelian; cf. *EN* 1109b1–6. Cf. Sen. *Ep.* 123. 13:
'Riches, pleasures, beauty, office, and other such alluring things
attract us; labour, death, pain, ignominy, and a frugal diet repel us.
We should therefore discipline ourselves in order not to fear the
one nor desire the other. Let us strive in the opposite direction, and
retreat from the things that invite us, while meeting the hostile
things head on.' For other Stoic parallels see Bonhöffer 1894: 42
nn. 10–11, 151 n. 16. On logic's role in meeting sophisms, alluded
to in §6, cf. 1. 7. 11 with comment. On preconceptions and their
place in Stoic epistemology see comment ad 1. 22.

Death (§§7–9) was indifferent in the Stoic scheme of things (DL 7. 102), though 'dispreferred' (DL 7. 106). For statements of the idea in E cf. 2. 19. 13, 4. 1. 132–8. For the terms of the enthymeme that he formulates in §7 to prove that death is not evil, cf. Sen. *Ep.* 77. 19: 'Are you not unaware that death is among life's duties?'; *NQ* 6. 32. 12: 'Death is a duty and an obligation for mortals.' The paraphrase of Sarpedon in §8 is based on Homer's *Iliad* 12. 322–8. Sarpedon corresponds to Aristotle's 'godlike man'; note E's pointed reference to him as 'the son of Zeus'. According to Aristotle (*EN* 1145a27) such a person is 'rarely found'; E similarly characterizes his virtue as 'beyond us'. But his example shows us what man is capable of, and even if we do not defy death, as Sarpedon did, we can at least accept it when the time comes. For the thought of the passage cf. 1. 2. 33–7, about Socrates, and 1. 6. 32–6, about Heracles, both notable heroes, but like Sarpedon, neither a realistic role model. The 'that' within our reach in §8 is glossed in §10 as dying without 'moaning and groaning'; cf. 1. 2. 21. With §9 cf. Xen. *Apol.* 23, where Socrates declines the option of exile on the grounds that he knows of 'no spot inaccessible to death'.

[In §7 all modern editors agree in adopting Meibom's emendation of *kalon* ('good') to *kakon* ('evil'). In §8 I also adopt Schweighäuser's insertion of *mē* to change 'Sarpedon' to 'not Sarpedon.']

With the aetiology of passion in §10, cf. 2. 17. 18, 3. 2. 3: 'A passion only arises when desire fails of its purpose, or aversion falls into what it would avoid.' As Bonhöffer (1890: 279) explains, this supports the orthodox Stoic definition of passion as 'corrupt opinion' (Plut. *De Virt. mor.* 447A), since wishing is based on the opinion that the object of desire is good. Thus we are referred back to the problem, broached at the beginning, of monitoring our impressions.

For the egoism E espouses in §§12–14 see comment ad 1. 19. 11–15. This is a notable example of his *Realphilosophie*. The interlocutor in §14 piously exclaims that it is wrong to blame the gods. E responds that, if conventional values are sound, it is reasonable to blame the gods, and a matter of indifference if they are angered in consequence, since any punishment they might inflict could hardly be worse than what we already suffer. E's main point, though, is that the goods we can be deprived of, and the evils we cannot avoid, are indifferent; thus we have no cause to reproach the gods on their account. The same idea is developed at 2. 22. 15–17, 4. 7. 8–11; *Ench.* 31. 4.

On §§15–21 see Bonhöffer 1890: 7–8, 129–30; 1894: 123. Following Schweighäuser (ii. 306–7), he interprets E as adopting a com-
promise position, approving debate with the Sceptics on questions
of knowledge, but only for those who have already reformed their
character. 'Convention' in §§15 and 20 is *sunētheia*, used here in
what Cherniss calls a 'semi-technical sense' to refer to confidence
in the evidence of the senses, as advocated by the Stoics and condemned by the Sceptics; cf. Plut. *St. rep.* 1036C and *Comm. not.*
1059B with Cherniss's notes. In §§17–20, E defends *sunētheia* in
the sense just defined. For the interpretation of §§20–1, we must
distinguish between supporting 'convention' in the sense of trusting
the senses, on the one hand, and defending their reliability against
Sceptic attack, on the other. The former E endorses for everyone,
the latter he reserves to those who have 'leisure' for technical arguments, i.e. people already free of harmful emotions. Such people
can devote time to epistemological research because they alone are
capable of thinking clearly; see comment ad 1. 4. 1.

[I depart from other editors in assigning §15 (beginning with
'For my part')–§16 to an interlocutor.]

The question mooted in §17 relates to ancient theories of cognition. As such, it concerns the epistemological issues around which
the whole discourse is loosely based. On the exact interpretation of
§17 see Bonhöffer 1890: 102–5. The question whether perception
takes place 'through the whole or a part' is first raised in Plato's
Theaetetus, 184b–d. In the Stoa it was complicated by the fact that
'the whole', i.e. the soul or 'ruling faculty' (*hēgemonikon*), comprised
each 'part', i.e. each sense-organ. Cf. Calcidius 220 (= LS 53G),
Aet. 4. 21. 1 (= LS 53H): 'The Stoics say that the highest part of
the soul is the commanding faculty, which produces impressions,
assents, sensations, and impulses.' Thus Stoics could not appeal
to the same easy division between soul and body that informs
Plato's solution to the problem. Seneca at *Ep.* 113. 23 adverts to
a related question within the Stoa, whether we walk with the feet,
or with that part of the commanding faculty that resides in the
feet. He betrays the same impatience with such controversies as E
evinces here.

§19 is directed at Sceptics. For the way they are refuted in §§18–
19, cf. 2. 20. 28; Plut. *In Col.* 1122E: 'Why does the man who
suspends judgement not go running off to a mountain rather than
the bath, or why does he not get up and walk to the wall instead

of the door, when he wishes to enter the market-place?' As Long
and Sedley (2. 444) remark, this style of argument harks back to
Aristotle's defence of the principle of non-contradiction at *Met.*
1008b12–16.

[In **§18** 'as to a target' (*pros skopon*) is Schweighäuser's emendation of the puzzling *proskpoptōn* in the MSS. Like other modern
editors, I have adopted it *faute de mieux*.]

CHAPTER 28

That We Should Not Be Angry with Men, and What Are the Small Things and the Great among Men

The compound title reflects a certain discursiveness on E's part. As
usual, rhetorical questions, or the questions of a suppositious interlocutor, help mark the transitions, since they function as a pretext
to head the argument in a new direction. One of the chief interests
of the piece attaches to the discussion of Euripides' *Medea* in §§7–9.
There was a tradition of Stoic comment on her case. E's remarks
provide insight into earlier treatments of the story, as well as having
interest in their own right.

The essay may be analysed thus:

§§1–6 A statement of ethical determinism, to the effect that impulses are strictly conditioned by our perception of the good, the
appropriate, etc.

§§7–9 This thesis upheld in the case of Medea, the traditional per-
sonification of *akrasia*.

§§10–13 The thesis extended to other figures of myth, with the focus
on the disproportion between a single false impression and its far-
reaching consequences.

§§14–25 A distinction made, based on the Stoic scheme of values,
implying that such consequences are not significant except in so far
as they alert us to an underlying failure in reason. In man's case,
actions should not be judged by their material consequences, but
by the judgements motivating them.

§§26–33 From the prevalence of disagreement over what is significant, E draws the inference that a standard must be devised and

systematically applied—to abstract disputes over values, as well as to individual impressions. The importance of finding such a stand- ard is highlighted by reiterating the point about how hazardous it is to assent to impressions carelessly—hence the need to address the problem at its source.

With §§1–4 compare 1. 18. 1–2, 2. 26. 7, 3. 3. 2, 3. 7. 13, 3. 22. 43. Other Stoic sources likewise affirm that manifest impressions force the mind to accept them. Cf. SE *M* 8. 316: 'As we have said, some things are clear, others are unclear, and clear are those that are apprehended involuntarily from the impression and from feeling, such as now, "It is day", and "This is a man", and the like. Unclear are those that are not of this sort.' For additional statements of this psychological determinism cf. SE *M* 7. 405; Cic. *Ac.* 2. 38; Plut. *In Col.* 1122C. E extends the principle to all three kinds of impression (or proposition): true, false, and unclear. For the threefold classifica- tion cf. 1. 7. 5, 1. 17. 1. This was a standard definition of dialectic within the Stoa: cf. DL 7. 42, 62; Hülser frs. 60–4.

Claims similar to E's were part of the Stoic arsenal in its battle against the Sceptics. But if judgements are invariably determined in accordance with the nature of the impression, or *lekton*, how does error arise? Cf. SE *PH* 2. 97–8: 'Some objects, according to the dogmatists, are clear and some are unclear. And of the unclear, some are unclear once and for all, some are unclear for the moment, some are unclear by nature. What comes to our knowledge of itself, such as "It is day", is clear. What is not of a nature to yield to our apprehension, such as whether the stars are even in number, is unclear once and for all. What has a clear nature but is obscured by external circumstances is unclear for the moment, such as the city of the Athenians is now to me. What is not of such a nature as to yield to our clear apprehension is naturally unclear, such as imper- ceptible pores.' As E accounts for the first two items in Sextus' list, error must arise from the latter two: things unclear for the moment and things unclear by nature. These do not compel the mind to react one way or the other, and so invite error.

As the passage from Sextus indicates, the question of whether the number of stars is odd or even was a stock example of some- thing about which only suspension of judgement was possible: cf. Cic. *Ac.* 2. 32, 110; SE *PH* 2. 90–1. As an example of something self-evident, the fact that it is day was also standard: cf. Cic. *Ac.* 2.

119, 128, 145; SE *PH* 2. 97. In §3 E invents a false correlative to the latter, the proposition 'It is now night' (when it is day).

E exploits the Stoic doctrine of the mind's determination by things that are clear or unclear 'once and for all' as fresh evidence for the Platonic belief that 'the soul is unwillingly deprived of the truth' (*Soph.* 228c; cf. *Rep.* 382a, 413a, 589c; this is cited again at 2. 22. 36, and also quoted by Marcus in this form at 7. 63). The inference derives from E's teleological and functionalist view of nature. As he says elsewhere, the profession (*epangelia*) of reason is to 'affirm the true, reject the false, and suspend judgement about what is unclear' (1. 7. 5). The regularity with which the mind does this in response to certain impressions supports this belief, although it is only a partial proof.

In §5 the necessity of our nature demonstrated in our mental responses is here extended from the sphere of impressions to the sphere of action. This is the critical point for what follows. For the correlation E draws between the incentives to thought and action see Annas 1992: 93: 'It seems as though there is a certain parallelism between action and perception; in both cases there is an appearance, and what is up to the rational agent is to accept or reject it.' Instead of assenting to the proposition that 'It is day', one assents to the proposition that 'This is advantageous', or 'This is proper', and impulse results. Cf. Stob. 2. 88. 1: 'The Stoics say that all impulses are assents, but that the ones issuing in action contain a motivating element'; cf. SE *M* 7. 405; Plut. *In Col.* 1122C. For the same parallel as here between the true and the good, the one compelling cognitive assent, the other hormetic impulse, cf. 1. 18. 1–2 and 3. 3. 2–4. It is doubtful, however, if there exist things as self-evidently proper or advantageous as the proposition 'It is day' is clear. Note that E does not give analogous examples. He draws the parallel in order to lend colour to the ethical determinism on which the essay is based. On this passage see also the remarks of Imbert 1980: 215–16; and Long 1991*b*: 113–18 (repr. in part in Hard 1995: 342–4).

E has expounded his brand of determinism. He has argued that it is the soul's nature always to accept the truth, and be attracted toward what is proper. In §7 he proceeds to illustrate this principle with reference to the figure of Medea. Note that she is introduced defensively ('But what of her who says . . . ?'). This suggests that E recognizes in her a threat to his thesis. As someone whose crimes supposedly stemmed not from ignorance of right or wrong, but from anger and a lust for revenge, she posed a special challenge to rationalism. E accepts the standard interpretation up to a point, but makes a distinction that enables him to bring it in line with Stoic psychology. It is reasonable to suppose that his interpretation is consistent with Chrysippus' account of Medea's behaviour (as Nussbaum 1993: 128 and Dillon 1997: 214 also assume).

For evidence of the old Stoics' reverence for poetry cf. DL 7. 4, 175, 200: it reflects their concern to ground their doctrine in common belief. For discussion of Stoic use of the poets see Gill 1983; Long 1992; Nussbaum 1993; Tieleman 1996: 219–48. The verses E quotes are from Euripides' *Medea*, lines 1078–9. They may be part of a large interpolation into the text (see Dillon 1997: 218 n. 12), but this is immaterial for our purposes, because Chrysippus had treated them as genuine. Medea's case is cited again and discussed at 2. 17. 19–22, where E calls the slaughter of her children 'the act of a great spirit'. Stoics evidently found her to be a good philosophical example. Sources report that Chrysippus quoted the play *in extenso* (DL 7. 180; cf. 7. 166). Galen in *On the Views of Hippocrates and Plato* (*PHP*) indicates that he appealed to it chiefly as a proof-text for his psychology. From *PHP* 4. 6. 19 (= *SVF* 3. 473 *in fine*) we learn that he cited these same two lines in the fourth book of his work *On the Passions*. They are also quoted in Alcin. *Epit.* 24. 3 and Calcidius 183, evidence that they were commonplace in discussions of the passions and parts of the soul. (This is the reason, apparently, that E does not bother to identify their source; for similar informality cf. Verg. *Ecl.* 8. 47–50; Ovid, *Trist.* 2. 387–8; Plut. *De Vit. pud.* 533D; Simpl. *In Ench.* 68a.)

The lines have usually been treated as a *locus classicus* for the phenomenon of *akrasia*, incontinence or weakness of the will, the existence of which the Stoics, following Socrates, allegedly denied (see Rickert 1987; Price 1995: 2–5). The traditional view is that if Medea is acratic, then the conflict within her is between reason and *thumos*, the seat of the emotions. At *PHP* 5. 6. 34–7 (= LS 65I) Cleanthes is credited with an imaginary dialogue between reason and *thumos*, a polarity assumed in this interpretation. Galen ad loc. says that this makes their use by Chrysippus the more surprising, since 'he does not perceive that in quoting it he is testifying against himself'. But of course this is only Galen's opinion. He is committed to the view that the lines refute Chrysippus' unified view of the soul and show that emotions operate independently of reason.

Varieties of psychological tension are hinted at in a handful of Stoic texts (e.g. Sen. *Ep.* 21. 1, 95. 37; E 4. 1. 147). But they do not represent the faculties of the soul as competing on equal terms. They should be interpreted in light of the Stoic opinion that all human impulses are rational, and that emotions are opinions or judgements (DL 7. 111; Plut. *De Virt. mor.* 446F).

Galen says that Chrysippus invoked Medea as a victim of passion (*pathos*: *PHP* 4. 2. 27). Chrysippus characterized her passion as an impulse that is excessive (*pleonazousa*), and compared it with the legs of a running man (*PHP* 4. 2. 16–18, 4. 4. 24, 4. 6. 35). Like the legs of the runner, the inertial force of the excessive impulse resists subsequent efforts to control it. Chrysippus actually called emotions *akrateis*, 'out of control' (*PHP* 4. 4. 24). Yet, in the opinion of Gill (1983: 141), 'Chrysippus does not take her words as involving a complete denial of (rational) intentionality on Medea's part.' His point can be supported with reference to what E says here: 'the gratification of her *thumos* in taking vengeance on her husband she regards as more profitable than saving her children'. In other words, her crimes were acts of passion, but her passion grew out of a conscious decision to gratify her outraged sense of justice. E accepts for argument's sake the traditional view, assumed also in Euripides' lines, that *thumos* is a distinct faculty of the soul. But he insists that her action was determined by reason. He presents Medea's decision to kill her children in terms as blunt and paradoxical as possible, as a question of what is 'more profitable'. This shocking phrase describes a purely rational, cold-blooded act.

E's discussion is truncated. But it can be supplemented by reference to the independent evidence for Chrysippus' reading, a reading which to some extent E probably assumes. Chrysippus could have emphasized that Medea's behaviour is cunning and rational to a degree throughout—a point certainly made by members of the Academy to discredit the Stoic claim that virtue is the perfection of reason. Cf. Cic. *ND* 3. 66–78, esp. 68: 'Medea was criminal, but she was also perfectly rational'; and 71: 'Medea and Atreus, characters of heroic legend, planned their atrocious crimes with a cool calculation of profit and loss.' Medea does not act impulsively, but after prolonged deliberation, deliberation which in Euripides' version takes up the better part of the play. Medea was a complex creation, whose behaviour could be analysed in either of two ways. As a witch, she is known and feared for her 'wisdom' (cf. *sophē* at *Med.*

285). But as a woman scorned, she is prey to emotions that make her irrational (*Med.* 1079). I suggest that Chrysippus focused on the former.

If Chrysippus gave most weight to Medea's rationality, then the interpretation of Medea upheld in the Academy and transmitted by Cicero has special force as a response to him. (The Stoic arguments that Cotta the Academic is rebutting have unfortunately dropped out of Cicero's text.) It might seem improbable that Chrysippus would have highlighted Medea's rationality in view of the contradiction alleged by his critics. But if there was a contradiction, it pertained to his ethics, not his psychology. Using opponents' premises to expose self-contradictions was in any case standard practice, especially in refuting the Stoics, who boasted that their philosophy was all of a piece (cf. Plut. *St. rep.*, *passim*, and see Annas 1993: 281). For a modern reading of the play that highlights Medea's rationality, see Foley 1989. For further background see Campbell 1985; Gosling 1990: 48–68; Nussbaum 1994: 439–83; Price 1995: 145–78; Joyce 1995.

'That we should not be angry with men' is a consequence of the main argument. In defining virtue as the perfection of reason (Cic. *Laws* 1. 25; Plut. *De Virt. mor.* 441B–C), Stoics identified with the Socratic (and Platonic) belief that virtue is knowledge; for the background cf. Arist. *EN* 1145b21–9. A corollary is that vice is ignorance, and wrongdoing involuntary, since the wrongdoer does not know better. Aristotle (or pseudo-Aristotle) *MM* 1187a7–10 drew the determinist implications of that view. In **§8–9** E accepts those implications, and adds another: moral correction is a matter of showing the wrongdoer the error of his ways. Once he grasps the truth, he must adjust his behaviour accordingly. In the meantime, we cannot blame him for our own failure to enlighten him. The discourse resembles Seneca's argument against anger at *De Ira* 2. 9–10. Cf. Marc. 8. 14: 'Whoever you meet, say to yourself at once: "What are his doctrines concerning good and bad things?" For if he has doctrines of a certain sort concerning pleasure and pain and their sources, and fame and its absence, and death and life, I will not think it remarkable or strange if he acts as he does. I will remember that he is compelled to act in this way.' Long and Sedley (1. 385) note that such passages urging pity rather than censure of the morally depraved are common in Marcus and E, and 'indicate that committed Stoics tempered the harshness of their absolute moral categories by a charitable attitude towards those whose values are mistaken'. The whole of 1. 18, 2. 26, and 4. 6 should be compared, as well as 2. 26. 3–7, 4. 1. 147; *Ench.* 42; Muson. 56. 3–6; Marc. 4. 16, 5. 17, 7. 22, 9. 42. 2, 10. 30, 11. 18. 3, 11.

Pity was condemned in earlier Stoicism as a species of distress (*lupē*), because distress was a species of passion (*pathos*); cf. *SVF* 3. 412–16. Later Stoics still express misgiving; cf. Sen. *Clem.* 2. 4. 4–2. 6, arguing that the wise man will never stoop to pity, but will act dispassionately to assist others in need. This doctrine could be criticized as heartless (cf. Sen. *Clem.* 2. 5. 2; *SVF* 3. 450), but was entailed not only by the Stoic view of the passions, but by their revision of values. E endorses the view that virtue, the only real good, lies within one's power, so that there are in principle no grounds for pity. But he sanctions pity when a person is confused about basic moral truths. Cf. 1. 18. 3–4, 9: ' "Thieves . . . are what they are, and gaolbirds." What does "thieves and gaolbirds" mean? They are mistaken about what is good and evil. So should one be angry with them, or pity them? . . . Man, if you must be affected in a way contrary to nature by the evil of another, pity, do not hate him.' Because pity is a passion, it is 'contrary to nature' (cf. 3. 22. 13, 3. 24. 43, 4. 1. 4). But since men err involuntarily, pity could be considered an appropriate response; cf. 1. 17. 14; Marc. 2. 13, 7. 26; Boeth. *Cons.* 4M4. 12.

In **§§11–13** E again has recourse to poetry to enforce his ethical (or psychological) determinism. The myth of Helen's abduction by Paris was adduced by others in discussions of fate and free will: cf. Gorgias, *Helen* (DK B11), Alcin. *Epit.* 26. 2. For the thought that evil entails its own punishment cf. 2. 10. 26; Plut. *De Sera num.* 551E; *St. rep.* 1041D; Marc. 4. 26. The related claim that it is worse to do wrong than suffer it was originally another Socratic 'paradox': cf. *Grg.* 469b; *Crito* 49b; see Vlastos 1991: 200–32. '[B]ut the *Odyssey* as well' (**§13**) means, of course, as the sequel to the *Iliad*: rather a sardonic jest.

In **§14** the argument takes an abrupt turn. The question from a suppositious interlocutor launches E in a different direction (I follow Schenkl's and Souilhé's punctuation). What E says involves a partial retraction of what he said earlier, in that formerly he magnified the ills attendant on ignorance, whereas now he makes light of them. The reason is that he does not want to be seen assigning too much importance to externals. And so he catches himself, inserts a

factitious objection, and launches a different argument (see introductory comment on this section).

Plotinus at 1. 4. 7. 31–3 denies that 'the wise man will consider
loss of power and the destruction of his city a great thing,' a passage
that Graeser (1972: 82) believes is indebted to the one here. The
terms of comparison in §§15–18 are perhaps meant to recall the
tragedy of Ajax, who attacked sheep and cattle, thinking they were
Greek chieftains; and the comic battle of pygmies and storks. E
creates an effect of mock bombast by the repetition of *polla* ('many');
forms of *polus* were catchwords of the epic style, as evidenced by
the opening lines of the *Iliad* and the *Odyssey*, the parody of the
manner in the opening of the *Margites* ('he knew many things, all of
them badly'); and contrarily in the verses of Archilochus, implicitly
critical of Homer, opposing quantity to quality: 'The fox knows
many things, but the hedgehog one great thing' (fr. 201 West; cf. fr.
126). Like Archilochus, E is not impressed by mere numbers.

§§19–23: that something (man, in this case) is to be identified
with the thing that sets it apart is an assumption underlying many
ancient ethical arguments. It informs the so-called *ergon* argument at
Pl. *Rep.* 352e–354a and Arist. *EN* 1097b28–1098a17. And it influenced Chrysippus in formulating the end for man as living in agreement with nature, 'particularly human nature' (DL 7. 89). E views
this difference under two aspects: intelligence, or, as in §§20 and
23, distinctive qualities like faithfulness and the social instinct. This
list of qualities is repeated with variations several times in E; cf.
2. 4. 2, 3. 7. 36, etc.; see Bonhöffer 1894: 129–30. The assumption
that these qualities are unique in man's case lies behind the negative use of animal metaphors in E and Marcus (cf. §9 above, and see
note ad 1. 3. 7–9). It is open to the objection that they are manifest
throughout the animal kingdom, a point actually made by Stoics in
Cynic mode to argue that they are 'natural' in this universal sense
(cf. Cic. *Fin.* 3. 62; for irrational animals as the standard of natural
behaviour cf. Plut. *Am. prol.* 439B–E; see LS 1. 352). Stoics, then,
had to add that mankind exhibits qualities like the social instinct
more consistently (cf. Cic. *Fin.* 3. 63, 5. 65; *Laws.* 1. 28; the point is
similar to Arist. *Pol.* 1253a7; cf. Plut. *Soll. an.* 963a). The 'social
instinct' (*to koinōnikon* in §20) is a prominent theme in Stoic ethics,
related to the topic of the brotherhood of man: cf. *SVF* 3. 340–8,
628; Hierocles 11. 14–15. '[U]nderstanding' is *parakolouthein*, the
verb from *parakolouthēsis*, as at 1. 6. 15; see note ad loc. These

qualities are not so much virtues as seeds of virtue; as such, they owe something to the ethics of Panaetius. '[R]everent of others' (**§23**) is Greek *aidēmōn*, from the noun *aidōs*; 'faithful' is *piston*, from *pistis*. For the importance Panaetius attached to these cf. Cic. *Off.* 1. 23, 39, 127 (in Cicero's Latin, *verecundia* and *fides*, respectively). 'Decent' in **§23** is *to kosmion*. This was the seed of *sōphrosunē*, or self-control, according to Panaetius; cf. Cic. *Off.* 1. 15. Panaetius' influence on Seneca is also evident in this respect; cf. the litany of positive qualities rehearsed at *De Ira* 1. 5.

The argument in **§§22–5** turns on the distinction between the consequences of an action and its motive. It leads to the conclusion that Paris was already lost when he was living in apparent bliss with Helen, and Achilles, too, was in a bad way almost from the start. This paradoxical perspective, characteristically Stoic, turns tragedy on its head. '[A]dd this opinion' in **§27** is *prosdoxazō*, a technical term in Hellenistic epistemology. Epicurus regarded sense perceptions as infallible, and blamed error on additional opinions that go beyond the appearances (DL 10. 50, 62; Lucr. 4. 65, 468, 816). Pyrrhonists held that it is only by superfluous opinion, and therefore wrongly, that things perceived by the senses in a certain way are judged to be good or bad in their nature (*PH* 3. 236; *M* 11. 158, 166). Cf. 2. 11. 6–8.

My translation of **§22** assumes the text of Souilhé. On Achilles etc. see note on 1. 22. 5–8. For 'mere woman' in **§24** E uses the diminutive *korasidion*; cf. *muliercula* at Cic. *TD* 1. 37, 5.103, 112; *Off.* 2.57, etc. In the view of Graeser (1972: 82) **§26** is imitated by Plotinus at 1. 4. 7. 31–3.

Preoccupation with a criterion of truth, reflected in **§§28–30**, was a dominant feature of Hellenistic epistemology. The analogy with artificial criteria was standard; see note ad 1. 17. 6–7. It may derive from Plato's description of the hedonic calculus at *Prot.* 356b–357e. For E, articulated preconceptions played the role of criteria *par excellence*; cf. 1. 22 *passim*. But is the analogy to cut-and-dried things like weight and length fair, and can there be comparable certainty in moral matters? E's confidence may seem naïve in contrast with the judiciousness of Aristotle (cf. *EN* 1094b11–28). But Aristotle admits *orthos logos* as a standard (*EE* 1249a21–b3); and E does not say that his standard needs to be as precise as artificial criteria, only that it is ultimately more important. On the need to scrutinize impressions carefully before assenting to them see note ad 1. 1. 12. 'At random' translates *eikēi*, a heedless frame of mind that Marcus continually inveighs against: cf. 1. 7. 3, 21, 27; 2. 5; 4. 2, etc.

[At **§31** the text has been questioned. Schweighäuser, followed by Oldfather and Souilhé, preferred to delete *mē* ('not'). Souilhé emended *mē* to *monōi*. In that case we might paraphrase, 'Am I so much better than Achilles and Agamemnon, that they came to grief by following their impressions, yet I (alone) imagine I can get away with the same thing?' But the *mē* is necessary for the implied contrast between Achilles and Agamemnon (who follow their impressions unquestioningly), and E, who does not. We may paraphrase: 'Am I better than those heroes of legend in not being satisfied with what was good enough for them?' E's attitude toward tragedy and tragic figures is mainly negative, which favours the received reading. For *kai* used similarly (i.e. in an adversative sense) cf. 1. 6. 36, 1. 19. 2–3.]

CHAPTER 29

On Steadfastness

The longest discourse in Book I, and the fourth longest in the corpus, weaves together three themes: (1) the independence of moral character; (2) the primacy of practice over theory; (3) the impossibility of getting everyone to adopt philosophical principles. Socrates, who best wedded theory to practice, is featured prominently here. Analysis:

§§1–8 The essence of the good is moral character, and is in our power to control.

§§9–15 This is no contradiction, but rather a confirmation, of the law of nature dictating that the stronger always prevails over the weaker. But we should be careful to distinguish in what respect a thing is stronger.

§§16–21 The *exemplum Socratis* invoked to make the point that tyrants and the like are stronger with respect to the body, but weaker—powerless in fact—over other people's minds.

§§22–6 It may be that tyrants and others do not understand this, but suppose that they get the better of a person's mind when they merely subdue the body. But we know better.

§§27–9 The option of suicide in such circumstances alluded to, with the usual caveats.

§§30–2 It is unreasonable to expect everyone to adopt philosophical beliefs; those who do not should be treated with condescension, like children.

§§33–49 Circumstances test our principles, but the philosopher accepts with equanimity every circumstance he confronts. He will not, however, accept them to the extent of identifying with them. Circumstances are the material, not the essence, of moral character.

§§50–4 The point of §§22–6 and §§30–2 restated with new rhetorical arguments.

§§55–63 Philosophy is both theoretical and practical; we should not cling to theory from fear of applying its lessons.

§§64–6 Socrates again appealed to in support of the discourse's third theme, that the principles embodied in its first will never command universal, or even majority, assent. We should accept this fact, and consider ourselves among the elect.

'[M]oral character' in **§1** is Greek *prohairesis*; see comment ad 1. 1. 23. For the thought cf. 1. 8. 16, 1. 25. 1, 2. 1. 4–6, 2. 10. 25, 2. 13. 10, 2. 16. 1, 3. 10. 18. This is what E at 4. 12. 7 calls one of his 'general principles' (*katholika*). It works a variation on the Stoic doctrine that virtue alone is good, vice bad (cf. DL 7. 101, etc.). Virtue (*aretē*) is a term E rarely uses (see Bonhöffer 1894: 16–17)— possibly because the old Stoic conception of virtue was extreme and controversial. *Prohairesis*, or, as here, *prohairesis* of 'a certain kind,' mostly replaces it in E's vocabulary.

'Externals' in **§2** correspond to what Stoics otherwise called 'indifferents' (*adiaphora*); although neither good nor bad *per se*, how they are used is good or bad, and determines one's character accordingly. E refers to them as 'materials'. This derives from the Stoic designation of the indifferents that have value or disvalue as the 'material of virtue' (Plut. *Comm. not.* 1069E). Cf. Cic. *Fin.* 3. 61: 'For the primary things either in accordance with or contrary to nature fall under the judgement and choice of the wise man, and make up as it were the material of wisdom.' E develops the idea at greater length at 2. 5. 1–8 and 2. 6. 1–2. See also comment at 1. 20. 3.

With **§§4–8** compare 1. 1. 23–5, 1. 24. 12–13, and 1. 25. 19, with comments ad loc. For the thought of the passage cf. Cic. *PS* 16–18.

[The translation in **§5** assumes, with Oldfather and Souilhé, Wolf's emendation of *mē kalē* ('does not call') to *me kalē* ('calls me'). The attempt of Radt (1990: 370) to defend the received reading by comparison with 4. 1. 48 is desperate.]

With the advice in **§§9–10** to render unto Caesar what is Caesar's compare Sen. *Ep.* 73. 1: 'I think they are wrong who suppose that serious devotees of philosophy are mutinous and rebellious, scornful of their magistrates or of their kings, by whom the state is governed.' Yet E is not really concerned with the philosopher's attitude toward temporal authority; his point is simply that the latter has power over the body, not the mind. Inasmuch as this doctrine could embolden one to defy tyrants when they threaten physical violence, his attitude was, in fact, potentially subversive. But in the extant diatribes E is found approving only a kind of passive resistance when a philosopher's own principles are under attack; cf. 1. 2. 19–24.

[In **§9** Schweighäuser proposed changing *tōn ekeinōn* to *hōn ekeinoi*, which has been adopted by all subsequent editors, and is assumed here.]

With the statement in **§12** that *prohairesis* conquers itself, cf. 1. 17. 26 with note. With the 'law' in **§§13–15** cf. §19 below, 3. 17. 6, 4. 7. 36. It is identical with the Sophistic principle defended by Callicles at Pl. *Grg.* 483c–d. E adopts the Socratic gambit of conceding this law, but distinguishing: superior numbers can constrain physical entities like the body, but it is possible to have a 'majority of one' where the judgement of a superior mind is concerned (*Laches* 184e). Compare the turn Seneca gives the principle at *Ep.* 95. 4.

On Socrates' significance for E (**§§16–19**) see Döring 1979: 43–79 and Long 1988: 150–1; and cf. §§29 and 65–6 below. His references to Socrates are collected as Giannantoni I C 515–30. With **§16** cf. 1. 1. 23 and Pl. *Phd.* 115c–116a, on the difference between 'Socrates' and Socrates' body. The first quote in **§18** is a paraphrase of Pl. *Apol.* 30c, which E cites repeatedly and Vlastos (1991: 219) calls E's 'favourite text'; cf. 2. 2. 15, 2. 23. 21; it is quoted in this form at Plut. *De Tranq. an.* 475E. The second comes from Pl. *Crito* 43d, with the alteration of a single word (*estō* to *ginesthō*), as at 1. 4. 24. E cites it here to support his contention that Socrates regarded death as indifferent. It appears in a slightly different light in the original, however. The 'law of nature' in **§19** is a restatement of the law elaborated in §§13–15 above. Cf. Pl. *Apol.* 30d: 'I

don't think it is lawful for a better man to be harmed by a worse.'
The principle is developed at length in Plato's *Gorgias*. With §21
cf. 1. 18. 15. On the use of Platonic themes in §§16–21 see Jagu
1946: 53–4.

[There are two emendations assumed in the translation of §16:
sōmation ('poor body') for *pragmation* ('poor thing'); and *apopsuchēi*
('expire') for *apophugēi* ('flee'). The former appears in the Sala-
manca edition (on which see Schenkl, pp. xcv–xcvii), the latter was
suggested by Wolf. §18 adopts Schweighäuser's necessary change
of *proschōmen* to *prosschōmen* ('pay attention').]

The point of §§22–6 is made concisely at 1. 15. 2: 'Philosophy
does not promise to secure for a man any external thing. If it did, it
would be taking on something outside its proper subject-matter.'
This being the case, we have no cause to be disenchanted with
philosophy for failing to protect us against misfortunes like imprisonment. But philosophy enables us to accept such adversity calmly.
§27 indicates that it makes no difference to the philosopher whether
he is in prison or not; cf. comment ad 1. 12. 23.

With §28 compare 1. 25. 7 and 14. This and the following section
invoke the option of suicide. E's judicious attitude, discouraging
'irrational' suicide, agrees with the teaching of other Stoics; cf. 1. 2.
2 with comment. Our passage also owes a clear debt to Pl. *Phd.*
61b–62e (cf. 1. 9. 10–17 with comment), although it ignores the
unqualified ban on suicide there in favour of the more subtle Stoic
position. For the idea that god needs us, cf. Marc. 6. 42. For the
metaphor of retreat in §29 cf. Cic. *Cato* 73, and see comment ad
1. 9. 22–6.

§§30–2 return to the idea in §§22–6, that the world does not
comprehend the paradoxical doctrines E promotes concerning the
indifference of external circumstances. But this is no reason to
waver in one's views; cf. 1. 25. 32–3. Seneca too often warns against
the influence of vulgar opinion; cf. *Ep.* 44. 6, 67. 12; *De Otio* 1. 3.
For the metaphor of the Saturnalia and the need to indulge people
on such occasions, cf. 1. 25. 8. The putative response to the children in §31 presumably stems from a pedantic adherence to Stoic
principles; see comment ad §§2–3 above.

[Following Wolf, and all subsequent editors, 'he doesn't want
(*mē . . . thelēi*)' in §32 has been emended to 'you don't want (*mē . . .
thelēis*)'.]

§§33-45 develop the contrast, frequent in E, between theory and practice; see comment ad 1. 4. 6–17, and 1. 26. 3–4. Cf. 2. 16. 34–5: 'What did you learn at school? Why did you represent yourself as a philosopher when you might have told the truth, and said, "I have studied a few introductions and read a bit of Chrysippus, but I never passed the threshold of philosopher. What claim have I to the calling of Socrates, who lived and died as he did?"' '[A]ny such difficulty' in **§33** refers back to **§22**. The graduate in **§34** craves a more difficult problem to display his logical acuity; the ethical lessons learned in school are also meant to be tested in practice. A more figurative use of the analogy with logic appears below in **§40**. The idea that difficult circumstances could even be welcomed, as athletes welcome a worthy opponent, was a favourite with Seneca; cf. *Prov.*, *passim*, and see comment ad 1. 6. 36. On the metaphor of 'travail' in **§36**, see comment ad 1. 22. 17–21; on the comparison of life to the Olympics cf. 1. 18. 21–2 and 1. 24. 1–2, with comment. On 'the gladiators of Caesar' in **§37** see Grant 1967: 35–50; on pp. 38–9 he notes that from the time of the emperor Claudius on, 'the leading gladiatorial training centres were imperially owned'. Presumably 'my athlete' in **§38** means 'my favourite athlete'. For the comparison of philosophy with gladiatorial combat, or training, cf. Sen. *Ep.* 37. With **§39** cf. 1. 12. 17, 2. 5. 11, 1. 6. 30.

[The translation of **§34** assumes Schweighäuser's approved change of *eulogon* ('reasonable') to *euluton* ('easy'). I have also followed other editors in assuming that the second, redundant *ouk* in **§35** should be deleted.]

With the figure in **§40**, comparing life to a problem in logic, cf. 1. 25. 11–13. '[H]ypothetical' is Greek *tropikon*. This was the distinctively Stoic designation of what otherwise, following Aristotle, they called the hypothetical argument; cf. Alex. Aphr. *In Arist. An. pr.* 262. 28–265. 26 (= Hülser fr. 1082); see Frede 1974: 101 n. 25. 'Consequence' is Greek *epiphora*, which denotes the conclusion of an argument; cf. DL 7. 45, 76–7, and see Frede 1974: 118 n. 2.

For the idea in **§§41-5** that one's position in life is adventitious, and analogous to an actor's mask and costume, cf. Pl. *Rep.* 577a–b; Lucr. 3. 57–8; see comment ad 1. 24. 15; 1. 25. 8–10. **§44**, like §27, suggests that good fortune, represented here by a governorship, could be as much a test of one's character as poverty or obscurity. Cf. 4. 4. 2: 'What difference is there between the desire to be a

senator, and not to be a senator? Or the desire to hold office, or not
to hold office?' Both are 'circumstances'; cf. 1. 24. 1 with comment.
The use of 'witness' (*martus*) in **§§46–9** parallels E's use of 'spy' at
1. 24. 6–7. See Kittel 1967: iv. 480–1 on E's use of *martus*, and its
(superficial) resemblance to the early Christian use of the word,
usually translated (or transliterated) 'martyr'.

[The translation of **§45** assumes Meibom's emendation of *proselthe*
to *proelthe*; in **§49** Wolf's change of *prosagagein* to *proagagein* has
been adopted, and for the same reason: the dramatic metaphor for
life informs the whole passage, as Radt (1990: 371) noticed.]

§§50–4 again develops the theme of §§22–7 and 30–2, with a
Socratic argument from the arts similar to that at 1. 19. 3–4. With
§50 cf. 2. 1. 26, 3. 8. 5. The hypothetical charge recalls the one
brought against Socrates; cf. Pl. *Apol.* 26c. With **§51** cf. *Ench.* 42:
'For if anyone should suppose that a true composite judgement is
false, the composite judgement is not harmed, but the person who
is deceived about it is harmed.' '[C]onditional' is Greek *sunēmmenon*.
Cf. DL 7. 71: 'A conditional, as Chrysippus says in his *Dialectical
Treatises* and Diogenes in his *Dialectical Handbook*, is a proposition
linked by the connective "if". This connective indicates that the
second follows from the first. For example, "If it is day, it is light." '
See Frede 1974: 80 n. 18.

The idea in **§§54–63** is that philosophizing is necessary and practical, whatever scoffers might think. But it is only practical when it
is actually applied in everyday life. This is one of E's distinctive
themes, as Bonhöffer 1890: 9–10 notes; cf. 1. 26. 3–4 with comment. That philosophy should wed theory to practice is a characteristically Stoic perspective. Cf. Sen. *Ep.* 95. 10: 'Philosophy is at
once contemplative and active, it both investigates and acts.' See
comment ad 1. 6. 21. With **§57** see comment ad 1. 1. 18–32. The
comparison in **§§58–63** of the philosophical life—what E calls *to
theōrein* in **§§58–9**—to watching a play is a variation on the old
analogy of philosophy to spectatorship at the Olympic games. It
may have originated with Pythagoras, but was formalized in the
Academy; see Guthrie 1962: i.164–6. The additional simile of the
slave, and the underlying idea in the section, are Stoic, however.
Cf. Cic. *TD* 5. 52: 'The man who can be affected by distress must
also be affected by fear, for fear is the anxious expectation of future
distress. The man affected by fear must also be affected by dread,

nervousness, panic, and cowardice, so that in consequence he is sometimes conquered . . . , and not only conquered but actually enslaved.'
Thus E reworks an old analogy to accommodate both sides of
philosophy as the Stoics perceived it, the theoretical as well as the
practical; see comment on 1. 10. 7–12.

§§64–6 restates the principle developed in §§22–7, 30–2, and
50–4 above, that people who are hostile to philosophy should be
ignored, or at best humoured; cf. 1. 22. 18–21. Ultimately these
passages derive from the famous digression in Plato's *Theaetetus*
173c–176a, concerning the inability of the world to understand the
philosopher. For the impact of this passage down through the
centuries see Burnyeat 1990: 35. The reference to Socrates in **§65**
derives from Pl. *Phd.* 116d, the reference in **§66** from 117d.

CHAPTER 30

What We Should Have Ready in Circumstances

After Chapter 29, one of the longest discourses in the corpus, Book
I ends with a decrescendo, with one of the shortest. Chapter 30
reprises E's familiar principles in the form of an imaginary dialogue
with god. It ends on a wry note, only partly facetious, suggesting
that E's students will find his constant dwelling on the same themes
to have been unnecessary.

'Another' in **§1** is of course god; the same oblique expression is
found at 1. 25. 13. In **§§2–5** god catechizes the philosopher on his
beliefs. On these beliefs, a summary of E's philosophy *in nuce*, cf. 1.
25. 1 and 1. 29. 1–2, with comments; also 2. 16. 1. On the injunction to 'follow [god]', identified in **§4** as 'the goal of life', cf. 1. 12. 5,
with comment.

In **§§6–7** E suggests that experience will confirm at first hand
what was said immediately above (and frequently elsewhere), that
'[t]hings independent of moral character' should not be feared,
since they cannot harm a person. By this time E has made this point

so often that he fears he may have inadvertently magnified the significance of such things in his pupils' minds, which would tend to encourage an attitude opposite to the one intended. So E takes another tack, prospectively ascribing to his students the disdainful attitude toward externals that he actually wants to instill. For the thought cf. 2. 6. 23; for similar use of psychology on E's part cf. 1. 9. 10–17, 1. 10. 12–13.

BIBLIOGRAPHY

A. Texts and Translations of Epictetus Cited in the Introduction and Commentary

CARTER, E. (1758). *All the Works of Epictetus, which are now Extant, Consisting of his Discourses, Preserved by Arrian, in Four Books, the Enchiridion, and Fragments* (London).

CASSANMAGNANO, C. (1982). *Epitteto: Diatribe, Manuale, Frammenti* (Milan).

HARD, R. (1995). *Epictetus: The Discourses*, ed. with an introduction and notes by C. Gill (London and Rutland, Vt.).

KORAES, A. (1827). *Arrian's Four Books of the Diatribes of Epictetus* (Paris).

MEIBOM, M. (1711). *Epicteti Manuale et Sententiae* (Copenhagen).

OLDFATHER, W. A. (1925–8). *Epictetus: The Discourses as Reported by Arrian, the Manual, and Fragments* (2 vols., London and Cambridge, Mass.).

SCHENKL, H. (1916). *Epicteti Dissertationes ab Arriano Digestae*, 2nd edn. (Leipzig).

SCHWEIGHÄUSER, J. (1799–1800). *Epicteteae Philosophiae Monumenta* (5 vols., Leipzig).

SOUILHÉ, J. (1948–65). *Épictète: Entretiens* (4 vols., Paris).

STELLWAG, H. W. F. (1933). *Epictetus: Het Eerste Boek der Diatriben* (Amsterdam).

UPTON, J. (1739–41). *Epicteti Quae Supersunt Dissertationes ab Arriano Collectae* (2 vols., London).

WOLF, H. (1560–3). *Arriani Commentariorum de Epicteti Disputationibus Libri IV* (Basel).

B. Secondary Literature

ABEL, K. (1983). 'Das Propatheia-theorem: ein Beitrag zur stoischen Affektenlehre', *Hermes*, 111: 78–97.

ALESSE, F. (1994). *Panezio di Rodi e la Tradizione Stoica* (Naples).

AMANN, J. (1931). *Die Zeusrede des Ailios Aristeides* (Stuttgart).

ANNAS, J. (1992). *Hellenistic Philosophy of Mind* (Berkeley).

—— (1993). *The Morality of Happiness* (Oxford).

—— and BARNES, J. (1985). *The Modes of Scepticism* (Cambridge).

ATHERTON, C. (1988). 'Hand Over Fist: The Failure of Stoic Rhetoric', *CQ* 38: 392–427.

—— (1993). *The Stoics on Ambiguity* (Cambridge).

---

236   BIBILIOGRAPHY

BABUT, D. (1969). *Plutarque et le Stoicisme* (Paris).
BALDRY, H. C. (1965). *The Unity of Mankind in Greek Thought* (Cambridge).
BALTES, M., and DÖRRIE, H. (1993). *Der Platonismus im 2. und 3. Jahrhundert nach Christus* (Stuttgart).
BARNES, J. (1980). 'Proof Destroyed', in Schofield *et al.*: 161–81.
—— (1982*a*). 'Medicine, Experience and Logic', in Barnes *et al.*: 24–68.
—— (1982*b*). *The Presocratic Philosophers* (London and New York).
—— (1990*a*). 'La διαφωνία pyrrhonienne', in A. J. Voelke (ed.), *Le Scepticisme antique* (Geneva), 97–106.
—— (1990*b*). 'Pyrrhonism, Belief and Causation. Observations on the Scepticism of Sextus Empiricus', in *Aufstieg und Niedergang der Römischen Welt* (Berlin), ii. 36. 4: 2608–95.
—— (1990*c*). 'Some Ways of Scepticism', in S. Everson, (ed.), *Companions to Ancient Thought I: Epistemology* (Cambridge), 204–24.
—— (1990*d*). *The Toils of Scepticism* (Cambridge).
—— (1993*a*). 'Galen and the Utility of Logic', in J. Rollesch and D. Nickel (eds.), *Galen und das Hellenistische Erbe* (Stuttgart), 33–52.
—— (1993*b*). 'Imperial Plato', *Apeiron*, 26: 129–51.
—— (1995) (ed.). *The Cambridge Companion to Aristotle* (Cambridge).
—— (1997). *Logic and the Imperial Stoa* (Leiden).
—— and GRIFFIN, M. (1989) (eds.). *Philosophia Togata* (Oxford).
—— *et al.* (1982) (eds.). *Science and Speculation* (Cambridge).
BARNEY, R. (1992). 'Appearances and Impressions', *Phronesis*, 37: 283–313.
BARTH, M., and BLANKE, H. (1994). *Anchor Bible: Colossians* (New York).
BETT, R. (1997). *Sextus Empiricus: Against the Ethicists* (Oxford).
BILLERBECK, M. (1978). *Epiktet: vom Kynismus* (Leiden).
—— (1979). *Der Kyniker Demetrius. Ein Beitrag zur Geschichte der frühkaiserzeitlichen Popularphilosophie* (Leiden).
BLACK, M., and GEACH, P. (1952) (eds.). *Translations from the Philosophical Writings of Gottlob Frege* (Oxford).
BOBZIEN, S. (1986). *Die stoische Modallogik* (Würzburg).
—— (1996). 'Stoic Conceptions of Freedom and their Relation to Ethics', in R. Sorabji (ed.), *Aristotle and After* (*BICS* supplement 68), 1–19.
BONHÖFFER, A. (1890). *Epictet und die Stoa* (Stuttgart).
—— (1894). *Die Ethik des Stoikers Epictet* (Stuttgart).
BOSWORTH, A. B. (1988). *From Arrian to Alexander* (Oxford).
BOTROS, S. (1985). 'Freedom, Causality, Fatalism and Early Stoic Philosophy', *Phronesis*, 30: 274–304.
BOWERSOCK, G. W. (1973). 'Greek Intellectuals and the Imperial Cult', in *Culte des Souverains*. Entretiens Hardt XIX (Geneva), 179–206.
BOYANCÉ, P. (1936). *Études sur le Songe de Scipion* (Bordeaux).

BRADLEY, K. R. (1986). 'Seneca and Slavery', *Classica et Mediaevalia*, 37: 161–72.

BRANCACCI, A. (1985). *Rhetorike Philosophousa* (Naples).

—— (1990). *Oikeios Logos: La Filosofia del linguaggio di Antistene* (Naples).

BRENNAN, T. (1996). 'Epicurus on Sex, Marriage, and Children', *CP* 91: 346–53.

BRUNSCHWIG, J., and NUSSBAUM, M. (1993) (eds.). *Passions and Perceptions* (Cambridge).

BRUNT, P. A. (1973). 'Aspects of the Social Thought of Dio Chrysostom and of the Stoics', *PCPS* 199: 9–34.

—— (1975). 'Stoicism and the Principate', *PBSR* 43: 7–39.

—— (1977). 'From Epictetus to Arrian', *Athenaeum*, 55: 19–48.

BURNYEAT, M. (1976). 'Protagoras and Self-Refutation in Later Greek Philosophy', *PR* 85: 44–69.

—— (1980). 'Can the Sceptic Live his Scepticism?', in Schofield *et al.*: 20–53.

—— (1983) (ed.). *The Skeptical Tradition* (Berkeley).

—— (1990). *The Theaetetus of Plato* (Indianapolis and Cambridge).

—— (1994). 'Enthymeme: Aristotle on the Logic of Persuasion', in D. J. Furley and A. Nehamas (eds.), *Aristotle's Rhetoric* (Princeton), 3–55.

BURY, R. G. (1894). '*Δύναμις* and *Φύσις* in Plato', *CR* 8: 297–300.

CAMPBELL, K. (1985). 'Self-Mastery and Stoic Ethics', *Philosophy*, 60: 327–40.

CHERNISS, H. (1976) (ed.). *Plutarch's Moralia*, xiii (Cambridge).

—— and HELMBOLD, W. C. (1957) (eds.). *Plutarch's Moralia*, xii (Cambridge).

CHILTON, C. W. (1960). 'Did Epicurus Approve of Marriage?', *Phronesis*, 5: 71–4.

CHROUST, A.-H. (1972). 'Late Hellenistic "Textbook Definitions" of Philosophy', *Laval Théologique et Philosophique*, 28: 15–25.

DE LACY, P. (1977). 'The Four Stoic *personae*', *ICS* 2: 163–72.

DENNISTON, J. D. (1966). *The Greek Particles*, 2nd edn. (Oxford).

DE STE CROIX, G. E. M. (1981). *The Class Struggle in the Ancient World* (Ithaca, NY).

DIBELIUS, M. (1956). *Studies in the Acts of the Apostles* (New York).

DIHLE, A. (1982). *The Theory of Will in Classical Antiquity* (Berkeley).

DILLON, J. (1983). '*Metriopatheia* and *Apatheia*: Some Reflections on a Controversy in Later Greek Ethics', in J. Anton and A. Preus (eds.), *Essays in Ancient Greek Philosophy* (Albany, NY), ii. 508–17.

—— (1993). *Alcinous: The Handbook of Platonism* (Oxford).

—— (1997). 'Medea among the Philosophers', in J. J. Clauss and S. I. Johnston (eds.), *Medea: Essays on Medea in Myth, Literature, Philosophy, and Art* (Princeton), 211–18.

DILLON, J., and LONG, A. A. (1988) (eds.). *The Question of Eclecticism* (Berkeley).

DOBBIN, R. (1991). 'Προαίρεσις in Epictetus', *AP* 11: 111–35.

DODDS, E. R. (1951). *The Greeks and the Irrational* (Berkeley).

DÖRING, K. (1979). *Exemplum Socratis.*, Hermes Einzelschrift 42 (Wiesbaden).

DÖRRIE, H. (1977). 'Der Begriff "Pronoia" in Stoa und Platonismus', *Freiburger Zeitschrift für Philosophie und Theologie*, 24: 60–87.

DUHOT, J.-J. (1989). *La Conception stoicienne de la causalité* (Paris).

EDELSTEIN, L., and KIDD, I. G. (1972, 1988) (eds.). *Posidonius* (2 vols., Cambridge).

ENGBERG-PEDERSEN, T. (1990). *The Stoic Theory of Oikeiôsis* (Aarhus).

ERSKINE, A. (1990). *The Hellenistic Stoa: Political Thought and Action* (Ithaca, NY).

FARQUHARSON, A. S. L. (1944). *The Meditations of the Emperor Marcus Antoninus* (2 vols., Oxford).

FLASHAR, H., and GIGON, O. (1986) (eds.). *Aspects de la philosophie hellénistique* (Geneva).

Fondation Hardt, *Entretiens sur l'antiquité classique* XXXII (Geneva).

FOLEY, H. (1989). 'Medea's Divided Self', *CA* 8: 61–85.

FORTENBAUGH, W. W. (1983) (ed.). *On Stoic and Peripatetic Ethics: The Work of Arius Didymus* (New Brunswick, NJ).

FREDE, M. (1974). *Die stoische Logik. Abhandlungen der Akademie der Wissenschaften in Göttingen, philologisch-historische Klasse 88* (Göttingen).

—— (1986). 'The Stoic Doctrine of the Affections of the Soul', in Schofield and Striker: 93–110.

FURLEY, D. (1980). 'Self-Movers', in A. Rorty (ed.), *Essays on Aristotle's Ethics* (Berkeley), 55–67.

GALINSKY, K. (1990). 'Hercules in the Aeneid', in S. Harrison (ed.), *Oxford Readings in Vergil's Aeneid* (Oxford), 277–94.

GALLOP, D. (1975). *Plato: Phaedo* (Oxford).

GARNSEY, P. (1994). 'Philo Judaeus and Slave Theory', *SCI* 13: 30–45.

GIANNANTONI, G. (1990). *Socratis et Socraticorum Reliquiae* (4 vols., Naples).

GILL, C. (1983). 'Did Chrysippus Understand Medea?', *Phronesis*, 28: 136–49.

—— (1988). 'Personhood and Personality: The Four *personae* Theory in Cicero, *De Officiis* I', *OSAP* 5: 169–99.

GILL, M. L., and LENNOX, J. G. (1994) (eds.). *Self-Motion* (Princeton).

GOLDSCHMIDT, V. (1953). *Le Système Stoïcien et l'idée de temps* (Paris).

GOSLING, J. (1990). *Weakness of the Will* (London).

GOTTSCHALK, H. B. (1980). *Herakleides of Pontus* (Oxford).

—— (1987). 'Aristotelian Philosophy in the Roman World', in *Aufstieg und Niedergang der Römischen Welt* (Berlin), ii. 36. 2: 1079–1174.

GOULET-CAZÉ, M.-O. (1986). *L'Ascèse cynique* (Paris).

GRAESER, A. (1972). *Plotinus and the Stoics* (Leiden).

GRANT, M. (1967). *Gladiators* (London).

GRIFFIN, M. (1976). *Seneca, A Philosopher in Politics*, repr., with additions, 1991 (Oxford).

—— (1984). *Nero: The End of a Dynasty* (London).

—— (1986). 'The Stoics on Suicide', *G&R* 33: 64–77, 192–202.

GUTHRIE, W. K. C. (1962–81). *A History of Greek Philosophy* (6 vols., Cambridge).

HADOT, I. (1996). *Simplicius. Commentaire sur le Manuel d'Épictète* (Leiden).

HADOT, P. (1978). 'Un Clé des *Pensées* de Marc-Aurèle: les trois *topoi* philosophiques selon Épictète', *Les Études philosophiques*, 33: 65–83.

HAHM, D. (1977). *The Origins of Stoic Cosmology* (Columbus, Oh.).

—— (1991). 'A Neglected Stoic Argument for Human Responsibility', *ICS* 17: 23–48.

—— (1994). 'Self-Motion in Stoic Philosophy', in Gill and Lennox: 175–225.

HANKINSON, J. (1989). 'Galen and the Best of all Possible Worlds', *CQ* 39: 206–27.

HARDIE, W. F. R. (1980). *Aristotle's Ethical Theory*, 2nd edn. (Oxford).

HEADLAM, W. (1922). *Herodas: The Mimnes and Fragments*, ed. A. D. Knox, repr. 1966 (Cambridge).

HERSHBELL, J. (1986). 'The Stoicism of Epictetus', in *Aufstieg und Niedergang der Römischen Welt* (Berlin), ii. 36. 3: 2148–63.

HIJMANS, B. L. (1959). *Askesis: Notes on Epictetus' Educational System* (Assen).

HIRZEL, R. (1895). *Der Dialog: ein literarhistorischer Versuch* (Leipzig).

HOSSENFELDER, M. (1986). 'Epicurus—hedonist malgré lui', in Schofield and Striker: 245–63.

HOVEN, R. (1971). *Stoicisme et Stoiciens face au problème de l'au-delà* (Paris).

HÜLSER, K. (1987–88). *Die Fragmente zur Dialektik der Stoiker* (4 vols., Stuttgart).

IERODIAKONOU, K. (1993). 'The Stoic Division of Philosophy', *Phronesis*, 38: 57–74.

IMBERT, C. (1980). 'Stoic Logic and Alexandrian Poetics', in Schofield et al. 182–216.

INWOOD, B. (1983). 'The Two Forms of *oikeiôsis* in Arius and the Stoa', in Fortenbaugh: 190–201.

—— (1984). 'Hierocles: Theory and Argument in the Second Century A.D.', *OSAP* 2: 151–84.

—— (1985). *Ethics and Human Action in Early Stoicism* (Oxford).

—— (1986). 'Goal and Target in Stoicism', *JP* 83: 547–56.

—— (1993). 'Seneca and Psychological Dualism', in Brunschwig and Nussbaum: 150–83.

IOPPOLO, A.-M. (1980). *Aristone di Chio e lo stoicismo antico* (Rome).

—— (1986). *Opinione e Scienza: il dibattito tra Stoici e Accademici nel III e II secolo a.C.* (Naples).

IRWIN, T. (1986). 'Stoic and Aristotelian Conceptions of Happiness', in Schofield and Striker: 205–44.

—— (1988). *Aristotle's First Principles* (Oxford).

JAEGER, W. (1948). *Aristotle: Fundamentals of the History of his Development*, 2nd edn. (Oxford).

JAGU, A. (1946). *Épictète et Platon* (Paris).

JOYCE, R. (1995). 'Early Stoicism and Akrasia', *Phronesis*, 40: 315–35.

KERFERD, G. B. (1978). 'What Does the Wise Man Know?', in Rist 1978*b*: 125–36.

KIDD, I. G. (1971). 'Stoic Intermediates and the End for Man', in Long 1971*c*: 150–72.

—— (1978). 'Moral Actions and Rules in Stoic Ethics', in Rist 1978*b*: 247–58.

—— (1995). 'Some Philosophical Demons', *BICS* n.s. 2: 217–24.

KITTEL, G. (1967) (ed.). *Theological Dictionary of the New Testament* (10 vols., Grand Rapids, Mich.).

KOESTER, H. (1982). *History, Culture and Religion of the Hellenistic Age* (2 vols., Berlin).

KRÄMER, H.-J. (1972). *Platonismus und hellenistische Philosophie* (Berlin).

LAKMANN, M.-L. (1995). *Der Platoniker Tauros in der Darstellung des Aulus Gellius* (Leiden).

LAKS, A., and SCHOFIELD, M. (1995) (eds.). *Justice and Generosity* (Cambridge).

LAPIDGE, M. (1973). '*Archai* and *Stoicheia*: A Problem in Stoic Cosmology', *Phronesis*, 18: 240–78.

LATTE, K. (1960). *Römische Religionsgeschichte* (Munich).

LONG, A. A. (1967). 'Carneades and the Stoic Telos', *Phronesis*, 12: 59–90.

—— (1968*a*). 'Aristotle's Legacy to Stoic Ethics', *BICS* 15: 72–85.

—— (1968*b*). 'The Stoic Concept of Evil', *PQ* 18: 329–43.

—— (1970*a*). 'The Logical Basis of Stoic Ethics', *PAS* 71: 85–104 (= Long 1996*c*: 134–55).

—— (1970*b*). 'Stoic Determinism and Alexander of Aphrodisias De Fato (i–xiv)', *AGP* 52: 247–68.

—— (1971*a*). 'Freedom and Determinism in the Stoic Theory of Human Action', in Long 1971*c*: 173–99.

—— (1971*b*). 'Language and Thought in Stoicism', in Long 1971*c*: 75–113.

—— (1971*c*) (ed.). *Problems in Stoicism* (London).

—— (1974). *Hellenistic Philosophy* (London).

—— (1975). 'Heraclitus and Stoicism', *Philosophia*, 5: 133–56 (= Long 1996*c*: 35–57).

—— (1978). 'Dialectic and the Stoic Sage', in Rist 1978b: 101–24 (= Long 1996c: 85–106).

—— (1980). 'Stoa and Sceptical Academy: Origins and Growth of a Tradition', *LCM* 5: 161–74.

—— (1981). 'Aristotle and the History of Greek Scepticism', in D. J. O'Meara (ed.), *Studies in Aristotle* (Washington), 79–106.

—— (1982a). 'Astrology: Arguments *pro* and *contra*', in Barnes *et al.* 1982: 165–92.

—— (1982b). 'Epictetus and Marcus Aurelius', in T. J. Luce (ed.), *Ancient Writers* (New York), 985–1002.

—— (1982c): 'Soul and Body in Stoicism', *Phronesis*, 27: 34–57 (= Long 1996c: 224–49).

—— (1983). 'Greek Ethics after MacIntyre and the Stoic Community of Reason', *AP* 3: 184–99 (= Long 1996c: 156–78).

—— (1985). 'The Stoics on World-Conflagration and Everlasting Recurrence', *SJP* 23 suppl.: 13–38.

—— (1986). 'Pleasure and Social Utility—The Virtues of Being Epicurean', in Flashar and Gigon: 283–324.

—— (1988). 'Socrates in Hellenistic Philosophy', *CQ* 38: 150–71 (= Long 1996c: 1–34).

—— (1989). 'Stoic Eudaimonism', *Proceedings of the Boston Area Colloquium in Ancient Philosophy*, 4: 77–101 (= Long 1996c: 179–201).

—— (1991a). 'The Harmonics of Stoic Virtue', *OSAP* suppl. vol.: 97–116 (= Long 1996c: 202–23).

—— (1991b). 'Representation and the Self in Stoicism', in S. Everson (ed.), *Companions to Ancient Thought: Psychology* (Cambridge), 102–20 (= Long 1996c: 264–84).

—— (1992). 'Stoic Readings of Homer', in R. Lamberton and J. J. Keaney (eds.), *Homer's Ancient Readers* (Princeton), 41–66 (= Long 1996c: 58–84).

—— (1996a). 'Notes on Hierocles Stoicus *apud* Stobaeum', in M. Serena Funghi (ed.), *Odoi Dizesios. Le Vie della Ricerca: Studi in onore di Francesco Adorno* (Florence), 299–309.

—— (1996b). 'Stoic Psychology and the Elucidation of Language', in G. Manetti (ed.), *Knowledge through Signs. Ancient Semiotic Theories and Practices* (Brussels), 109–31.

—— (1996c). *Stoic Studies* (Cambridge).

LUSCHNATT, O. (1958). 'Das Problem der ethischen Fortschritts in der alten Stoa', *Philologus*, 102: 178–214.

MACMULLEN, R. (1966). *Enemies of the Roman Order* (Cambridge).

MANNING, C. E. (1986). 'Stoicism and Slavery in the Roman Empire', in *Aufstieg und Niedergang der Römischen Welt* (Berlin), ii. 36. 3: 1518–43.

MANSFELD, J. (1979). 'Providence and the Destruction of the Universe in Early Stoic Thought', in M. J. Vermaseren (ed.), *Studies in Hellenistic Religions* (Leiden), 129–88.

MARTIN, D. A. (1990). *Slavery as Salvation: The Metaphor of Slavery of Pauline Christianity* (New Haven).

MATTINGLY, H. (1966). *The Man in the Roman Street* (New York).

MAYOR, J. E. B. (1886–9). *Thirteen Satires of Juvenal*, 4th edn. (London).

MILANI, P. A. (1972). *La Schiavitu nel Pensiero Politico: dai Greci al Basso Medio Evo* (Milan).

MILLAR, F. (1965). 'Epictetus and the Imperial Court', *JRS* 55: 141–8.

MOLES, J. (1995). 'The Cynics and Politics', in Laks and Schofield: 129–58.

MORAUX, P. (1973). *Der Aristotelismus bei den Griechen*, i (Berlin).

—— (1984). *Der Aristotelismus bei den Griechien*, ii (Berlin).

MUELLER, I. (1978). 'An Introduction to Stoic Logic', in Rist 1978*b*: 1–26.

MÜLLER, R. (1968). '*Bios theōrētikos* bei Antiochus von Askalon und Cicero', *Helikon*, 8: 222–37.

NOCK, A. D. (1972). *Essays in Religion and the Ancient World* (2 vols., Oxford).

NUSSBAUM, M. (1986). *The Fragility of Goodness: Luck and Ethics in Greek Tragedy and Philosophy* (Cambridge).

—— (1990) (ed.). *The Poetics of Therapy* (*Apeiron*, 23. 4) (Edmonton).

—— (1993). 'Poetry and the Passions: Two Stoic Views', in Brunschwig and Nussbaum: 97–149.

—— (1994). *The Therapy of Desire: Theory and Practice in Hellenistic Ethics* (Princeton).

OBBINK, D. (1989). 'The Atheism of Epicurus', *GRBS*, 29: 187–223.

—— (1992). 'What All Men Believe—Must Be True: Common Conceptions and *consensio omnium* in Aristotle and Later Hellenistic Philosophy', *OSAP* 10: 193–231.

OLDFATHER, W. (1921). 'Richard Bentley's Critical Notes on Arrian's *Discourses of Epictetus*', *TAPA* 1921: 41–52.

O'MEARA, D. (1994). 'Faut-il philosopher?—le voyage d'une question dans le monde antique', in A. Kessler, T. Ricklin, and G. Wurst (eds.), *Perigrina Curiositas* (Göttingen), 1–12.

PEASE, A. S. (1941). 'Caeli enarrant', *HTR* 34: 163–200.

PÉPIN, J. (1971). *Idées Grecques sur l'homme et sur Dieu* (Paris).

—— (1976). 'Prière et providence au 2ᵉ siècle', in *Images of Man: Studia G. Verbeke dicata* (Louvain), 111–25.

POHLENZ, M. (1964), *Die Stoa. Geschichte einer geistigen Bewegung*, 3rd edn. (2 vols., Göttingen).

POWELL, J. G. F. (1988). *Cicero: Cato Major de Senectute* (Cambridge).

PRICE, A. W. (1995). *Mental Conflict* (London and New York).

PUGLIA, E. (1988). *Aporie testuali ed esegetiche in Epicuro: (Ptterc. 1012) Demetrio Lacone* (Naples).

RADT, S. L. (1990). 'Zu Epiktets *Diatriben*', *Mnemosyne*, 43: 363–73.

REALE, G. (1989). *A History of Ancient Philosophy*, iv: *The Schools of the Imperial Age* (Albany, NY).

REINHARDT, K. (1921). *Poseidonius* (Munich).

—— (1926). *Kosmos und Sympathie* (Munich).

—— (1954). *Poseidonius von Apameia, der Rodier genannt*, in *Paulys Realencyclopädie der Classischen Altertumswissenschaft*. XXII, 1 (Stuttgart): 559–826.

REINHOLD, M. (1988). *From Republic to Empire* (Atlanta).

RICKERT, G. (1987). 'Akrasia and Euripides' Medea', *HSCP* 91: 91–117.

RIST, J. M. (1969). *Stoic Philosophy* (Cambridge).

—— (1978a). 'The Stoic Concept of Detachment', in Rist 1978b: 259–72.

—— (1978b) (ed.). *The Stoics* (Berkeley).

—— (1982). 'Are You a Stoic? The Case of Marcus Aurelius', in B. F. Meyer and E. P. Saunders (eds.), *Self-Definition in the Graeco-Roman World* (London), iii: 23–45.

ROBINSON, R. (1953). *Plato's Earlier Dialectic*, 2nd edn. (Oxford).

ROSENMEYER, T. (1989). *Seneca and Stoic Cosmology* (Berkeley).

ROSS, D. (1953). *Aristotle* (London).

RUSSELL, D. A. (1991). *Greek Prose* (Oxford).

—— (1992). *Dio Chrysostom: Orations VII, XII and XXXVI* (Cambridge).

RUTHERFORD, R. B. (1989). *The Meditations of Marcus Aurelius: A Study* (Oxford).

SAMBURSKY, S. (1959). *Physics of the Stoics* (Princeton).

SANDBACH, F. H. (1930). '*ENNOIA* and *ΠΡΟΛΗΨΙΣ* in the Stoic Theory of Knowledge', *CQ* 24: 44–51.

—— (1975). *The Stoics* (London).

SCHOFIELD, M. (1980). 'Preconceptions, Argument, and God', in Schofield *et al.*: 283–308.

—— (1983). 'The Syllogisms of Zeno of Citium', *Phronesis*, 28: 31–58.

—— (1986). 'Cicero For and Against Divination', *JRS* 76: 47–65.

—— (1991). *The Stoic Idea of the City* (Cambridge).

—— (1995). 'Two Stoic Approaches to Justice', in Laks and Schofield: 191–212.

—— and STRIKER, G. (1986) (eds.). *The Norms of Nature* (Cambridge).

—— *et al.* (1980) (eds.). *Doubt and Dogmatism* (Oxford).

SEDLEY, D. (1989). 'Philosophical Allegiance in the Greco-Roman World', in Barnes and Griffin: 97–119.

—— (1991). 'Is Aristotle's Teleology Anthropocentric?', *Phronesis*, 36: 179–96.

SEDLEY, D. (1993). 'Chrysippus on Psychophysical Causality', in Brunschwig and Nussbaum: 313–31.

SHARPLES, R. W. (1983). *Alexander of Aphrodisias: On Fate* (London).

—— (1986). 'Soft Determinism and Freedom in Early Stoicism', *Phronesis* 31: 266–79.

—— (1987). 'Alexander of Aphrodisias: Scholasticism and Innovation', in *Aufstieg und Niedergang der Römischen Welt* (Berlin), ii. 36. 1: 1176–1243.

—— (1991). *Cicero On Fate & Boethius The Consolation of Philosophy* (Warminster).

SMITH, M. (1975). *Cena Trimalchionis* (Oxford).

SOLMSEN, F. (1960). *Aristotle's System of the Physical World* (Ithaca, NY).

—— (1963). 'Nature as Craftsman in Greek Thought', *JHI* 24: 332–55.

SORABJI, R. (1980). *Necessity, Cause, and Blame* (Ithaca, NY).

SPANNEUT, M. (1962). 'Epiktet', in *Reallexicon für Antike und Christentum* (Stuttgart): v. cols. 599–681.

STADTER, P. (1980). *Arrian of Nicomedia* (Chapel Hill, NC).

STANTON, G. R. (1968). 'The Cosmopolitan Ideas of Epictetus and Marcus Aurelius', *Phronesis*, 13: 183–95.

STARR, C. G., Jun., (1949). 'Epictetus and the Tyrant', *CP* 44: 20–9.

STOCKDALE, J. (1995). 'Testing Epictetus' Doctrines in a Laboratory of Human Behaviour', *BICS* NS 2: 1–13.

STRIKER, G. (1974). '*Κριτήριον τῆς ἀληθίας*', *Nachrichten der Akademie der Wissenschaften in Göttingen*, Phil.-hist. Kl.: 47–110.

—— (1983). 'The Role of *oikeiosis* in Stoic Ethics', *OSAP* 1: 145–67 (= Striker 1996: 281–97).

—— (1986). 'Antipater, or the Art of Living', in Schofield and Striker: 185–204 (= Striker 1996: 298–315).

—— (1991). 'Following Nature: A Study in Stoic Ethics', *OSAP* 9: 1–73.

—— (1996). *Essays on Hellenistic Epistemology and Ethics* (Cambridge).

SUMMERS, W. C. (1910). *Select Letters of Seneca* (London).

TALANGA, J. (1986). *Zukunftsurteile und Fatum* (Bonn).

TAYLOR, C. C. W. (1995). 'Politics', in Barnes 1995: 233–58.

THEILER, W. (1924). *Zur Geschichte der teleologischen Naturbetrachtung bis auf Aristoteles* (Zurich).

—— (1930). *Die Vorbereitung des Neuplatonismus* (Berlin).

—— (1982). *Poseidonius: Die Fragmente* (2 vols., Berlin).

TIELEMAN, T. (1996). *Galen and Chrysippus on the Soul* (Leiden).

TODD, R. B. (1973). 'The Stoic Common Notions', *SO* 48: 47–75.

—— (1978). 'Monism and Immanence', in Rist 1978b: 137–60.

USENER, H. (1887). *Epicurea* (Leipzig).

VAN DER WAERDT, P. (1991). 'Politics and Philosophy in Stoicism', *OSAP* 9: 185–211.

VAN STRAATEN, M. (1962). *Panaetii Rhodii Fragmenta* (Leiden).

VLASTOS, G. (1981). *Platonic Studies*, 2nd edn. (Princeton).

—— (1991). *Socrates, Ironist and Moral Philosopher* (Cambridge).

—— (1994). *Socratic Studies* (Cambridge).

VON ARNIM, H. (1905–23). *Stoicorum Veterum Fragmenta* (4 vols., Leipzig).

WHITAKER, J. (1987). 'Platonic Philosophy in the Early Empire', in *Aufstieg und Niedergang der Römische Welt* (Berlin and New York), ii. 36. 1: 81–123.

WILAMOWITZ-MOELLENDORFF, U. von (1902). *Griechesches Lesebuch* (2 vols., Berlin).

WIRTH, T. (1967). 'Arrians Erinnerungen an Epiktet', *MH* 24: 149–89, 197–216.

WOODMAN, A. J. (1983). *Velleius Paterculus: The Caesarian and Augustan Narratives* (Cambridge).

ZANKER, P. (1995). *The Mask of Socrates: The Image of the Intellectual in Antiquity* (Berkeley).

INDEX NOMINUM

INDEX LOCORUM

Note: Only the more important discussions are cited.

SUBJECT INDEX